Social Justice through Pedagogies of Multiliteracies

Social Justice through Pedagogies of Multiliteracies explores the ways in which pedagogies of multiliteracies can be used to promote and achieve situated forms of social justice, especially for minoritized L2 learners.

This edited collection focuses on pedagogies of multiliteracies that seek to develop and strengthen L2 learner identity and agency within and outside formal educational contexts in bilingual, multilingual, multimodal, community, language, and teacher education. The volume contextualizes agency and identity around questions, ideologies, and issues related to language, gender, sex, sexuality, body, race, and ethnicity. Contributions illustrate the design and implementation of pedagogies of multiliteracies through a diverse range of modalities and settings: linguistic landscapes, graphic novels, picturebooks, photovoice, text, and imagery through instructor- and student-developed materials. The volume acknowledges, enacts, and builds upon the responsibility of L2 educators to develop pedagogies of multiliteracies that reflect the life experiences, identities, and needs of minoritized L2 individuals in the curriculum in order to realize the social justice aim of L2 education.

Social Justice through Pedagogies of Multiliteracies will be of interest to L2 researchers, teachers, and teacher educators.

Vander Tavares is an Associate Professor in education at Inland Norway University of Applied Sciences, Norway, and holds a PhD in linguistics and applied linguistics from York University, Canada. His research interests include language teacher identity development, critical second language education, internationalization of higher education, and identity in multilingual/multicultural contexts.

Multiliteracies and Second Language Education
Series Editor: Gabriela C. Zapata,
University of Nottingham, UK

The *Multiliteracies and Second Language Education* series explores different aspects of the incorporation of the multiliteracies framework and related approaches such as Learning by Design in L2 education. Topics covered include teacher education and L2 learning in diverse instructional environments and in relation with contemporary social issues (e.g., diversity, equity, and inclusion; identity).

Learning by Design and Second Language Teaching
Theory, Research, and Practice
Gabriela C. Zapata

Multiliteracies in International Educational Contexts
Towards Education Justice
Edited by Gabriela C. Zapata, Mary Kalantzis and Bill Cope

Social Justice through Pedagogies of Multiliteracies
Developing and Strengthening L2 Learner Agency and Identity
Edited by Vander Tavares

For more information about this series please visit: https://www.routledge.com/Multiliteracies-and-Second-Language-Education/book-series/MSLE

Social Justice through Pedagogies of Multiliteracies
Developing and Strengthening L2 Learner Agency and Identity

Edited by Vander Tavares

LONDON AND NEW YORK

Designed cover image: Ignatiev/Getty Images

First published 2025
by Routledge
4 Park Square, Milton Park, Abingdon, Oxon OX14 4RN

and by Routledge
605 Third Avenue, New York, NY 10158

Routledge is an imprint of the Taylor & Francis Group, an informa business

© 2025 selection and editorial matter, Vander Tavares; individual chapters, the contributors

The right of Vander Tavares to be identified as the author of the editorial material, and of the authors for their individual chapters, has been asserted in accordance with sections 77 and 78 of the Copyright, Designs and Patents Act 1988.

All rights reserved. No part of this book may be reprinted or reproduced or utilised in any form or by any electronic, mechanical, or other means, now known or hereafter invented, including photocopying and recording, or in any information storage or retrieval system, without permission in writing from the publishers.

Trademark notice: Product or corporate names may be trademarks or registered trademarks, and are used only for identification and explanation without intent to infringe.

British Library Cataloguing-in-Publication Data
A catalogue record for this book is available from the British Library

ISBN: 978-1-032-57313-7 (hbk)
ISBN: 978-1-032-56789-1 (pbk)
ISBN: 978-1-003-43884-7 (ebk)

DOI: 10.4324/9781003438847

Typeset in Galliard
by KnowledgeWorks Global Ltd.

Contents

List of Contributors	*viii*
Introduction: Social Justice in L2 Education through Pedagogies of Multiliteracies VANDER TAVARES	1

PART I
Exploring Agency and Identity Development in Student-Led Projects — 19

1 **Photovoice: A Multiliteracies Approach to Facilitate Identity Reflection and Self-Advocacy for Multilingual Students with Communication Disorders** — 21
TOBY LOEWENSTEIN AND ROBIN DANZAK

2 **Multiliteracies and Student-Created Materials Design: Learner Engagement and Agency in the EFL Classroom** — 41
KEN MIZUSAWA AND TAMAS KISS

PART II
Multiliteracies Pedagogies for Inclusion in Diverse Communities — 59

3 **Multiliteracies for Social Inclusion and Plurilingual Identity Construction: Repositioning the Self in a Superdiverse Language Learning Environment** — 61
BARBARA SPINELLI

vi *Contents*

4 Drawing on Cope and Kalantzis' Transpositional
Grammar to Explore L2 Identities through
Multiliteracies 82
SUSAN M. HOLLOWAY

PART III
Critical Literacies Development through
Linguistic Landscapes 99

5 Reading Japanese Linguistic Landscapes for
Critical Multiliteracies: Nurturing Agency
and Criticality for Social Justice 101
YURI KUMAGAI

6 L2 Learners Engaging with Linguistic Landscapes in the
Classroom: Developing Criticality and Inspiring Agency 120
MÓNICA LOURENÇO AND SÍLVIA MELO-PFEIFER

PART IV
Multiliteracies for Social Justice in Teacher
Education Contexts 139

7 Building Deaf Agency through the Teaching and
Learning of 'English Grammar Games' 141
JENNY WEBSTER, ULRIKE ZESHAN, NIRAV PAL,
AND DEEPU MANAVALAMAMUNI

8 Coming-of-Age Graphic Novels in L2 Education:
Reflecting on Social Justice from a Feminist Perspective 163
DOLORES MIRALLES-ALBEROLA, MARGARIDA CASTELLANO-SANZ,
AND AGUSTÍN REYES-TORRES

PART V
Practitioner Reflections on Students' and Teachers'
Critical Literacies Development 181

9 Becoming Critically Literate about the Other(ed):
Proposing Disruptions and Innovations to a
Portuguese as a Foreign Language Course 183
VANDER TAVARES

Contents vii

10 Critical Literacy for Korean Language Learning and
Teaching: Exploring and Expanding Its Possibilities 201
JOOWON SUH

Index *217*

List of Contributors

Margarida Castellano-Sanz is an Assistant Professor in the Department of Languages and Literature Education at the Universitat de València, Spain. She holds a PhD in Language, Literature and Culture from the Universitat de València. She has done research at the Universidad Nacional Autónoma de México and the Queen Mary University of London. She is the author of the book *Les altres catalanes. Memòria, identitat i autobiografia en la literatura d'immigració* (2018) and has also published several journal articles related to postcolonial literature, identity construction, and multimodal approaches in L2 teaching.

Robin L. Danzak's research has examined bilingual writing and its intersection with identity and the immigrant experience through dynamic projects with multilingual-multicultural adolescents and adults. Eager to explore arts-based qualitative methods, she is currently working on understanding the adoption experience through visual and narrative inquiry. Robin is an Associate Professor of Communication Sciences & Disorders at Emerson College in Boston, USA.

Susan M. Holloway is an Associate Professor in the Faculty of Education at the University of Windsor, Canada. Her research interests include critical literacy, multiliteracies, socio-cultural perspectives on second language acquisition theory, adult education, teacher education, and critical theory. She is currently the Principal Investigator on a SSHRC Insight grant.

Tamas Kiss works as an Associate Professor at Sunway University, Centre for English Language Studies, Malaysia. He has been involved with language teacher education programs in Europe, the Middle East, South Asia, Latin America, and South East Asia. He has delivered one-off talks and directed longer, intensive teacher development courses in more than 20 countries, including Hungary, the Philippines, Lithuania, Pakistan, Iraq, Hong Kong, Singapore, Ukraine, Mexico, and Nepal. He co-authored *Creativity and English Language Teaching: From inspiration to implementation* (2018, Palgrave Macmillan) with Alan Maley.

List of Contributors ix

Yuri Kumagai (EdD) is a Senior Lecturer of Japanese at Smith College, USA. Her specializations are critical literacy and multiliteracies in world language education. Her research interests include language ideologies, semiotic landscapes, and translingual practices. She publishes journal articles and book chapters in English and Japanese. Her recent publications include: "'Ekkyō-bungaku' as crossing the border of language" (*Global Education Effect*, Routledge, 2020), "Translingual Practices in a Monolingual Society: Discourses, Learners' and language choices." (Journal of Bilingual Education and Bilingualism, 2020).

Toby Loewenstein is currently a speech and language pathologist providing outpatient pediatric care at Boston Children's Hospital, USA. She obtained her Master of Elementary Education from University of Missouri – St. Louis in August, 2015. She spent five years as a classroom teacher, teaching in a preschool special education inclusion classroom and a kindergarten general education classroom. She then obtained her Master of Science in Communication Sciences and Disorders from Emerson College in 2021.

Mónica Lourenço is an Assistant Professor at the Faculty of Arts and Humanities of the University of Coimbra, Portugal. She has a PhD in Didactics and Teacher Education and over 15 years of experience teaching and supervising students in the field of language education and early language learning. Her main research interests include global citizenship education, teacher education, linguistic and cultural diversity, plurilingualism and early language learning. From 2019 to 2022 she was the institutional coordinator of the Erasmus+ project *LoCALL – Local Linguistic Landscapes for Global Language Education in the School Context*.

Deepu Manavalamamuni was a research assistant for the Peer-to-Peer Deaf Multiliteracies project and played a pivotal role in training and coordinating the deaf tutors delivering classes in India.

Sílvia Melo-Pfeifer is a Full Professor at the Faculty of Education, at the University of Hamburg, Germany. She works in the fields of French and Spanish initial teacher education and research on pluralistic approaches in language and teacher education, heritage language development, and arts-based approaches in teacher education and research. She was the international coordinator of the Erasmus+ project *LoCALL – Local Linguistic Landscapes for Global Language Education in the School Context* and is currently coordinating the Erasmus+ project *CoMMITTEd – Covid, Migrants and Minorities in Teacher Education: A Fake News Observatory to promote Critical Thinking and Digital Literacy in Times of Crisis.*

Dolores Miralles-Alberola received her PhD in Latin American Literature with a Designated Emphasis on Native American Studies from the University of California, Davis. Currently, she is an Assistant Professor at the University of Alicante, Spain. Her research interests focus mainly on the

x *List of Contributors*

inclusion of intercultural literature in the teaching of languages from a critical literacy perspective. She has published diverse academic articles on resistance literature, film, and Native American children's literature in English language education. She is a member of the research group Lit(T)erart.

Ken Mizusawa is a Lecturer in the English Language and Literature Academic Group and Programme Leader for the Postgraduate Diploma in Education (PGDE) in Literature at the National Institute of Education (NIE), an institute of Nanyang Technological University, Singapore, and a playwright represented by Playmarket, New Zealand. He has published a number of textbooks. He has co-authored the two-volume series, *Integrating Language and Literature* (2016), and authored *Mastering Visual Literacy* (2018). He is the editor of *Something Old, Something New, Something Borrowed* (2018).

Nirav Pal is a language and literacy trainer and a teacher in a primary school for deaf children in India. He taught English and multiliteracies skills to deaf children and trainee tutors for three years as a member of the Peer-to-Peer Deaf Multiliteracies project.

Agustín Reyes-Torres is an Associate Professor in the Department of Languages and Literature Education at the Universitat de València, Spain. He holds an M.A. in Comparative Literature from the University of Iowa and a PhD in English Philology from the Universitat de València. He has lectured an extensive range of courses and conducted research fellowships at the University of Virginia, Boston College and Middlebury Language Schools. His publications include a significant number of journal articles on second language teaching, postcolonial studies, multicultural literature, and the use of multimodal resources in L2.

Barbara Spinelli is a Senior Lecturer in Italian at Columbia University, USA. She worked as Researcher in Educational Linguistics at the University for Foreigners in Perugia, Italy. She collaborated with the Centre for Language Assessment and Certifications as a teacher trainer and language tester. She was involved in research projects promoted by the European Commission and the Council of Europe as language expert. She has published book chapters as well as articles in international research journals. She is the co-author of the *Profilo della lingua Italiana: Livelli A1, A2, B1, B2 del QCER* (Rizzoli Education).

Joowon Suh (Ed.D., Teachers College, Columbia University) is Senior Lecturer and Director of the Korean Language Program in the Department of East Asian Languages and Cultures at Columbia University, USA. She co-authored KLEAR Integrated Korean Workbook Series and revised its Textbook Series 2nd and 3rd Edition, published by University of Hawaii Press. She served as the 9th President of the American Association of Teachers of Korean (2018–2021). Her research interests include Korean linguistics and language pedagogy, discourse analysis, sociolinguistics, and pragmatics.

Vander Tavares is an Associate Professor in education at Inland Norway University of Applied Sciences, Norway, and holds a PhD in linguistics and applied linguistics from York University, Canada. His research interests include language teacher identity development, critical second language education, internationalization of higher education, and identity in multilingual/multicultural contexts. He is the author of *International Students in Higher Education: Language, Identity, and Experience from a Holistic Perspective* (Rowman & Littlefield), editor of *Social Justice, Decoloniality, and Southern Epistemologies within Language Education* (Routledge).

Jenny Webster is a research associate at the University of Central Lancashire, UK. She focuses on deaf multiliteracies, sign multilingualism, and sign language endangerment, as well as supporting the Research Centre for Migration, Diaspora and Exile. She also edits publications for the European Union of the Deaf, International Telecommunication Union, and UNESCO.

Ulrike Zeshan is a Professor of Sign Language Linguistics at the University of Central Lancashire, UK. Her team has pioneered research in deaf literacy and multiliteracies, the comparative study of sign languages, and the multilingualism of deaf signers. She is a member of the European Academy of Sciences and was awarded an Honorary OBE.

Introduction

Social Justice in L2 Education through Pedagogies of Multiliteracies

Vander Tavares

The conceptual shift from literacy (as singular and fixed) to literacies (as plural and evolving) is often associated with the seminal work of the New London Group (1996; NLG henceforth). Prior to their proposed approach toward a pedagogy of multiliteracies, literacy was predominantly discussed from a perspective of cognitive linguistics, with overwhelming emphasis placed not only on literacy as linguistic comprehension and production but also on these functions within a *single* language: typically, the "national" language (Cope & Kalantzis, 2015). Indeed, the ways in which the focus on a single language—the dominant, "standard," officialized one—displaced or invisibilized multiple literacies within linguistically diverse contexts was one of the main guiding forces behind the NLG's 1996 proposal. The other was the changing nature of texts brought about by new information and multimedia technologies (Cope & Kalantzis, 2023). Viewing both forces as interconnected, the NLG members discussed the need to reconceptualize literacies in a fast-changing world and, accordingly, the pedagogies needed to support the development of *multiple literacies.*

This initial paragraph, albeit brief, helps to broadly delineate possible paths toward social justice in the genesis of NLG's (1996) pedagogy of multiliteracies. Even for highly "monolingual" settings, the recognition of literacy as being constituted by multiple varieties and registers within the same language makes room for the problematization of what groups of speakers are politically included in or excluded from the "standard" language (Tollefson, 2007). Moreover, literacy as reading and writing in the "standard" language has a mutually reaffirming ideological association with monolingualism and monoculturalism, since all three constructs work to protect the boundaries between singularity and plurality. The NLG's proposal for *multiliteracies* also broadened the concept of meaning: how it is made, processed, and conveyed. That is, the NLG scholars posited that we needed to move away from a focus solely on linguistic meaning to incorporate other modes of meaning-making, such as visual, auditory, gestural, and spatial, and thus recognize the multimodal nature of communication. Much of this reconceptualization reflected the changing nature of contemporary workplaces and their reliance on new media and technologies, and the need to prepare learners to effectively function in them.

DOI: 10.4324/9781003438847-1

2 V. Tavares

In addition to the workplace, formal settings of education have become increasingly more diverse when it comes to learners' profiles and backgrounds. Historically, however, institutions of education have "managed its context of human diversity by exclusion (e.g., separate schools), assimilation (e.g., one-size-fits-all, sink-or-swim education), or more recently and aspirationally, practices of inclusion" (Tzirides et al., 2023, p. 260). The NLG (1996) made an explicit acknowledgment of the importance of legitimizing learners' diverse lived experiences through the concept of "lifeworlds"—a combination of individual experiences located within and across the learner's working, personal, and public lives that involve different multimodal and sociocultural resources. Teaching and learning that conceptually depart from pedagogies of multiliteracies have the potential to recognize and value diverse "lifeworlds," thereby strengthening the social justice imperative in education by confronting mechanisms that replicate social inequality through exclusion and the assimilation of difference.

Although not in the context of additional language (L2) education, the 1996 manifesto identified the central mechanism of marginalization of L2 learners. That is, the notion of deficit. The call to reposition learners' multiple identities and languages "as a resource for learning" (NLG, 1996, p. 72) intersects incontestably with ongoing attempts in L2 research and practice that seek to rupture with the assimilation of L2 learners grounded in linguistic discrimination. From an assimilationist perspective, linguistic and cultural diversity are considered forms of interference, deficit, and even failure, whether in schools or the workplace, for those using an L2 (Nguyen & Hajek, 2022; Park, 2016). Of course, since the L2 is part of a learner's identity, linguistic deficit does not operate alone: it is fused with race, ethnicity, and nationality, among other aspects, within a complex hierarchy of power. Speaking to the need to build on diversity, the NLG (1996) argued that pedagogy must be based on "an epistemology of pluralism that provides access [to social power] without people having to erase or leave behind different subjectivities" (p. 72).

A pedagogy of multiliteracies repositions learners from "empty vessels" to meaning makers through a range of representational resources and for different, situated purposes. Paulo Freire (2018) argued that in traditional education, which he referred to as banking education, learners are made passive recipients of decontextualized, fragmented information that is not only completely irrelevant to their social worlds but also fabricated by authoritarian teachers. From a perspective of multiliteracies (NLG, 1996), learners are "active designers—makers—of social futures" (p. 64). Design is, in fact, a key concept in the pedagogy of multiliteracies, both as a noun and a verb. Learners draw on *available designs*—the "grammars" of semiotic systems—to shape new meanings that are in constant communication with one another. The NLG termed this process as *designing*. Designing leads to the *redesigned*: a new, transformed meaning constructed by learners in a particular time and space.

The redesigned is the outcome of an active process through which learners—the designers—"reconstruct and renegotiate their identities" as they intermix cultural resources and identity-related choices in a subjectivity-based process (NLG, 1996, p. 76). The redesigned not only reflects the identity of the designer but also becomes a new meaning-making resource or a new available design. In comparison with a model of L2 education enveloped in the notion of deficit, the concept of design, with its interrelated components, is a new ground on which the learner role is reinvented: one anchored in agency and identity. Hepple et al. (2014) explained that a pedagogy of multiliteracies is an "approach to literacy based on student-led, generative, joint activities supported by strategic assistance, rather than the traditional 'remediation' practices" (p. 227). As a relatively transformative approach to teaching and learning literacies, a pedagogy of multiliteracies supports learner creativity and ownership.

To explain how a pedagogy of multiliteracies unfolds, the NLG (1996) proposed four factors. *Situated practice* is learning that includes learners' present and past experiences as well as an integration of learners' communities and discourses from outside the school. Situated practice takes place within a community of learners, both experts and novices. *Overt instruction* has to do with scaffolding by a teacher or expert member so that learners can identify and capitalize on features of their experiences that matter, especially through the use of metalanguages. *Critical framing,* as the name suggests, is meant to help learners approach and problematize their knowledge from different perspectives where power is present. Lastly, *transformed practice* centers on the application of new understandings from a reflective stance. These factors are offered in the context of an increasingly complex landscape of literacies that requires learners to learn not only multiple literacies but also the how and why of what they learn as they create new meanings and identities.

In 2009, Cope and Kalantzis reflected on multiliteracies in light of a more complex sociopolitical landscape at the time since the first NLG (1996) publication. Their reflections led to numerous "updates" to some of the key tenets of a pedagogy of multiliteracies, thereby demonstrating the need for literacies and pedagogies to remain responsive to contextual changes, particularly technological innovation and cultural diversity. In the domain of modalities of meaning, Cope and Kalantzis (2009) proposed that the linguistic element should be seen as two essentially different modes: oral and written languages. Additionally, the "tactile" was integrated to account for touch, smell, and taste and to therefore bring another facet of bodily meaning-making into the approach. The four instructional components of the NLG's pedagogy of multiliteracies (i.e., *situated practice, overt instruction, critical framing,* and *transformed practice*) were also reformulated as knowledge processes or "things you can do to know" (Kalantzis et al., 2016, p. 74), renamed as *experiencing, conceptualizing, analyzing,* and *applying* (see below), and conceived of as processes within the *Learning by Design* framework (Cope & Kalantzis,

4   V. Tavares

2015). In the same 2009 paper, the increased multimodal nature of everyday human experience was centrally acknowledged.

- Experiencing: the situated process of navigating experiences, both inside as well as outside the classroom, and between the familiar and the unfamiliar, becoming transformative when it moves the learner into new domains of action and meaning;
- Conceptualizing: the knowledge process through which learners develop concepts for and links between their lived and academic experiences;
- Analyzing: the capacity to evaluate something functionally (e.g., cause and effect, evidence, sequence of argumentation) and critically (e.g., identifying biases, hidden meanings, political interests);
- Applying: the practical application of knowledge based on learning, whether to test something in "the real world" or to intervene through creativity and innovation.

A *multiliteracies* framework with its focus on design, multimodality, technology, and diversity has further revealed the complexities, challenges, and opportunities of teaching and learning in the twenty-first century. Multimodality-inspired research has shed light on the ways in which teachers' (unintended) embodied pedagogy—gestures, spaces, movements, and tools—influences the design of learners' experiences by complementing linguistic meaning (Lim, 2021). Research has also identified the affordances of a multiliteracies-based use of technology in improving the experiences of plurilingual learners and teachers across the educational landscape: early childhood education (Kim et al., 2021), secondary school (Cooper et al., 2013), post-secondary (Heng & Yeh, 2022), teacher education (Borsheim et al., 2008) and, notably, language education (see next section). Though the NLG's (1996) proposal originated in the Global North, their ideas have been proliferated in, contextualized by, also compared to perspectives from the Global South (Trigos-Carrillo & Rogers, 2017).

This introductory section discussed some of the main sociocultural concerns and conceptual tenets of a pedagogy of multiliteracies envisioned by the NLG (1996). Almost 30 years have passed since the proposal was first introduced. Since then, practitioners have adapted and adopted NLG's pedagogy of multiliteracies in its entirety or partially, across a range of educational fields, and in combination with other approaches to (literacies) education. Pedagogies of multiliteracies are not static because the world in which teachers and learners live is in constant change. Indeed, in the next section, an overview of the applications and implications of pedagogies of multiliteracies specifically in L2 education is presented. Subsequently, the theme of social justice in L2 education will be explored through the lens of two approaches that have come to the forefront of most recent L2 research and practice: translanguaging and plurilingualism. As it will be demonstrated, both approaches align with some of the ethical goals of pedagogies of multiliteracies in terms of strengthening L2 learner identity and agency through linguistic and cultural inclusion. This introductory chapter is concluded with a review of agency and identity, and of the organization of this volume.

From 1996 to the Present: A Panoramic View of Pedagogies of Multiliteracies within L2 Education

In L2 education, multiliteracies have often been discussed through classroom-based investigations, typically in terms of student-led project design. This body of research has not only been conceptually contextualized through the seminal and updated formulations but also contributed to their fine-tuning over the years. Generally speaking, these studies have punctuated the affordances of pedagogies of multiliteracies in relation to L2 students' (simultaneous) literacy and language development in ways that reflect learner ownership, agency, and equally important, learner identity, in activities in the L2 classroom linked to experiences from outside. For instance, language and literacy have been developed with English language learners through videos (Yeh, 2018), drama (Ntelioglou, 2012), digital multimodal texts (Chen, 2020; Kustini, 2019; Zhang & Yu, 2022), graphic stories (Danzak, 2011), clay figures and movie-making (Hepple et al., 2014), podcasts (Toohey et al., 2012), and art museums (Arshavskaya, 2021), though this is not a comprehensive account.

A diversity of modes, modalities, and literacies represent only one instructional facet of pedagogies of multiliteracies in L2 education. Along with those, pedagogies of multiliteracies have also been implemented within a diverse range of language instruction contexts (Kumagai et al., 2015). These include, but are not limited to, Chinese (Kim & Xing, 2019; Wang & Li, 2022), Japanese (Kumagai & Iwasaki, 2015), German (Warren & Winkler, 2016), Italian (Spinelli, 2015), Spanish (Zapata, 2023), and French (Michelson & Dupuy, 2014). A clear feature of studies based on pedagogies of multiliteracies is that there is never only one modality, resource, or literacy in place: they are always plural and interweaved in one another. Indeed, research on the potential and importance of multiliteracies reveals its role in simultaneously developing critical, intercultural, linguistic, and technological competence (Paesani & Menke, 2023).

Pedagogies of multiliteracies in L2 education have been implemented with a diverse range of L2 learner groups. These have included refugee, heritage, local and transnational, older adult, college and university students, teacher students, and teacher educators, to cite a few, across numerous languages (see Lotherington & Jenson, 2011, for an overview). Noteworthy here are not only the distinct linguistic and literacy needs of each L2 learner group but also their lived experiences that epistemologically impact meaning-making and knowledge co-construction (Anstey & Bull, 2018). Diversity has, in fact, become a guiding principle in contemporary education. However, pedagogies of multiliteracies explicitly attempt to invite and integrate diversity into L2 education from an equity perspective that originates in the learner. Burke and Hardware (2015) stressed that a pedagogy of multiliteracies "offers

6   *V. Tavares*

minority students more points of reference since it uses their lifeworlds as teaching resources considerably more than traditional forms" (p. 146). The same authors go further in saying that a pedagogy of multiliteracies *honors* L2 learners' cultural and linguistic diversities.

Recent research has also demonstrated the potential of pedagogies of multiliteracies to confront language ideologies in L2 education. Classroom-based studies have illuminated the ways in which tenets of pedagogies of multiliteracies, such as multimodality in meaning-making, contribute to validating the already-existing multi-semiotic practices of L2 teachers and learners, thereby promoting a sense of empowerment for those minoritized by exclusive, ideology-inspired language policies (e.g., Chen & Tsou, 2021; Lim, 2022). Lin et al. (2021) argued that, in its current conception, pedagogies of multiliteracies contribute meaningfully to "destabilizing, crossing and ultimately deconstructing various boundaries that are sociohistorically constructed" (p. 16). From an L2 education perspective, the ongoing developments in pedagogies of multiliteracies help synchronize it with those stemming from plurilingual and translingual approaches. In a move toward equity, these approaches emphasize semiotic and linguistic hybridity rather than parallelisms (Lin et al., 2021).

Pedagogies of multiliteracies have driven enormous theoretical, methodological, and practical progress in L2 education. Nevertheless, scholars continue to identify challenges for their systematization so that they may become the "new" pedagogical foundation, rather than often an individual choice by the teacher, in L2 education (Paesani & Allen, 2020). These challenges include comprehensive training of L2 teachers, which "requires models of professional development that emphasize the long-term development of conceptual knowledge and strategies rather than one-off training opportunities," reconceptualizing L2 teaching materials and textbooks, which tend to have a focus on grammar through traditional modes (e.g., text and imagery), in addition to better dialogue between stakeholders of L2 education (Warner & Dupuy, 2018, p. 122). Zapata (2022) has identified major conceptual interconnections between a pedagogy of multiliteracies and other pedagogical frameworks. However, despite the overlap, such frameworks still need better integration by educational organizations, teacher groups, and academic institutions.

Reconceptualizing L2 Education through Social Justice-Oriented Pedagogies

Rethinking L2 education from and for social justice demands continuous reflection and action in all domains: teaching, learning, and research. To begin with, working toward equity requires that we revisit conventional concepts and labels used in L2 education. For instance, scholars have underscored both the subtle and explicit ways in which the categorization of "nonnative speaker" has been embedded in notions of deficit, signaling gap, and partiality compared

Social Justice in L2 Education   7

to an imagined "native" speaker who is supposedly not only linguistically but also intellectually superior (Tavares, 2021). The "native" speaker, as is the case with English and many other "modern" European languages, has also been constructed as a White speaker of the language, therefore delegitimizing racialized speakers within the "mainstream" (Kubota & Lin, 2006; Tavares, 2022). Furthermore, the dichotomy of native/nonnative itself is problematic in the sense that it misrepresents the linguistic proficiency and identity of *all* speakers (Ellis, 2016; Faez, 2011).

These critical perspectives have contributed powerfully to improving L2 education scholarship. Yet, the use of the "native" and "nonnative" labels is still widespread, perpetuating biases rooted in native-speakerism and monolingualism. These biases have also permeated into other areas of L2 education, such as traditional bilingual education and research, through the assumption that languages and language practices exist as two completely separate systems in the speaker (Franceschini, 2011; García, 2017). In this volume, "L2" is used as *additional language* within the "multilingual turn," where the sequence of acquisition is not taken to evoke correlation with fluency or the speaker's affective "relationships" with a language. Among other aims, the "multilingual turn" questions "what counts as (legitimate) language and as (legitimate) practices" and promotes "heteroglossic practices that value students' repertoires and experiences" (Melo-Pfeifer, 2018, p. 208).

The most significant development within the "multilingual turn" concerns the L2 learner and their lived experiences of language. In harmony with such a conceptual change, multilingualism at the individual level is better represented through the perspective of plurilingualism, which holistically integrates the varied linguistic and cultural knowledges of learners and positions these as assets for language teaching and learning, thereby validating what L2 learners already know (Chen et al., 2022). In doing so, the L2 classroom is reconciled as an integral part of the social reality of learners, rather than a discrete educational space wherein linguistic and cultural interaction is curtailed. Language proficiency is in the learner's linguistic-cultural repertoire—a hybrid "place"—which they draw from to navigate different life experiences. Plurilingualism recognizes that language proficiency is situated, relative, and variable.

Translanguaging has also transformed the landscape of L2 education as a radically inclusive pedagogical approach. Otheguy et al. (2015) defined this concept as "the deployment of a speaker's full linguistic repertoire without regard to watchful adherence to the socially and politically defined boundaries of named languages" (p. 281). Conceptually, translanguaging accounts "for the complex, semiotic language practices and pedagogies of bi-/multi-lingual communities who transcend between and beyond the systems that make up their complete linguistic repertoires" (Prada & Turnbull, 2018, p. 13). Pedagogical perspectives based on translanguaging have major implications for L2 education, including the ways in which languages are (socially) defined, taught, and learned. By extension, a learner's identity is understood more inclusively

8   *V. Tavares*

as translanguaging works to empower learners by de-foreignizing their (trans)
lingual, community-, and home-based practices (García & Wei, 2014).

Other issues related to promoting educational equity in L2 education are
broader and therefore affect all forms of education and schooling. Elitism,
linguicism, racism, sexism, and other forms of discrimination, unequal access,
and bias are complex and operate at different levels of interaction between
individuals, institutions, and cultures. Education informed by social justice is
thus urgently necessary and "requires an examination of systems of power and
oppression combined with a prolonged emphasis on social change and student
agency in and outside of the classroom" (Hackman, 2005, p. 104). This kind
of engagement is essential also for a critical L2 education in which L2 learners
of a minoritized background are often assigned linguistically and politically
inferiorized positions based on their diverse backgrounds and life experiences
that differ from the "mainstream." Kayi-Aydar (2022) has argued that social
justice can only be achieved when "diverse (cultural) identities are recognized,
accepted, and appreciated" (p. 150). This volume makes a contribution toward
this goal as social justice also characterizes a pillar of multiliteracies education.

Guiding Concepts: Agency and Identity

Agency is a construct that is interdisciplinary in nature and typically examined in conjunction with something else, such as identity or motivation, in
L2 education. Much theorization on agency in more recent L2 education
research has embraced a sociocultural perspective in which the sociocultural
environment contextualizes and mediates, in complex but relativized ways, a
learner's enactment of agency (Kalaja et al., 2016). In this sense, it is possible
to characterize agency as a kind of social act or practice, whether linguistic
or behavioral, that produces an observable effect. Mercer (2012) has drawn
attention to the need to consider variance within and across individuals in
addition to the sociocultural context in conceptualizations of learner agency.
She maintains that "whilst an individual's capacity to act is widely accepted as
being socioculturally, contextually and interpersonally mediated, it also needs
to be understood in terms of a person's physical, cognitive, affective, and mo-
tivational capacities to act" (p. 42). These positions exemplify different theoretical facets of agency, whose relevance will oscillate depending on the object
of study.

In this volume, these dimensions are appreciated, but not exclusively, in
light of the diversity of settings, languages, learners, and concerns in the investigations. Agency may be therefore best understood in relation to contextualized forms of empowerment—as the desire and "capability of individual
human beings to make choices and act on these choices in a way that *makes a
difference in their lives*" (Martin, 2004, p. 135, emphasis added). When considering agency, one particular factor—whether of the individual or of the
context—may be much more pertinent and consequential in a given setting
than another as the focus is on the interplay between agency and change for

the individual L2 learner. However, although Martin's (2004) definition is quoted in a number of papers, it is critical to add *the other* in such a definition. Thus, agency is not acting in a way that makes a difference only in one's life but also in the lives of others. This is especially true for those learners who hold more power and are therefore able to influence the lives of others. The *desire* to act and to make change is also important to note as agency departs from some kind of emotion (Benesch, 2018).

In a similar vein to agency, identity has been one of the most theorized constructs in qualitative research in L2 education and applied linguistics since the early 2000s. This trend is informed by theoretical, conceptual, and methodological approaches that break from formative perspectives on the construct, which have been often defined or at least significantly influenced by models in psychology and psycholinguistics. Stimulated first by the "social turn" in second language acquisition research (Block, 2003), scholarly discussions on identity continue to flourish, evolve, and unveil important areas that were previously left unattended due to the predominance of more widely accepted prescriptive and decontextualized positions. The "social turn" foregrounds the sociocultural, historical, and political facets of language use, and consequently, of L2 teaching and learning, in a field whose foundation constructed L2 acquisition overwhelmingly as individual and cognitive processes (Atkinson, 2011; Lantolf, 2000), positioning the L2 learner as almost entirely responsible for their own linguistic development.

Post-structuralist perspectives have drawn attention to the complexities of identity as a construct by examining its relationship to language. Norton (2010), for instance, spoke of the inextricability of language and identity by arguing that "it is through language that a person negotiates a sense of self within and across a range of sites at different points in time" (pp. 350–351). Centering on the politics of language, she posits that "it is through language that a person gains access to – or is denied access to – powerful social networks that give learners the opportunity to speak" (pp. 350–351). At the core of such a position is identity construction as a dynamic, situated, and negotiated practice. Identity is therefore maintained, undone, and redone by the self and others in social interaction (Pavlenko & Blackledge, 2004). From a post-structuralist point of view, identity is neither fixed nor unitary but rather characterized by multiple sociological units and affiliations along with individual traits. Identity positions not only change over time but also intersect. As such, identity is a site of both congruence and tension for the individual (Eslamdoost et al., 2020; Kinginger, 2013; Melo-Pfeifer & Tavares, forthcoming). Post-structuralist perspectives are plural and function as a conceptual magnifying glass.

Anstey and Bull (2018) emphasized that experiences both in and outside schools are intertwined in the development of one's literacy identity. These experiences contribute to the kinds of resources about literacy and literate practices L2 learners bring into the classroom. Literacy identity includes "social and cultural resources, technological experiences, all previous life experiences as well specific literacy knowledge" experienced by the L2 learner (Anstey & Bull, 2018, p. 67). To make meaning and interpret new knowledge, L2 learners draw on their literacy identities; however, they may not be aware of them or be encouraged to use them strategically. In many L2 education contexts, learners' life experiences from outside the school have been unacknowledged or even devalued for they "deviate" from those of the dominant school culture. Of major concern here is discrimination in the form of language policy wherein the use of other languages by L2 learners has been and continues to be banned or penalized (Macedo & Bartolomé, 2014). An L2 is, on this account, deemed a deficit, rather than an asset within the learner's repertoire of resources for L2 literacy development.

Affirming L2 learner identity rests on visualizing learners holistically and taking into account the sociopolitical contexts in which learners' experiences unfold. This is the position espoused in this volume. Many of the chapters in this volume advance investigations within and reflections on the L2 classroom, where representations of identity are co-constructed in social interaction through the implementation of pedagogies of multiliteracies. Multimodal texts, understood broadly, for instance, offer learners opportunities to express themselves and (re)define their identities in their own ways. As Danzak (2011) reminds us by referencing a multimodal narrative study with immigrant teens in the English language learning classroom, an L2 learning experience that provides the adequate resources, combined with individual support and a welcoming learning environment, "affords a voice to students who are frequently silenced in the traditional, monolingual, English-speaking classroom" (p. 196). L2 learning is meaningful when learners' (literacy) identities are not only involved but also further developed in the process, though it is important to also scaffold such processes outside and beyond the use of texts, sequences, and structures (Leander & Boldt, 2013).

This Volume: Organization and Main Themes

This volume broadens our understanding of the potential of pedagogies of multiliteracies in L2 education by exploring the ways in which they can be incorporated into L2 instructional contexts to promote and achieve situated forms of social justice, especially for minoritized L2 learners. It does so by focusing on practices and reflections that seek to develop and strengthen L2 learner identity and agency within and outside formal educational contexts. The ensuing contributions illustrate the design and implementation of pedagogies of multiliteracies through a diverse range of modalities and settings: linguistic landscapes, community engagement, graphic novels, picturebooks, photovoice, text, and imagery. The main goal of this volume is to acknowledge, enact, and build upon the responsibility of L2 educators to develop pedagogies of multiliteracies that reflect the life experiences, identities, and needs of minoritized L2 individuals in the curriculum in order to realize the social justice aim of L2 education.

Social Justice in L2 Education 11

In Chapter 1, Toby Loewenstein and Robin L. Danzak present a qualitative study that utilized photovoice as a multiliteracies approach to empower multilingual students aged 11–14 with communication disorders. Loewenstein and Danzak worked with the students from grades 5 to 9 to create and discuss images and captions that represented their experiences with communication and speech-language therapy (SLT). To achieve photovoice's aim of enacting change, the participants also created a collective video of their photographs to share with professionals and students in the field of SLT. Study outcomes revealed the participants' unique perspectives on communication challenges, a growth mindset to SLT, and a desire to generalize skills. Responses to the video suggested that viewers were impacted to take action by incorporating multiliteracies approaches in their professional practice. The authors discuss implications around the use of photovoice as a multiliteracies teaching strategy and offer concrete suggestions for educators and professionals.

In Chapter 2, Ken Mizusawa and Tamas Kiss examine how secondary school students in India, Nepal, Malaysia, and Indonesia were guided in the design of their own personally relevant ELT materials via a regional project that leveraged on learners' out-of-school literacies and cultural capital through a focus on multiliteracies. The authors report that the participants' communication practices were constrained by conventional approaches to material design and, when given the opportunity, they were able to communicate their ideas in symbolically rich ways that empowered them and granted them agency. Through their findings, Mizusawa and Kiss problematize how standardized ELT materials can lead to social and cultural inequity, as they often promote a Western-centric, monomodal idea of English and fail to account for the global proliferation of English and its dynamic use in various technology-mediated communication settings.

In Chapter 3, Barbara Spinelli considers how the increasing complexity of multilingual and multicultural language learning communities has refocused language education toward issues of identity and subjectivities. Spinelli describes how diverse learners in a multilingual post-secondary Italian language classroom have the capacity to actively position themselves and redesign the perception of their multilingual identity through a pedagogical awareness-raising journey starting from a digital oral pluri-biography shared in the classroom with their peers. The results of this case study show how this recursive reflective process can facilitate learners' dynamic positioning and identify what variables can affect it, such as family, language policy, social status, social space, different migration experiences, and self-reflection practices. Additionally, the findings suggest that the re-negotiation of learners' multilingual identities can challenge predetermined social categorizations and develop social, multiple, and critical literacies.

In Chapter 4, Susan M. Holloway uses a social justice lens to explore the ways in which L2 learners are better able to succeed in learning a new language when they feel emotionally and socially supported through literacy practices shaped by the principles articulated within a pedagogy of multiliteracies.

12   V. Tavares

Holloway draws upon Kalantzis and Cope's conceptualization of agency, participation, and design to contribute to a transpositional grammar of meaning-making. In this study, high schools and government language learning councils, museums, art galleries, and other community-based organizations are included as sites to expand thinking about how multiliteracies and multimodality can be adopted to significantly increase L2 learners' abilities to engage in language learning. The participants include teachers, students, adult educators, and learners as well as policy makers and administrators. Through this research, Holloway investigates ways in which L2 learners are best supported to succeed through multiliteracies pedagogies.

In Chapter 5, Yuri Kumagai introduces a virtual linguistic landscape project within a second-year Japanese language course at a US liberal arts college. The project aims at providing students with an experience to analyze features such as what languages and other modes are used on public signs, inclusion/exclusion, power relationship between different languages/people, and what suggestions can be made to transform signs to better serve a greater population. Students explored the public signage visible from the streets of a Japanese city using Google Street View. They then collected signs and engaged in multiple layers of analyses inspired by the four knowledge processes of *Learning by Design* and the four resource models of critical literacy. Based on the analysis of students' multimodal essays on WordPress and answers to post-project questionnaires and interviews, Kumagai demonstrates that the project nurtured students' multiliteracies and encouraged them to become critical participants in their own multilingual, multimodal textual world.

In Chapter 6, Mónica Lourenço and Sílvia Melo-Pfeifer report on the results of a multiple case study that aimed to investigate how L2 learners (re)build their own identity and agency through the exploration of linguistic landscapes in two lower secondary school settings in Germany. Data were collected in the context of student practicum by two pre-service teachers of Spanish as an L2. In both cases, data included audio recordings of classroom interactions, students' drawings of their linguistic biographies and their ideal linguistic landscapes, and photographs they took of the linguistic landscape. Results suggest that that students were able to (re)discover and accept their and others' plurilingual repertoires and multilingual identities, to unveil situations of linguistic (in)equity as well as possibilities to exert their agency. Lourenço and Melo-Pfeifer problematize the notion of student agency and define "agency-oriented pedagogy" around the principles of action-research, participation, positionality, and criticality.

In Chapter 7, Jenny Webster, Ulrike Zeshan, Nirav Pal, and Deepu Manavalamamuni examine data provided by two deaf master trainers and a group of deaf trainee tutors in India who were learning about "English Grammar Games" (EGGs). A common approach for teaching English to deaf signers is to explain the "rules" of English in sign language. EGGs may facilitate this with a linguistic rationale that also builds L2 learner agency. Each game starts with a "real-life English" text, and players must find parts of it that match abstract grammatical structures given as prompts. The authors evaluate the schedules, videos, reports, and feedback from this training. They find that using EGGs enables deaf instructors without any background in English language or TESOL to teach their deaf peers because the materials and the game choreography provide an easy access point where formal knowledge of grammar is not needed. This points to the potential for democratization of teaching and learning in this community through using EGGs and multiliteracies.

In Chapter 8, Dolores Miralles-Alberola, Margarida Castellano Sanz, and Agustín Reyes-Torres work with pedagogies conceptually anchored in multiliteracies to enhance students' understanding of social justice from a feminist perspective. To this end, multicultural coming-of-age stories in the form of graphic novels offer teachers key elements to engage students in readings that not only strengthen their intercultural awareness but also facilitate reflection on social justice in its recognitive, redistributive, and representative dimensions. By providing a *Learning by Design* reading unit based on the coming-of-age graphic novels *We're All Just Fine* (2023) by Ana Penyas, *The Waiting* (2021) by Keum Suk, and *A Girl Called Echo* (2017) by Katherena Vermette, the authors demonstrate the ways in which L2 students can discuss, think, and write critically over a variety of texts dealing with social issues that still affect women from different countries.

In Chapter 9, Vander Tavares reflects on curricular changes to the prevailing ideological configuration of a Portuguese as a foreign language course taught by the author at an institution of higher education in a major Canadian city. In the context of Portuguese as an international language, patterns of deficit have contributed to inferiorizing or invisibilizing certain groups of Portuguese language speakers, especially those from the African continent. Drawing on critical literacy and critical awareness, Tavares proposes disruptions and innovations meant to evoke experiences of becoming critically literate about such injustices for learners of Portuguese as an L2, which should involve possibilities to not only critically examine texts but to also take action in response to such engagements. This chapter underscores potential links between pedagogies of multiliteracies and social justice for minoritized groups in L2 education in the context of Portuguese as a foreign language.

In Chapter 10, Joowon Suh discusses critical literacy in connection with gender, class, race, ethnicity, and identity by reflecting on classroom practices in both Korean as a foreign language and as a second language settings within higher education. With the increasing awareness of diversity and multiculturalism found in Korean language learners, critical literacies in Korean language education have started to gain long overdue attention, slowly but steadily. Critical literacy, one of the two main axes of the multiliteracies pedagogy (the other being multimodality), emphasizes differing voices and stances represented in texts and challenging social issues addressed in the language classroom. In this chapter, the author explores how the notion and practice of critical literacy can be further developed and refined by implementing more controversial and contentious social justice-related issues to enact a multiliteracies pedagogy in Korean language education.

14 *V. Tavares*

This volume invites researchers, language teachers, teacher educators, curriculum designers, and graduate students in L2 education around the world to rethink and enhance pedagogy from a social justice perspective that is based on pedagogies of multiliteracies. The hope is that this volume can help inspire all involved in L2 education to work specifically toward empowering and strengthening L2 learner agency and identity through a creative and critical range of pedagogical possibilities, as the chapters in this volume so richly demonstrate.

References

Anstey, M., & Bull, G. (2018). *Foundations of multiliteracies: Reading, writing and talking in the 21st century*. Routledge.

Arshavskaya, E. (2021). Art museums as translanguaging spaces: ESL students, multimodality, and identities. *TESOL Journal, 13*(2). https://doi.org/10.1002/tesj.643

Atkinson, D. (Ed.) (2011). *Alternative approaches to second language acquisition*. Routledge.

Benesch, S. (2018). Emotions as agency: Feeling rules, emotion labor, and English language teachers' decision-making. *System, 79*, 60–69.

Block, D. (2003). *The social turn in second language acquisition*. Georgetown University Press.

Borsheim, C., Merritt, K., & Reed, D. (2008). Beyond technology for technology's sake: Advancing multiliteracies in the twenty-first century. *The Clearing House: A Journal of Educational Strategies, Issues and Ideas, 82*(2), 87–90.

Burke, A., & Hardware, S. (2015). Honouring ESL students' lived experiences in school learning with multiliteracies pedagogy. *Language, Culture and Curriculum, 28*(2), 143–157.

Chen, C. W. (2020). Composing print essays versus composing across modes: Students' multimodal choices and overall preferences. *Literacy, 55*(11), 25–38.

Chen, L., Karas, M., Shalizar, M., & Piccardo, E. (2022). From "promising controversies" to negotiated practices: A research synthesis of plurilingual pedagogy in global contexts. *TESL Canada Journal, 38*(2), 1–35.

Chen, F., & Tsou, W. (2021). Empowering local bilingual teachers through extending the pedagogy of multiliteracies in Taiwan's primary education. *OLBI Journal, 11*, 79–103.

Cooper, N., Lockyer, L., & Brown, I. (2013). Developing multiliteracies in a technology-mediated environment. *Educational Media International, 50*(2), 93–107.

Cope, B., & Kalantzis, M. (2009). "Multiliteracies": New literacies, new learning. *Pedagogies: An International Journal, 4*, 164–195.

Cope, B., & Kalantzis, M. (2015). The things you do to know: An introduction to the pedagogy of multiliteracies. In B. Cope & M. Kalantzis (Eds.), *A pedagogy of multiliteracies: Learning by design* (pp. 1–36). Palgrave Macmillan.

Cope, B., & Kalantzis, M. (2023). Towards education justice: The multiliteracies project revisited. In G. C. Zapata, M. Kalantzis, & Bill Cope (Eds.), *Towards education justice: Literacy, multiliteracies, and the design of social futures*. Routledge.

Danzak, R. L. (2011). Defining identities through multiliteracies: EL teens narrate their immigration experiences as graphic stories. *Journal of Adolescent & Adult Literacy, 55*(3), 187–196.

Ellis, E. M. (2016). "I may be a native speaker but I'm not monolingual": Reimagining all teachers' linguistic identities in TESOL. *TESOL Quarterly, 50*(3), 597–630.

Eslamdoost, S., King, K. A., & Tajeddin, Z. (2020). Professional identity conflict and (re)construction among English teachers in Iran. *Journal of Language, Identity & Education, 19*(5), 327–341.

Faez, F. (2011). Are you a native speaker of English? Moving beyond a simplistic dichotomy. *Critical Inquiry in Language Studies, 8*(4), 378–399.

Franceschini, R. (2011). Multilingualism and multicompetence: A conceptual view. *The Modern Language Journal, 95*, 344–355.

Freire, P. (2018). The banking concept of education. In E. B. Hilty (Ed.), *Thinking about schools* (pp. 117–127). Routledge.

García, O. (2017). Bilingual education. In F. Coulmas (Ed.), *The handbook of sociolinguistics* (pp. 405–420). Wiley-Blackwell.

García, O., & Wei, L. (2014). *Translanguaging: Language, bilingualism and education*. Palgrave Macmillan.

Hackman, H. W. (2005). Five essential components for social justice education. *Equity & Excellence in Education, 38*(2), 103–109.

Heng, L., & Yeh, H. C. (2022). Interweaving local cultural knowledge with global competencies in one higher education course: An internationalisation perspective. *Language, Culture and Curriculum, 35*(2), 151–166.

Hepple, E., Sockhill, M., Tan, A., & Alford, J. (2014). Multiliteracies pedagogy: Creating claymations with adolescent, post-beginner English language learners. *Journal of Adolescent & Adult Literacy, 58*(3), 219–229.

Kalaja, P., Barcelos, A. M. F., Aro, M., & Ruohotie-Lyhty, M. (2016). *Beliefs, agency and identity in foreign language learning and teaching*. Springer.

Kalantzis, M., Cope, B., Chan, E., & Dalley-Trim, L. (2016). *Literacies*. Cambridge University Press.

Kayi-Aydar, H. (2022). Multicultural social justice education through the lens of positioning: English Language learners in K-12 contexts. In M. Mantero, J. L. Watzke, & P. C. Miller (Eds.), *Language and social justice* (pp. 147–160). Information Age Publishing.

Kim, M. S., Meng, X., & Kim, M. (2021). Technology-enhanced multiliteracies teaching towards a culturally responsive curriculum: A multiliteracies approach to ECE. *Interactive Learning Environments*, 1–13. https://doi.org/10.1080/10494820.2020.1870503

Kim, M. S., & Xing, X. (2019). Appropriation of affordances of multiliteracies for Chinese literacy teaching in Canada. *Research and Practice in Technology Enhanced Learning, 14*(1), 1–14.

Kinginger, C. (2013). Identity and language learning in study abroad. *Foreign Language Annals, 46*(3), 339–358.

Kubota, R., & Lin, A. (2006). Race and TESOL: Introduction to concepts and theories. *TESOL Quarterly, 40*(3), 471–493.

Kumagai, Y., & Iwasaki, N. (2015). Reading words to read worlds: A genre-based critical multiliteracies curriculum in intermediate/advanced Japanese language education. In Y. Kumagai, A. López-Sánchez, & S. Wu (Eds.), *Multiliteracies in world language education* (pp. 109–131). Routledge.

Kumagai, Y., López-Sánchez, A., & Wu, S. (Eds.). (2015). *Multiliteracies in world language education*. Routledge.

Kustini, S. (2019). Looking at learner engagement in a digital multimodal-based instruction. In S. Madya et al. (Eds.), *English linguistics, literature, and language teaching in a changing era* (pp. 276–282). Routledge.

Lantolf, J. (Ed.). (2000). *Sociocultural theory and second language learning*. Oxford University Press.

Leander, K., & Boldt, G. (2013). Rereading "A pedagogy of multiliteracies" bodies, texts, and emergence. *Journal of Literacy Research, 45*(1), 22–46.

Lim, F. V. (2021). *Designing learning with embodied teaching: Perspectives from multimodality*. Routledge.

Lim, F. V. (2022). Thinking and talking about digital news in the Singapore secondary English classroom: A pilot study. *English Teaching & Learning*, 1–20. https://doi.org/10.1007/s42321-022-00134-5

Lin, A. M., Sohn, B. G., Geneviève, B., Keiko, T., & Levasseur, C. (2021). Introduction: Redesigning the pedagogy of multiliteracies II for acting in a society with uncertainties. *OLBI Journal, 11*, 15–27.

Lotherington, H., & Jenson, J. (2011). Teaching multimodal and digital literacy in L2 settings: New literacies, new basics, new pedagogies. *Annual Review of Applied Linguistics, 31*, 226–246.

Macedo, D., & Bartolomé, L. I. (2014). Multiculturalism permitted in English only. *International Multilingual Research Journal, 8*(1), 24–37.

Martin, J. (2004). Self-regulated learning, social cognitive theory, and agency. *Educational Psychologist, 39*(2), 135–145.

Melo-Pfeifer, S. (2018). The multilingual turn in foreign language education. In A. Bonnet, & P. Siemund (Eds.), *Foreign language education in multilingual classrooms* (pp. 191–212). John Benjamins.

Melo-Pfeifer, S., & Tavares, V. (Eds.). (forthcoming). *Language teacher identity: Confronting ideologies of language, race and ethnicity*. Wiley-Blackwell.

Mercer, S. (2012). The complexity of learner agency. *Apples-Journal of Applied Language Studies, 6*(2), 41–59.

Michelson, K., & Dupuy, B. (2014). Multi-storied lives: Global simulation as an approach to developing multiliteracies in an intermediate French course. *L2 Journal, 6*(1), 21–49.

New London Group (NLG) (1996). A pedagogy of multiliteracies: Designing social futures. *Harvard Educational Review, 66*, 60–92.

Nguyen, T. T. T., & Hajek, J. (2022). Making the case for linguicism: Revisiting theoretical concepts and terminologies in linguistic discrimination research. *International Journal of the Sociology of Language, 2022*(275), 187–220.

Norton, B. (2010). Language and identity. In N. Hornberger & S. K. MacKay (Eds.), *Sociolinguistics and language education* (pp. 349–369). Multilingual Matters.

Ntelioglou, M. B. Y. (2012). *Drama pedagogies, multiliteracies and embodied learning: Urban teachers and linguistically diverse students make meaning* (Doctoral dissertation). Ontario Institute for Studies in Education/University of Toronto, Toronto.

Otheguy, R., García, O., & Reid, W. (2015). Clarifying translanguaging and deconstructing named languages: A perspective from linguistics. *Applied Linguistics Review, 6*(3), 281–307.

Paesani, K., & Allen, H. W. (2020). Teacher development and multiliteracies pedagogy: Challenges and opportunities for postsecondary language programs. *Second Language Research & Practice, 1*(1), 124–138.

Paesani, K., & Menke, M. (2023). *Literacies in language education: A guide for teachers and teacher educators*. Georgetown University Press.

Park, M. Y. (2016). Resisting linguistic and ethnic marginalization: Voices of Southeast Asian marriage-migrant women in Korea. *Language and Intercultural Communication, 17*(2), 118–134.

Pavlenko, A., & Blackledge, A. (Eds.). (2004). *Negotiation of identities in multilingual contexts*. Multilingual Matters.

Prada, J., & Turnbull, B. (2018). The role of translanguaging in the multilingual turn: Driving philosophical and conceptual renewal in language education. *EuroAmerican Journal of Applied Linguistics and Languages, 5*(2), 8–23.

Spinelli, B. (2015). Empowering students in the Italian classroom to learn vocabulary through a multiliteracies framework. In Y. Kumagai, A. López-Sánchez, & Wu (Eds.), *Multiliteracies in world language education* (pp. 182–208). Routledge.

Tavares, V. (2021). *International students in higher education: Language, identity, and experience from a holistic perspective*. Lexington Books.

Tavares, V. (2022). Neoliberalism, native-speakerism and the displacement of international students' languages and cultures. *Journal of Multilingual and Multicultural Development*, 1–14.

Tollefson, J. W. (2007). Ideology, language varieties, and ELT. In J. Cummins & C. Davidson (Eds.), *International handbook of English language teaching* (pp. 25–36). Springer.

Toohey, K., Dagenais, D., & Schulze, E. (2012). Second language learners making videos in three contexts. *Language and Literacy, 14*(2), 75–96.

Trigos-Carrillo, L., & Rogers, R. (2017). Latin American influences on multiliteracies: From epistemological diversity to cognitive justice. *Literacy Research: Theory, Method, and Practice, 66*(1), 373–388.

Tzirides, A., Cope, B., & Kalantzis, M. (2023). Contemporary contexts for learning: An overview, *International Encyclopedia of Education, 6*, 258–266, https://doi.org/10.1016/B978-0-12-818630-5.14034-5

Wang, D., & Li, D. (2022). Exploring multiliteracies and multimodal pedagogies in Chinese language teaching: A Teacher's one-year action learning circle. *International Journal of Computer-Assisted Language Learning and Teaching (IJCALLT), 12*(1), 1–19.

Warner, C., & Dupuy, B. (2018). Moving toward multiliteracies in foreign language teaching: Past and present perspectives… and beyond. *Foreign Language Annals, 51*(1), 116–128.

Warren, M., & Winkler, C. (2016). Developing multiliteracies through genre in the beginner German classroom. In Y. Kumagai, A. López-Sánchez, & Wu (Eds.), *Multiliteracies in world language education* (pp. 29–57). Routledge.

Yeh, H. C. (2018). Exploring the perceived benefits of the process of multimodal video making in developing multiliteracies. *Language, Learning and Technology, 22*(2), 28–37.

Zapata, G. (2022). *Learning by design and second language teaching: Theory, research, and practice*. Routledge.

Zapata, G. (2023). Self-discovery and healing in Nepantla: Multimodality and learning by design in a mixed Spanish University classroom. *The International Journal of Pedagogy and Curriculum, 30*(1), 17–35.

Zhang, E. D., & Yu, S. (2022). Implementing digital multimodal composing in L2 writing instruction: A focus on developing L2 student writers. *Innovation in Language Learning and Teaching*, 1–9.

Part I

Exploring Agency and Identity Development in Student-Led Projects

1 Photovoice

A Multiliteracies Approach to Facilitate Identity Reflection and Self-Advocacy for Multilingual Students with Communication Disorders

Toby Loewenstein and Robin Danzak

Introduction

In this chapter, we introduce photovoice as a multiliteracies approach to engage multilingual[1] students with communication disorders to reflect on their experiences, self-advocate, and share their perspectives with educational professionals. Photovoice is a participatory action research method whereby participants take photographs that represent their life experiences, elaborating with written or oral descriptions (Wang, 1999). It has been used as a research method to understand the needs and assets of diverse groups and communities, empower marginalized groups to represent their viewpoints, and advocate for change by sharing photographs and stories with policy makers and advocates (Wang & Burris, 1994).

Photovoice has been linked to social justice frameworks, particularly Paulo Freire's critical pedagogy and feminist theory, as well as documentary photography (Wang & Burris, 1994). However, photovoice also reflects a multiliteracies lens, especially when used as a pedagogical tool. For example, Rajendram et al. (2022) presented rich examples of how photovoice can be used to engage multilingual learners through a translanguaging (i.e., multilingual students' strategic use of more than one language to learn and engage with content) and multiliteracies approach. These authors highlighted photovoice as a tool for storytelling and critical dialogue that "draws on linguistic, visual, and audio modes by utilizing technology to facilitate the communication of home languages" (p. 13), thus promoting multilingualism and affirming students' identities.

Indeed, the use of photographs for self-expression has been found to be a positive and empowering experience for participants (James et al., 2015; Ripat et al., 2020) and can lead to the development of skills such as self-awareness, social consciousness, goal setting, problem-solving, decision-making, reflecting, self-advocating, critical thinking, and critical analysis (Blackman & Fairey, 2007; Danzak, 2015). A core feature of photovoice is its purpose as a tool for self-reflection and self-advocacy. Once students better understand themselves and their needs, they can advocate for change by sharing photographs and stories with policy makers and advocates (McBrien & Day, 2012; Palibroda et al., 2009;

DOI: 10.4324/9781003438847-3

22   *T. Loewenstein and R. Danzak*

Ripat et al., 2020; Strack et al., 2004; Wang, 1999; Wang & Burris, 1997). Along these lines, photovoice has been used with multilingual and disabled[2] students within schools, programs, and camps to better understand their experiences and support changes in pursuit of equity and justice.

Photovoice and Multilingual Students

Within many research studies, photovoice has empowered multilingual students to self-advocate for change. Rotich (2014) used photovoice with 16 adolescent Montagnard (indigenous people from the central highlands of Vietnam) immigrant youth to support the students in communicating barriers they faced to physical activity. Students took photographs that represented environmental barriers (e.g., lack of access), sociocultural barriers (e.g., family and cultural views on physical activity), and socio-demographic barriers (e.g., lack of control over leisure time, financial and language barriers). Similarly, McBrien and Day (2012) used photography with 17 refugee adolescents to capture their daily experiences. They found that taking photographs provided a voice to the students and increased their self-awareness. These students, who were also multilingual and acquiring English, were able to communicate complicated, abstract ideas with the support of photographs and metaphors.

Furthermore, Streng et al. (2004) and Graziano (2011) used photovoice with multilingual students to explore their immigration experiences and educational realities. These projects empowered multilingual students to "identify, describe, discuss, organize themselves and others, and then act upon the issues affecting them" (Streng et al., 2004, p. 412) as well as "to have input in the collection and dissemination of data and gain pride and ownership of their work" (Graziano, 2011, p. 14). Finally, Greene (2015) also used photographs to engage 19 multilingual middle school students who were first- or second-generation immigrants in discussions around local changes to immigration policy. Students were asked to bring in images related to the theme of "What feels safe? What feels unsafe?" They then wrote titles and descriptions for their images. Greene concluded that the photographs facilitated both critical dialogue and language development for these participants.

Photovoice and Students with Disabilities

Photovoice also has been used to elicit perspectives of disabled students to promote self-reflection and self-advocacy. Photovoice has served as an accessible method of learning and communication for this population because it allows for a visual mode of communication, can be adapted to meet the needs of students, and encourages students to communicate their own authentic viewpoints rather than relying on those of adult proxies (e.g., parents and teachers).

Whitney (2006) used photovoice with 13 high school students with learning disabilities. The teens were tasked with taking photographs and sharing short narratives to express who they are as learners and their future goals. The project was presented to the students as a way for them to both discover more about themselves as learners and to influence teachers and school personnel to meet their needs. For Whitney, photovoice was "a promising practice for students with disabilities because it provides multiple modes for communication and can open our eyes to the forces behind students' engagement and disengagement in school" (p. 14).

Miller and Kurth (2021) used photovoice with six girls of color (ages 11–21) with intellectual disability and speech/language impairment. The girls were tasked with taking photographs of spaces that they enjoyed in school and helpful learning tools. The resulting themes included adult surveillance and limitations around writing tools, decision-making, and access to electronic devices for academic activities. The participants also expressed a need for learning tools in math and science.

Additionally, photovoice has been used to elicit the perspectives of autistic students. Regarding this population, Danker et al. (2019) noted that interviews have not always been an effective method due to language and literacy challenges. In their work with 16 autistic high school students, these authors found that photographs served as accessible, concrete visual prompts to support discussion while simultaneously reducing the expectation of eye contact, as the focus of the conversation was the photograph. They were also able to adapt photovoice to the needs of the students. Photovoice has also been used with autistic students to better understand connections among an individual's sensory experience, mental health, and social experiences (Clément et al., 2022), as well as to better understand how autistic students felt about transitioning from primary to secondary school (Hoy et al., 2018).

Finally, Seed (2016) used photovoice during a weekend camp for families with children with disabilities and found that the method was effective for "individuals with a wide range of intellectual, developmental and physical disabilities to participate in the evaluation without the need for a proxy to speak on their behalf" (Seed, 2016, p. 34). This author also noted that the flexibility and adaptability of photovoice as a method made it accessible to a wide range of individuals who are often left out of studies that use standardized methodologies.

Photovoice and Multilingual Disabled Students

While past research studies have shown the effectiveness of the use of the photovoice method with multilingual learners or learners with disabilities, no published studies using photovoice with students who identify as both multilingual and disabled have been found at this point. Therefore, the research presented here is unique in its use of the photovoice method as a multiliteracies approach with multilingual adolescents with communication disorders.

Method

This study applied the qualitative methodology of photovoice (Wang & Burris, 1994) as a multiliteracies practice for multilingual students diagnosed with communication disorders. There are three main goals of the photovoice method: (1) for individuals to think about and document strengths and areas of concern; (2) to promote dialogue about issues based on the photographs; and (3) to enact change (Wang & Burris, 1997). This research was approved by the authors' Institutional Review Board and took place in 2020–2021.

Participant Co-Researchers

Due to the participatory nature of this method, participants are considered participant co-researchers (PCRs); the primary researcher (first author) will be referred to as the facilitator. Four students took part as PCRs, as described in Table 1.1. Inclusion criteria for participation were: ages 9–18; speak or are exposed to another language or dialect in addition to Mainstream American English; currently receive speech-language therapy (SLT) or have within the last two years and have received speech or language services for at least one year; speak and understand enough English to enable full participation; and have internet and device capabilities to attend Zoom meetings and take and send pictures to the facilitator. Due to the COVID-19 pandemic, the entire photovoice process took place online. PCRs were recruited from across the country via emails to speech-language pathologists (SLPs) and teachers and social media posts.

Photovoice Procedures and Data Collection

Data included PCR background survey, photographs and captions, transcriptions of all meetings, the photovoice video exhibit of PCRs' photos, and viewers' reactions to the photovoice video exhibit gathered on a Google Form.

Table 1.1 Participant co-researcher demographics

Name[a]	Age	Grade	PCR birthplace	Parent birthplace	Multilingual repertoire	Self-reported SLT[b] goals
Amelia	11	5	Russia	Argentina	Understands Spanish, primarily speaks English	Speech articulation
Spencer	12	7	CA	India	Understands Malayalam, primarily speaks English	Speech articulation
Riku	14	9	CA	Japan	Understands and speaks English and Japanese	Communication (diagnosis of autism)
Adam	14	9	MA	Lebanon	Understands Arabic, primarily speaks English	Social communication (diagnosis of autism)

[a] All names are pseudonyms
[b] SLT = speech-language therapy

Table 1.2 Alignment of photovoice goals, research procedures, and multiliteracies components

Photovoice goal	Procedures of current research (described below)	Related multiliteracies component[a]
1 Document community's strengths and areas of concerns	1 Introductory meeting 2 Photography	1 Overt instruction 2 Situated practice
2 Create a dialogue about issues based on the photographs	3 One-on-one photograph discussion meeting 4 Two peer discussion group meetings	3 Critical framing
3 Enact change	5 Photovoice video exhibit	4 Transformed practice

[a] See the Introductory chapter of this volume for a description of the multiliteracies components

The following sections explain the photovoice process and data collection chronologically as they were implemented in this study. While the timelines, specific number of meetings, and content of meetings vary from one photovoice project to the next, there are several main components that remain consistent. These components align with the three main goals of photovoice, as well as the four instructional components of multiliteracies (New London Group, 1996), as described in Table 1.2 (see also the introductory chapter for an explanation of these components).

Overt Instruction: Introductory Meetings

For the overt instruction component, the PCRs met one-on-one with the facilitator prior to taking photographs for the project. Within these 30-minute recorded Zoom meetings, the facilitator introduced the project to the PCRs and provided guidance regarding how to complete the project. The meetings consisted of a warm-up game to establish rapport, a PCR background survey (demographics, language background, SLT history), a review of project goals and timeline, photography tips and guidelines, including the need to get consent from individuals who might appear in the photos, and sharing of the photography prompts (see below). Due to the varying ages and language abilities of the PCRs, the introductory meetings were modified to meet their needs. Parents were invited to attend these meetings to learn about the project and support their children as needed.

Situated Practice: Photography

At the end of the introductory meeting, the PCRs were given prompts for their photo assignment. The photography portion of the project acted as the situated practice component of multiliteracies because the PCRs were bringing their personal experiences and lives into the learning process by taking photographs

26 T. Loewenstein and R. Danzak

within their homes and communities. They were instructed to take pictures of the following:

1 A person you like to talk to
2 How you feel about talking to people at home
3 How you feel about talking to people at school
4 What's hard about talking
5 Something special about you
6 How you feel in speech class
7 What you learn in speech class
8 The best part of speech class
9 The worst part of speech class
10 A way you and your speech teacher are the same
11 A way you and your speech teacher are different

They were told to take photos with a phone or camera, but that they could also find photos online if needed. The PCRs were asked to text or email the photos along with the prompt number or a brief explanation of the image.

Critical Framing: One-on-One Photograph Discussion Meeting and Peer Discussion Groups

Once all of the PCRs had collected photographs in response to the prompts, they engaged in one-on-one meetings with the facilitator and group discussion meetings with other PCRs, all recorded on Zoom. These meetings served as the critical framing component, as PCRs interpreted their own photographs and analyzed themes across photographs. In the one-on-one meetings, the facilitator and each PCR discussed their photographs and captions. In these opportunities, the PCRs were prompted to talk about their images using a modified version of the PHOTO approach (Hergenrather et al., 2009). PHOTO is an acronym representing five discussion points: describe your *Picture*; what is *Happening* in your picture; why did you take a picture *Of* this; what does this picture *Tell* us about your life; and how can this picture provide *Opportunities* for us to improve life. One PCR sent captions for his photos in advance. After sharing about each photo, the remaining PCRs composed captions to help others better understand their pictures. One participant, Adam, did not share photographs for each prompt and instead was verbally interviewed using the PHOTO prompts, and his oral responses were included in the data analysis.

PCRs were then asked if there were any photos they wished they could have taken (Woodgate et al., 2017). This was particularly relevant because of the COVID-19 pandemic, which limited students' access to people and places they might have wanted to photograph. PCRs were invited to choose their three most meaningful photographs and were asked if there was anything they didn't want included in a presentation or paper about this project. Next, three of the four students (Amelia, Spencer, Riku) partook in two 1-hour group discussion

Zoom meetings. The facilitator presented all of their photographs to them, randomly assembled, and prompted them to share reactions, thoughts, photos they wanted to learn more about, and any photos they noticed were similar. Students were then presented with their photographs for each prompt and asked to find similarities and differences among the images and captions to elicit themes.

The remainder of the second group meeting was spent reflecting on the project as a whole. To elicit thoughts and opinions on the photovoice experience, each PCR was asked the following questions: What were your favorite and least favorite parts of the photovoice project? What is one new thing you learned during this photovoice project? What would you like people to learn from your photos and captions? Would you do a project like this again? Why or why not? What are three words to describe your experiences during this project? Anything else you want to share? They were given the choice to respond or to pass.

Transformed Practice: Photovoice Video Exhibit and Viewer Survey

Finally, within the transformed practice component of multiliteracies, the PCRs collaborated to create a video exhibit to share their takeaways with others. The aim was to share their work with those in power to effect change. Within the group discussion groups, PCRs were asked how they might share their work with other people. The facilitator presented several choices (i.e., creating a video, hosting a Zoom presentation, creating a website) and asked the PCRs if they had any ideas. For the video presentation, the facilitator shared an example created by students of similar ages (PhotovoiceWorldwide, 2020). The PCRs decided on a video slideshow.

Due to time constraints, the facilitator put together basic slides of the PCRs' photos, similar to the example video. During the meeting, the PCRs helped create a slide explaining what they did for the project. They expressed approval for the way the photos were laid out on the slides and were given an opportunity to remove pictures if they wanted to. They also worked together to come up with a title for the presentation. The slideshow was then converted into a movie with music.

The photovoice video exhibit was sent out to professors, researchers, graduate students, and undergraduate students at the authors' college, school SLPs who supervise the college's graduate students, and the PCRs and their parents (with an invitation to share with their friends and families if they chose). A brief survey (on Google Forms) was included with the video link to collect thoughts and reactions from viewers. The survey collected information on the individual's role, what they learned or took away from the video photo exhibit they watched, and how the video photo exhibit may impact them or their actions.

Thematic Analysis

The typical photovoice approach encourages PCRs to determine the common themes of their work. In this study, PCRs were prompted to identify

28 *T. Loewenstein and R. Danzak*

similarities among their photographs. Their comments and discussion were included in transcripts that were analyzed to extract themes. The present study utilized thematic analysis (Braun & Clarke, 2006) to determine themes from the data: photographs, captions, and transcripts from individual and group meetings. Using Dedoose (2024), codes were created and applied to images and text excerpts following an inductive approach (Braun & Clarke, 2006); that is, they emerged from the data without a pre-existing coding scheme. Coded photos and transcripts were reviewed several times, in conjunction with Dedoose's data analysis tools, to collapse related codes together into main themes. The photovoice video exhibit survey responses were analyzed separately but with the same steps of thematic analysis (Braun & Clarke, 2006).

For purposes of reliability, a graduate research assistant was trained on the code application and independently coded 50 out of 102 total excerpts coded in the data. To compute inter-coder agreement, Dedoose calculated the pooled Cohen's kappa (Cohen, 1960), a respected agreement measure that accounts for the rate of agreement expected by chance. The result was 0.85, indicating very good agreement (Landis & Koch, 1977). The facilitator and assistant then met to discuss discrepancies and reached a 100% consensus.

Findings

Results from the qualitative analysis of the photos and meeting transcriptions revealed themes apparent in the PCRs' experiences and perspectives. Themes are organized into two categories: *a posteriori* (created after data collection) and *a priori* (created before the data were collected) (Constas, 1992). Three main themes that emerged a posteriori are discussed first. Then, *a priori* themes that were influenced by the facilitator-generated photo prompts are reviewed. Finally, themes identified in the photovoice exhibit survey responses are presented.

Perspectives and Experiences on Communication and Speech-Language Therapy: A Posteriori Themes

Three main a posteriori themes that emerged from the data: (1) *communication challenges,* (2) *growth mindset,* and (3) *generalizing skills.* The theme *communication challenges* included difficulties with understanding and speaking. For example, Riku shared, "Uh because I don't understand what's the people talking about." Amelia shared a picture of her and her dog (see Figure 1.1) with the caption, "It's hard for me to say things because sometimes I feel like people are confused or don't really know what I'm saying. The dog doesn't understand what I'm saying."

Communication challenges also included the PCRs' internal reactions to their communication difficulties, including choosing not to talk and feelings of frustration with being corrected by someone else. For example, Amelia explained, "I feel so-so talking to people at my school because like I get like

Figure 1.1 Amelia's photo: Communicating with her dog

sometimes a little nervous or like shy or like something because I get scared I'm going to mess a word like and they're not gonna really understand" (see Figure 1.2). Spencer shared his frustrations with being corrected, "It's because it's kinda frustrating when you don't get something right when you keep on getting the wrong answer multiple times."

Growth mindset is the understanding that one's abilities can improve and grow and that mistakes can be learning opportunities. The PCRs discussed mistakes, persevering, and improving. Spencer shared a meme with the text, "Mistakes help me improve" (see Figure 1.3). He elaborated, "It's like mistakes always help you improve. Like it's okay to get mistakes. Sometimes it's better to get mistakes than to be right all the time. That'll help you improve." In the group discussion, Amelia added, "I do make some mistakes but like I just keep saying the sound until I get it right."

Finally, the PCRs expressed a desire to *generalize their skills* beyond SLT, as well as generalizing skills to more than one speech target. Spencer shared, "I've been going to speech for quite a while. I just want to get out of speech and do my own thing. Like I told you, it would be easier if I could just talk and listen to what I'm saying other than practicing and saying it over and over again." Amelia also shared that she self-corrects her speech in conversation when a communication partner doesn't understand her, "I don't feel like sad

Figure 1.2 Amelia's photo: Feeling so-so when speaking

Figure 1.3 Spencer's photo: Growth mindset

Figure 1.4 Spencer's photo: Repetitive nature of speech class

or mad when they don't understand … I just like keep saying [it until] I say it the right way ….". In response to the prompt, "The worst part of speech class," Spencer shared a meme with the text, "Reset the Clock!" (see Figure 1.4). He explained, "When I go to speech class, we always have to do the same things like resetting the clock over and over again. Also, I would rather focus on more than one flaw." In this context, he was expressing a desire to generalize skills to multiple speech errors rather than focus on only one at a time.

Perspectives and Experiences on Communication and Speech-Language Therapy: A Priori Themes

Additional themes were created *a priori* – that is, before data collection (Constas, 1992), because they were driven by the photo prompts generated by the facilitator. The following topics were discussed as direct responses to the prompts: *communicating at home*, *communicating at school*, *speech class* (i.e., SLT), and *speech teacher*. Themes related to these topics are discussed below.

Communicating at Home and School

PCRs shared only positive feelings regarding communication at home. They mentioned feelings of belonging, calm, comfort, and happiness. Spencer talked about home as, "The place I belong." Amelia said, "I feel like I can like express like my feelings …." Riku shared an image of a solid blue rectangle with the caption, "Color is blue. Well because I can calm down." PCRs also expressed mostly positive feelings, and a few negative feelings, regarding communication at school. Riku and Adam shared that they feel happy when talking to people at school. Regarding negative feelings about communicating at school,

Riku said while working on a worksheet in school, "Sometimes I don't understand." As discussed earlier, Amelia expressed feelings of nervousness or shyness when talking to teachers and friends she does not know well at school.

Speech-Language Therapy

SLT was largely discussed positively. Positive topics discussed included playing games, reading favorite books, talking about PCR interests, improving, and communicating with others. For example, Riku shared his enjoyment of talking about an interest, Pokémon, during speech class: "I was good talking about Pokémon, and she showed it … and I showed my card for Pokémon." Additionally, Adam shared, "Communicating is the best part because I like to talk to people."

Negative feelings related to speech class occurred about half as many times as positive feelings. Negative topics discussed included: putting time and effort into speech class, repetitive practice, not receiving a prize, choosing not to talk, and feeling confused. Riku shared a picture of himself with the comment, "Sometimes I am confused with what the teacher says" (see Figure 1.5). Amelia shared a picture of her reaching into a prize box with the caption, "I want a prize like every day but sometimes we don't get prizes because we have to earn it" (see Figure 1.6). She also explained, "So basically like I don't

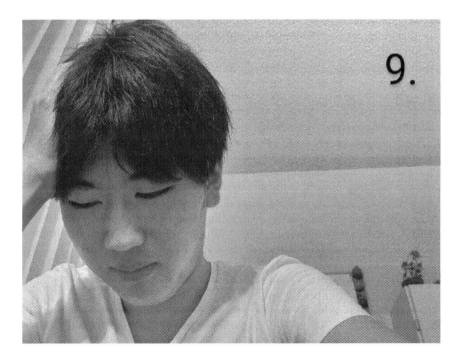

Figure 1.5 Riku's photo: Feeling confused at school

Figure 1.6 Amelia's photo: Prizes in speech class

like talking much in speech class. I do talk sometimes obviously when I have to like say the sounds but I don't talk that much. I have like three kids and the other kids always keep talking but I just always stay silent."

PCRs' Perceptions of Their Speech-Language Pathologists

As a way to probe for possible cultural-linguistic differences, PCRs were asked to take photographs of "A way you and your speech teacher are the same" and "A way you and your speech teacher are different." This presented as a relatively difficult set of prompts for them. Spencer did not come up with a response independently, and Riku misinterpreted the prompt to apply to the facilitator rather than his school SLP. Adam and Amelia responded with physical differences (i.e., clothes, height, glasses). Amelia's response to what was different between her and her SLP was they had different career goals (i.e., SLP vs. veterinarian).

34   *T. Loewenstein and R. Danzak*

Outcomes Related to Photovoice as a Method

Considering the novelty of using photovoice with participants who identify as both multilingual and disabled, as well as the self-reflective nature of the photovoice process, it is important to summarize the impact of the project on the PCRs themselves. Additionally, because the goal of photovoice is to invoke change, we also present the feedback from viewers of the students' video photo exhibit.

Regarding PCRs' reactions to the photovoice project, the students described the process of taking photos as both easy and hard. A common theme was enjoying the group aspect of the project more than one-on-one interviews with the facilitator. The students also expressed that they found it helpful to use photos to explain or share about themselves. When asked to think of three words to describe their experiences with the photovoice project, the PCRs generated the following words: great, coming together, happy, scared, difficult, fun, and proud of my picture.

With respect to the impacts of the video exhibit, 33 viewers completed the survey. These included primarily graduate students in Communication Sciences and Disorders (32%), SLPs (32%), and university staff or faculty (30%). Responses to an open-ended question about viewer takeaways were organized into the following themes: *utilizing other forms of expression to supplement language* (33 instances), *understanding clients' perspectives* (17), *client self-reflection* (8), *heterogeneity of clients* (8), *impacting practice* (8), and *SLT can be difficult for clients* (7).

Reflecting on the power of visual communication, one respondent stated that the video exhibit was "a great reminder that sometimes it is easier to express yourself using pictures, especially for students who might have trouble finding the right words for their feelings or pronouncing their words correctly." Another viewer commented how self-expression through creative means, "put[s] the client in the driver's seat." Regarding client perspectives and heterogeneity, one respondent commented that "Viewing the students' responses has made me think of the importance of understanding how the student perceives therapy and make adjustments accordingly;" another reported: "everyone's experience in speech therapy is different." Actions to take included identifying each student's individual needs, adjusting approaches to fit each learners' needs, and asking the learner how they learn best and what motivates them.

Finally, the video exhibit reminded professionals that SLT can be difficult for clients. One SLP shared that "It was a good reminder that the work we're asking of students is difficult for them and they can feel frustrated, especially if they don't feel like they're making progress."

Discussion

This study expands on previous research that applied photovoice with multilingual *or* disabled students to address students who are both multilingual *and* have language/communication disabilities. The intersectionality of multilingual students with communication disorders is an important area of research focus, as these students face challenges of both ableism and an ideology of monolingualism. As discussed, photovoice as a multiliteracies approach has many benefits for multilingual students with communication disorders including supporting communication with a visual modality, centering the student's message rather than a certain language, centering the experiences of the students and allowing them to build knowledge from those experiences, and allowing students a medium for self-reflection and self-advocacy (e.g., Graziano, 2011; McBrien & Day, 2012; Whitney, 2006).

Beyond these benefits, previous studies (Danker et al., 2019; Seed, 2016) as well as the present study suggest that the photovoice method allows for different levels of access. Specifically, each PCR within this study participated in a manner that allowed them to successfully contribute their thoughts and experiences. Amelia submitted photos of herself and her environment; Spencer used mostly internet memes rather than photographs; Adam provided spoken language responses within an interview modality rather than submitting photos for all prompts; and Riku benefitted from parental support during the meetings. However, all participants successfully participated in the project and provided positive feedback regarding participation in the project. The photovoice method's allowance for scaffolding and participation via various communication modalities makes it well-suited for multilingual students with communication disorders.

Finally, photovoice provides the benefit of bringing forward students' strengths by allowing them to communicate through means other than strictly reading and writing. Specifically, within this study, Riku, a student with difficulties related to language expression, had a passion for photography. In fact, participation in this study appealed to him because of his interest in photography, and he has since won awards for his art within photo contests. On the other hand, Spencer demonstrated strengths in the interpretation and use of popular culture memes to express his viewpoints. Overall, this project, as well as other photovoice projects (e.g., Danker et al., 2019; Seed, 2016), demonstrates how photovoice can be used as a multiliteracies approach to allow for participation via multiple modalities (e.g., visual, auditory, written) based on student strengths.

Photovoice as a Multiliteracies Pedagogical Tool

While photovoice has been used extensively in research studies as a tool to elicit individual and community viewpoints and experiences, the question remains of how this method can be best implemented as a pedagogical tool embedded within a curriculum. The present study has shed light on how this might work for students who are multilingual and disabled. Students with these identities are often pushed to the periphery in the US education system, which generally centers the English language and pedagogies designed for only certain types of learners. Within all the examples below, photovoice can be used with

36   T. Loewenstein and R. Danzak

multilingual and disabled students to center their experiences within the curriculum at various grade levels.

Eliciting Student Feedback

Photovoice can be used within schools to support student self-reflection and encourage students to be an active part of their education. Like in the present study and Miller and Kurth (2021), photovoice can invite students to share their viewpoints related to school or services they receive, what barriers exist to their education, and ideas for overcoming those barriers. Importantly, the present study expanded on previous work by including the voices of a rarely heard subgroup of students, multilingual students with disabilities, sharing feedback about their communication strengths and challenges, and how they negotiate these in the classroom context.

Engaging with Social Justice Topics

Photovoice is an excellent tool to use when learning about social justice issues that affect students' lives and communities. Although larger considerations of social justice were less emphasized in the present study, the facilitator repeatedly emphasized to the PCRs that they are the experts in their own experiences and therefore supported them in understanding that they have a right to share their opinions and advocate for themselves. In general, photovoice as a method empowers participants by encouraging them to use their voice to create change.

In the classroom context, similar to Greene's (2015) study, photovoice could be embedded within a social studies unit on immigration. Students may be asked to take pictures to bring their stories and life experiences to classroom discussions of immigration policies. Other ideas of centering social justice conversations around student experiences using photovoice include discussions of new laws and policies affecting their community (e.g., laws related to education, zoning, gender identity and gender-affirming care, voting rights, civil rights, and healthcare) within a civics or government class, discussions of climate change or biodiversity within a science class, or discussion of nutrition and food insecurity within a health class.

Teaching New Skills

Additionally, lessons can be made more meaningful by bringing in student experiences, through the use of photovoice, when learning new skills in the classroom. Within the present study, skills such as comparing and contrasting, analyzing photographs, and extracting common themes were taught and practiced.

There are endless ways to use photovoice in the classroom within daily lessons. For example, photovoice can be used to generate topics for writing assignments, thus bringing in student experiences to inspire their writing when learning to compose poems, personal essays, persuasive essays, etc. For multilingual classrooms, writing could be composed in multiple languages (see examples in Rajendram et al., 2022). Similarly, when learning about nonliteral language, students may be prompted to take photographs in their homes and communities that represent examples of metaphors and similes. Photovoice could be used when learning vocabulary words, as students could take pictures to define certain words. Within a science unit, students could take photographs of plants or animals in their environment as a starting point for learning about local animals and plants, scientific drawings, plant and animal anatomy, taxonomy, etc.

Photovoice as a Tool for Social Change

In addition to the personal benefits that photovoice may result in for individual students, a central aspect of photovoice is its impact on society. The third goal of photovoice is to enact change. In the present study, the PCRs achieved this by sharing their photos with graduate students and professionals in the field of Communication Sciences and Disorders in a video exhibit. Viewers' responses to the feedback survey suggested they would modify their practices based on what they learned from these students. This outcome is similar to previous photovoice research wherein the result is often to elicit ideas for actions. When those actions are put into practice, the result is social change. Therefore, in addition to using photovoice as a means to learning about the world around them, and how topics discussed in the classroom relate to their lived experiences, photovoice is also used to engage students in advocacy and social justice.

To extend the examples discussed above, students can use photovoice to make changes within their school based on their experiences. For example, they might advocate for healthier food in the cafeteria, sustainable practices in the school building, or more equitable access to technology for learning. Going beyond their classroom, students can effect change within their communities. After learning about immigration policy through the lens of their lived experiences, students can share their photographs with policy makers. Within a science unit on climate change, students can share documentation of the effects of climate change within their communities to share with policy makers. When educators facilitate student access to those with the power to make change, they empower the students to be an active part in social justice movements.

Conclusion

The research presented in this chapter showed the use of photovoice as a multiliteracies approach with multilingual adolescents with communication disorders. Three key themes emerged from photographs and discussions:

communication challenges, growth mindset, and generalizing skills. Students enjoyed the group aspect of the project, found it helpful to use photos to explain, and overall found the project challenging but enjoyable. Viewers of the photovoice exhibit were inspired to take action and change their practice. Educators can use photovoice in the classroom within a variety of disciplines, content units, and lessons to center learning on student experiences, allow different access points for students to enter meaningful conversations about topics related to their lives, and provide a tool to empower students to self-reflect and self-advocate for social change. Perhaps the key takeaway of this instance of photovoice as a multiliteracies application was engaging with students who were multilingual and disabled. The intersectionality of multilingualism and disability is an area that deserves increased consideration in multilingual education research. Photovoice offers an ideal forum to enhance the voices of these students, therefore providing educators with insights into their unique learning styles and abilities.

Notes

1 For the purposes of this chapter, multilingual encompasses individuals who speak and/or understand more than one language.
2 Some individuals prefer identity-first language ("disabled person") and others prefer person-first language ("person with a disability"). Best practice would be to use the terminology each individual prefers. For the purpose of this chapter, we will alternate between identity-first and person-first language.

References

Blackman, A., & Fairey, T. (2007). *The photovoice manual: A guide to designing and running participatory photography projects.* Photovoice.

Braun, V., & Clarke, V. (2006). Using thematic analysis in psychology. *Qualitative Research in Psychology, 3*(2), 77–101.

Clément, M., Lee, K., Park, M., Sinn, A., & Miyake, N. (2022). The need for sensory-friendly "zones": Learning from youth on the autism spectrum, their families, and autistic mentors using a participatory approach. *Frontiers in Psychology, 13.* https://doi.org/10.3389/fpsyg.2022.883331

Cohen, J. (1960). A coefficient of agreement for nominal scales. *Educational and Psychological Measurement, 20*(1), 37–46.

Constas, M. A. (1992). Qualitative analysis as a public event: The documentation of category development procedures. *American Educational Research Journal, 29*(2), 253–266.

Danker, J., Strnadová, I., & Cumming, T. M. (2019). Picture my well-being: Listening to the voices of students with autism spectrum disorder. *Research in Developmental Disabilities, 89,* 130–140.

Danzak, R. L. (2015). "Sometimes the perspective changes": Reflections on a photography workshop with multicultural students in Italy. *International Journal of Multicultural Education, 17*(3), 56–75.

Dedoose Version 9.2.007, cloud application for managing, analyzing, and presenting qualitative and mixed method research data (2024). Los Angeles, CA: SocioCultural Research Consultants, LLC. www.dedoose.com.

Graziano, K. J. (2011). Working with English language learners: Preservice teachers and photovoice. *International Journal of Multicultural Education, 13*(1), 1–19.

Greene, M. C. S. (2015). Reimagining: Using image and photovoice as curriculum with ELL adolescent immigrants to reimagine personal trajectories. *INTESOL Journal, 12*(2), 17–36.

Hergenrather, K. C., Rhodes, S. D., Cowan, C. A., Bardhoshi, G., & Pula, S. (2009). Photovoice as community-based participatory research: A qualitative review. *American Journal of Health Behavior, 33*(6), 686–698.

Hoy, K., Parsons, S., & Kovshoff, H. (2018). Inclusive school practices supporting the primary to secondary transition for autistic children: Pupil, teacher, and parental perspectives. *Advances in Autism.* https://doi.org/10.1108/AIA-05-2018-0016

James, N., Cowie, B., Bell, K., Deratnay, P., & Fourie, C. (2015). Revealing and acting on patient care experiences: Exploring the use of photovoice in practice development work through case study methodology. *International Practice Development Journal, 5*(11).

Landis, J., & Koch, G. (1977). The measurement of observer agreement for categorical data. *Biometrics, 33*(1), 159–174.

McBrien, J. L., & Day, R. (2012). From there to here: Using photography to explore perspectives of resettled refugee youth. *International Journal of Child, Youth and Family Studies, 4*(1), 546–568.

Miller, A. L., & Kurth, J. A. (2021). Photovoice research with disabled girls of color: Exposing how schools (re)produce inequities through school geographies and learning tools. *Disability & Society, 37*(8), 1362–1390.

New London Group. (1996). A pedagogy of multiliteracies: Designing social futures. *Harvard Educational Review, 66*(1), 60–92. https://doi.org/10.17763/haer.66.1.17370n67v22j160u

Palibroda, B., Krieg, B., Murdock, L., & Havelock, J. (2009). *A practical guide to photovoice: Sharing pictures, telling stories, and changing communities.* Prairie Women's Health Centre for Excellence. https://static1.squarespace.com/static/629994e184bdd264b27caafb/t/6320d111357994384c47b79c/1663095059477/a+practical+guide+pdf20.pdf

PhotovoiceWorldwide. (2020, August 20). *Young changemakers with a camera photovoice – summer 2020* [Video]. YouTube. https://www.youtube.com/watch?v=f8abMJGuCwM

Rajendram, S., Burton, J., & Wong, W. (2022). Online translanguaging and multiliteracies strategies to support K–12 multilingual learners: Identity texts, linguistic landscapes, and photovoice, *TESOL Journal, 13*, Article e685. https://doi.org/10.1002/tesj.685

Ripat, J., Woodgate, R. L., & Bennett, L. (2020). Attitudes faced by young adults using assistive technology as depicted through photovoice. *Disability and Rehabilitation: Assistive Technology, 15*(3), 314–321.

Rotich, J. P. (2014). Physical activity participation related challenges that adolescent Montagnard refugee youth encounter in America. *International Journal of Human Sciences, 11*(1), 45–54. https://doi.org/10.14687/ijhs.v11i1.2734

Seed, N. (2016). Photovoice: A participatory approach to disability service evaluation. *Evaluation Journal of Australia, 16*(2), 29–35.

Strack, R. W., Magill, C., & McDonagh, K. (2004). Engaging youth through photovoice. *Health Promotion Practice, 5*(1), 49–58.

Streng, J. M., Rhodes, S. D., Ayala, G. X., Eng, E., Arceo, R., & Phipps, S. (2004). Realidad Latina: Latino adolescents, their school, and a university use photovoice to examine and address the influence of immigration. *Journal of Interprofessional Care, 18*(4), 403–415.

Wang, C. (1999). Photovoice: A participatory action research strategy applied to women's health. *Journal of Women's Health, 8*, 185–192.

Wang, C., & Burris, M. A. (1994). Empowerment through photo novella: Portraits of participation. *Health Education Quarterly, 21*(2), 171–186.

Wang, C., & Burris, M. (1997). Photovoice: Concept, methodology, and use for participatory needs assessment. *Health Education and Behavior, 24*, 369–387.

Whitney, J. C. (2006). My education: Students with disabilities describe high school in pictures and words. *TEACHING Exceptional Children Plus, 3*(2), Article 1.

Woodgate, R. L., Zurba, M., & Tennent, P. (2017). Worth a thousand words? Advantages, challenges and opportunities in working with photovoice as a qualitative research method with youth and their families. *Forum: Qualitative Social Research, 18*(1).

2 Multiliteracies and Student-Created Materials Design

Learner Engagement and Agency in the EFL Classroom

Ken Mizusawa and Tamas Kiss

Introduction

Materials design is widely viewed as the exclusive purview of teachers, publishers, and curriculum experts given the pivotal role it plays in English Language Teaching (ELT) contexts (Lee, 2015). However, such a belief can lead to social inequity when we consider how exclusive, narrow, and subject-to-standardization ELT materials can be both linguistically and culturally (Block, 2004). Consequently, the materials design process can have the unintended effect of excluding and delegitimizing EL student voices and stifling any attempts at meaningful classroom interaction. As Baker (2012) notes: "For users of English to communicate effectively, they will need a mastery of more than the features of syntax, lexis, and phonology that are the traditional focus in ELT" (p. 63). We must thereby avoid fixed and unchanging representations of English in materials design as they are counterintuitive as much as inauthentic for our increasingly diverse, globally connected students (see Introduction; Jenkins, 2004; Mizusawa, 2021a).

What ELT materials typically promote is a Western, static, print-bound, and monomodal idea of English, "which wrongly hints at a uniformity or homogeneity among native speakers that does not in fact exist" (Nault, 2006, p. 315). They fail to account for the global proliferation of English (Block, 2004; Vettorel, 2018), its extended use in/across non-native contexts (Baker, 2012; Jenkins, 2004; Takahashi, 2014), and the dynamic and diverse character of modern multimodal technology-mediated communication in which it finds boundless expression (Glas et al., 2023; Mizusawa, 2021b; Sang, 2017). What our learners require therefore "is the ability to make use of linguistic and other communicative resources in the negotiation of meaning, roles, and relationships in the diverse sociocultural settings of intercultural communication through English" (Baker, 2012, p. 63). Yet, such priorities are generally ignored in favor of standardized, teacher-driven practices.

Learner Voice and Social Justice

Researchers recognize that entrenched practices in ELT in the Southeast Asian region and beyond urgently need to change, and change radically, despite the strong resistance from the teaching fraternity and education systems

DOI: 10.4324/9781003438847-4

(Glas et al., 2023; Kapur, 2021; Mizusawa & Kiss, 2020; Sulistyowardani et al., 2020). What still dominates is a teacher-centered approach to ELT that advocates for a formal and fixed understanding of British/American English which teachers alone believe in and value (Ambele & Boonsuk, 2021; Irham et al., 2022; Mizusawa & Kiss, 2020), rather than one that could empower young people to fully participate and prosper in a digitally connected world (Lim et al., 2022; Mizusawa, 2021b; Pang, 2020; Tan & Guo, 2014).

When EL is defined as an exclusive, strict, and denaturalized form of communication, students tend to struggle. In response, teachers default to a program of learning by rote, "fail proof" formulas, and memory work to help their students quickly "level up" to meet systemic demands for measurable progress and outcomes (Kiss & Mizusawa, 2018; Lim et al., 2021). This indicates that what happens in the classroom, whatever the intention, may be a barrier to student learning, engagement, and understanding. As Weninger (2018) explains: "In East/Southeast Asia, [...] English language education [...] is steeped in an instrumentalist rationale that stems from governments' internationalization agenda for national economic interests" (p. 3). This means that students should learn to communicate in a rather neutral and devoid of any cultural identity or membership. Under such conditions, the teachers' and the teaching materials' roles are to be content providers and the students' role to be consumers. This creates a social setting in which only teachers hold knowledge and power; teachers are "heard and validated" but the students are not (Kiss & Mizusawa, 2018, p. 63). In such classrooms the language knowledge learners master is at best discrete, non-transferable, decontextualized, and largely designed for classroom use. Basically, students are being made to use language in a functional manner prescribed by their teachers (Kalantzis & Cope, 2008; Mizusawa, 2021a).

There is no opportunity to foster meaningful interaction in such classrooms – with each other, the teacher, or the wider world. The teacher is thereby confusing efficiency with effectiveness, compliance with competence, and productivity with progress in making their pedagogical decisions. Students may be kept busy faithfully completing assigned tasks, but there may be little active engagement, social equity, or true language learning, which must be flexible, adaptable, and open-ended to meet 21st-century demands (Joseph Jeyaraj & Harland, 2016; Vettorel, 2018). The established ELT approach is accordingly one that relies on blind mimicry of teacher-endorsed norms and practices that lie well outside of the students' first-hand knowledge of real-world communication (in English or otherwise), places them helplessly on the margins instead of the center of the learning process, and denies them a legitimate voice with which to even contemplate self-expression in English (Kalantzis & Cope, 2008; Lim et al., 2021; Mizusawa & Kiss, 2020). Its continuation equates to a suppression of student motivation, participation, and voices (Irham et al., 2022; Lee, 2015).

Much of the blame for this lack of progress in ELT practices can be leveled at the widespread popularity of textbooks that (1) advocate for meeting high linguistic benchmarks based on Western ideals (Glas et al., 2023; Takahashi, 2014; Thurairaj & Roy, 2012; Vettorel, 2018), (2) rely heavily on assessment-driven practices to "accurately" measure student progress (Gregory & Clarke, 2003; Lim et al., 2021), and (3) often fail to acknowledge the cultural contexts of students in ways that aren't merely fleeting or tokenistic (Lee, 2015; Metboki, 2018; Nguyen et al., 2021).

Using language teaching materials that do not relate to the social, economic, or cultural classroom contexts in which they are extensively used is indeed problematic. "The fact, that a significant gap exists between the local students' knowledge of the world and the reality that the mandatory textbooks present" undermines the legitimacy of the learners' own cultural and social identities, rendering them virtually invisible – thus insignificant/inferior – when compared to majority groups (Kiss & Rimbar, 2021, p. 143). What is more, it can have the unintended effect of negatively skewing their worldview and identities by creating/reinforcing hierarchies, divisions, and inequities. If classrooms are not safe and equitable spaces, students will never be emboldened to take calculated risks, make meaningful decisions, and learn through trial and error. If ever in doubt, they will instinctively defer to the teacher's authority to best manage their learning.

To provide more context-relevant materials, sometimes teachers design their own. Yet, these are often inadequate to challenge the status quo. When teachers venture into materials design, they typically produce materials steeped in the traditions, ideologies, and content of published textbooks (Brown, 2022; Kiss & Mizusawa, 2018; Metboki, 2018; Mizusawa, 2021a). Clearly, to make the pursuit of social justice and student voices central to ELT, materials design must be robust enough to "counter dominant ideologies, address multiple publics, and create new forms of public participation" (Rogers, 2022, p. 14).

Given this enormous challenge, advocating for student-created materials design makes perfect sense. After all, students are not in any way beholden to the established norms of ELT materials design and are more likely to chart their own path. This is not to say that students are proficient at producing materials of a publication standard or that they fully understand the methodological approaches on which commercially produced materials are based. We acknowledge that student-produced materials are likely to be flawed, prone to error, and uninformed by strong (if any) pedagogical principles. However, students, given their familiarity with and place within today's multicultural, multilingual, and multimodal world, are better positioned to exploit its many resources and design ELT materials that reflect the communicative needs and lived experiences of young people.

Materials Design and Multiliteracies

The global standing of English in today's ever-changing world is beyond question (see Introduction; Nguyen et al., 2021). It has led to the emergence of different "Englishes" (Aoyama & Denton, 2022; Galloway & Rose, 2018;

44 *K. Mizusawa and T. Kiss*

Vettorel, 2018) and has also played a key role in the massive proliferation of technology-mediated communication (Glas et al., 2023). Yet, the formal recognition of such diverse and varied 21st-century forms of English has remained at best piecemeal in ELT materials design. As Block (2004) asserts: "there was seldom any suggestion in ELT circles that it might be problematic to package and transfer around the world ... one dominant methodology, and one particular type of pedagogical material" until very recently (p. 76). Such beliefs and practices originate from the long-presiding era of print. The power of mass distribution, standardization, and the monopoly held by Western publishers should never be underestimated. They ensured the propagation of a universally recognizable form of English (Kress, 2003; Nguyen et al., 2021; Thurairaj & Roy, 2012) and a near-exclusive focus on discrete and easily targeted language skills in ELT materials design (Mizusawa, 2021a; Weninger, 2018). Hence, we may suggest that current ELT materials are still very much a product of this print- and word-bound culture, whereas the communication practices we currently utilize are an outcome of digital culture, which are unbound and aligned to the image (Kress, 2003).

While the image continues to shape modern communication in dynamic and powerful ways, ELT materials have barely begun to acknowledge it as a legitimate mode of communication, let alone embrace the many implications of a 21st-century multimodal world that has made it central (Lim & Tan, 2021; Mizusawa, 2021a). This can partly be attributed to the constraints of print and partly to the role textbooks assign to images. First, in print, words have always been easier and cheaper to reproduce than images, which are cost-prohibitive for publishers, whereas online, images and words of any description can be effortlessly and carelessly shared by anybody at any time. Second, as Weninger and Kiss (2013) claim, images in most textbooks have an indexical role; they reinforce vocabulary presented in the materials in a visual format. Therefore, although they potentially carry multiple meanings, these are mostly neglected in classroom use due to a lack of tasks that would exploit them.

We argue that it is vital that images should have a more prominent place in ELT as meaning-making devices and not simply as decoration or indexical references. Visual media, if used appropriately, can act as a bridge between a student's in- and out-of-school literacies and provide a means for them to demonstrate their communicative competence through their prior/established knowledge and understanding of the online world (Tan & Guo, 2014).

Images are native to a student's daily communication practices. Students have an intuitive awareness of how they operate. They can more readily decipher and generate meaning using images, rather than in a language that is culturally removed from their everyday lives. Images can be the way students draw from and organize their multilingual and multicultural resources in service of materials design (Kiss & Weninger, 2013; Mizusawa, 2021b). They can also help blend and borrow all manner of media resources that students find online to strengthen and extend their communication practices in personal and powerful ways in and out of the classroom. Ours is not simply an image-driven

Multiliteracies and Student-Created Materials Design   45

culture but a convergence culture (Jenkins, 2006; Mizusawa, 2021b). Online, any end user is free to appropriate/misappropriate any image they find in service of their own content creation purposes. To communicate effectively in this world is "to change, to integrate, to mix, and to mash" (Davis et al., 2010, p. 194); a process which allows the learners to express themselves with limited linguistic resources and empowers them to create meaningfully communicate.

In addition, a multiliteracies-infused approach can help place a greater critical emphasis and awareness on the significance of students designing their own materials as a measure of student intentions, identities, and social futures (Leander & Boldt, 2013). Designing is a key component of the pedagogy of multiliteracies. "[T]he act of designing is an agentic bridge between convention and innovation, between the canonical and the new, between reproduction and creativity" (Garcia et al., 2018, p. 75). For students, designing must begin with the familiar (their existing knowledge and circumstances) and extend into the unfamiliar (what they need to know and understand to be successful at design). It is tied intimately to authorship, autonomy, and agency in a multimodal world. We should therefore evaluate the success of student-created materials design primarily by looking at its ability to: (1) operate as self-expression through which they negotiate on their own terms, roles, relationships, and responsibilities, (2) utilize and challenge communicative conventions and paradigms in innovative and meaningful ways, and (3) represent unique social and cultural identities that can be understood cross-culturally.

When a narrow range of language skills and their correct usage are no longer able to dominate the process of ELT materials design, and we venture instead into a multiliteracies-infused model of student-created materials design, new and vital opportunities begin to emerge. In our chapter, we examine how secondary students in socially deprived areas of India, Nepal, Malaysia, and Indonesia were facilitated to design their own linguistically and culturally relevant and varied ELT materials for each other via a regionally based research project that leveraged the students' out-of-school multicultural and multilingual capital through a focus on multiliteracies in accordance with growing research interest in the field in Southeast Asia (Kiss & Mizusawa, 2018; Lim et al., 2021; Mizusawa, 2021a; Mizusawa & Kiss, 2020; Putch-Behak et al., 2015; Rahman et al., 2022; Tan & Guo, 2014).

The Present Study

Research Questions

We asked the following Research Questions (RQs):

1 How do students express their social/cultural identities when designing multimodal language teaching/learning materials?
2 In what ways do students use ELT materials design to give voice to their lived experiences?

Education Context

We collected data from four different Southeast Asian countries where learners were severely disadvantaged due to their remote location, socioeconomic status, and the COVID-19 pandemic. The participating research countries shared some key similarities, despite their ethnic and cultural differences. They were all multicultural and multilingual societies, and their education systems were highly exam-driven.

Participants

Purposeful convenience sampling was used to identify two groups of research participants: EL teachers and EL learners. First, we approached secondary teachers working in urban poor neighborhoods and rural areas lacking even basic infrastructure. The sampling was thereby neither representative of the teaching population in the participating countries, nor the size or composition of their population. Nevertheless, the sampling provided adequate data for statistical analysis. See Table 2.1 for participant information.

In a survey, participants were asked to personally assess whether their schools could be identified as disadvantaged given their limited resources, location, or student profile. This was meant to ensure that the sample only contained participants from truly disadvantaged educational settings. However, each participant interpreted this question differently, relative to the context in which they worked. For example, one teacher labeled their school as being disadvantaged, although it had running water, electricity, and a computer lab with an internet connection, simply because it lacked the latest facilities (e.g., tablet computers, interactive whiteboards) that a neighboring school had. Other teachers considered their schools not to be disadvantaged because they had more than what other regional schools had. Their schools still lacked basic utilities and served impoverished students with illiterate parents. In response, we decided to use all valid data provided by teachers without further filters.

In the second research stage, select teachers – based on their previous experience with research, peer recognition, and status – were approached to facilitate their learners' design of multimodal ELT materials. Teachers from Malaysia (1), Indonesia (2), India (2), and Nepal (2) indicated their

Table 2.1 Teacher participants in different countries

Country	Frequency	Percent
India	62	30.2
Indonesia	51	24.9
Malaysia	37	18.0
Nepal	55	26.8
Total	205	100.0

Multiliteracies and Student-Created Materials Design   47

willingness to participate. Before their students embarked on the materials design journey, the authors conducted an online workshop for them covering: (1) the principles of materials design and (2) multimodal materials/communication, with a special emphasis on how different modalities can compensate for limited language ability. Altogether 25 sets of materials were produced by participating students, individually and in groups, with varying assistance from teachers.

All participating teachers signed an informed consent form, and their students and their parents/guardians were also asked to provide assent and consent to participate in the study which was approved by the Research Ethics Committee of Sunway University, Malaysia.

Data Collection

Questionnaire

A questionnaire served to gauge whether teachers consider their students capable and willing to design language teaching/learning materials for other learners. The instrument contained 25 closed-ended Likert-scale questions. A four-point scale (from strongly disagree to strongly agree) was used to discourage participants from "sitting on the fence." They also had to answer some open-ended questions, mainly concerning their learners' ability to design materials.

Student-Created Materials

The product of a teacher-assisted, but student-created, materials design process provided rich research data. Students were asked to produce multimodal texts without specific instructions on which modalities to use and/or combine. However, they were told that their teaching/learning materials would be used by fellow EL learners in the region. They were also informed that the materials should help introduce others to aspects of their culture and/or subcultures and develop EL skills. Accordingly, the students had to design multimodal texts that could be utilized to fulfill language learning tasks.

It was not surprising that student-created materials made heavy use of the linguistic design element. While some combined the verbal with the visual, others produced purely word-based materials despite clear instructions to do otherwise. This could indicate the students' lack of resources or simply their unfamiliarity with multimodal texts within their educational settings. They may not have had ready access to the simplest of digital tools or even regular internet access. They could be following available textbooks as a guide. Table 2.2 offers a summary of materials, together with basic information about from where they originate, their type/medium, and their ELT focus.

Only 12 materials out of the 25 were considered truly multimodal and thereby valid for analysis in this chapter.

48 *K. Mizusawa and T. Kiss*

Table 2.2 An inventory of student-designed materials

No.	Country	Name of activity	Type	ELT focus
1	Malaysia	Fried rice	Video	Vocabulary and writing, a focus on cohesive devices and instructional text, writing a recipe
2	Malaysia	Rice wrap	Video	Email writing
3	Malaysia	Bidayuh traditional dance	Video	Vocabulary and writing
4	Malaysia	Writing e-books (Ruth weekends)	Video	Speaking skills
5	India	A story: Snake in the garden	Audio	Listening comprehension
6	India	Festivals of India	Visual/Text	Reading comprehension
7	India	Writing a poem: Mother	Visual/Text	Creative writing
8	Nepal	Bashudev Dahai	Visual/Text	Mixed
9	Nepal	Tihar/Chhath festivals	Visual/Text	Reading, writing, vocabulary
10	Nepal	Pampha Adhikari	Visual/Text	Vocabulary and paragraph writing
11	Indonesia	Unit 1: How I started	Text	Reading, writing, vocabulary
12	Indonesia	Unit 2: Welcome to our home	Text	Mixed
13	Indonesia	I see my surroundings	Mainly text	Mixed
14	Indonesia	Tale as old as time	Text	Mixed
15	Indonesia	English book	Text	Mixed, grammar included
16	Indonesia	Vignettes of presidents	Text	Mixed
17	Indonesia	Literature: Poem	Text	Mixed, creative writing
18	Indonesia	Literature: Short story	Text	Mixed, creative writing
19	Indonesia	Indonesia through history	Text	Mixed
20	Indonesia	Entertainment: Unit 1	Visual/Text	Mixed
20	Indonesia	Entertainment: Unit 2	Mainly text	Mixed
21	Indonesia	Entertainment: Unit 3	Visual/Text	Mixed
22	Indonesia	Tourism: Unit 2 Reading	Text	Mostly reading
23	Indonesia	Tourism: Unit 2 Listening	Text (no audio provided)	Listening comprehension
24	Indonesia	Tourism: Unit 1 Listening	Text (no audio provided)	Listening comprehension
25	Indonesia	Tourism: Unit 1 Reading	Text	Mixed

Data Analysis

Questionnaire

For this chapter the questionnaire data were used to illustrate the general attitudes of teachers toward their learners' willingness and capabilities to design learning materials. Therefore, of the quantitative data we only present a select few, basic descriptive statistic results to offer a glimpse into the context of the student materials designers. The qualitative data were coded by two members of the research team to ensure reliability and validity. Open coding was followed by axial coding (Saldaña, 2021) to identify patterns in the data. Again, in this chapter we only use illustrative quotations as the focus is on the materials students produced.

Materials Analysis

Since most valid multimodal texts were based on visuals, they were examined via two methods for examining 21st-century visual media in classroom contexts (Mizusawa, 2018). This seemed appropriate as we were analyzing how and why students composed such texts to communicate their ideas. First, we looked at the compositional value of each individual image (if appropriate) according to what we may term their *style*, *elements*, and *characteristics*. In brief, style refers to the "distinctive look of visual media" (p. 86) which, in the case of student-created materials, will reflect the student's cultural influences, personal tastes, and available media tools and resources. Elements refer to the different parts/components that comprise an image, such as labels, captions, icons, headings, and objects within the frame. Characteristics point to the qualities of an image that reflect its purpose such as the use of genre conventions, online protocol, and established practices in ELT materials design. Second (and when appropriate), images were explored as meaning-making tools used in conjunction with other images. If students utilize not one but two images, they could be creating binary contrasts such as a before-and-after comparison. If students utilize three (or more) images, they are likely forming a pattern, offering choices, or telling a story with a beginning, middle, and end. Employing images in this manner reflects sophistication and a willingness to generate meaning through image arrangement or juxtaposition.

Findings

Teacher Questionnaire

Generally, participating teachers did not have much trust in their students' abilities to create ELT materials for other learners. They disagreed that students could do it (42.4%) and cited many reasons, but most commonly, they pointed to their students' weak language proficiency and a lack of resources

50   K. Mizusawa and T. Kiss

and time. As one participant put it, they are "time bound, getting resources, expenses in collecting materials and so on" (T205) would be too difficult.

Furthermore, they did not think the students would have the necessary skills to create texts and tasks, with 11.5% strongly disagreeing, and 44% disagreeing that their students would be capable of such an activity. Inadvertently, their qualitative survey answers hinted that students were still being taught EL in a teacher-fronted and functional manner. It also suggested that most classroom work was closely monitored and controlled by teachers. One participant commented that students need *more* teacher guidance and instruction, not less: "[Students] don't have enough knowledge to design teaching materials and need more guide [sic] from the teachers" (T67). Another lamented, alongside others, that their students' "lack of confidence" (T30) would likely prevent successful design work. They did not contemplate that engaging in materials design may build student confidence or was their job to create confidence-building opportunities where student voices could be heard and validated, where equal emphasis is placed on content (i.e., what the students want to say) and on form (i.e., how they express their meanings).

The teachers' negative perceptions of their learners were not justified as evidenced in the materials. In the following we will offer an in-depth analysis of three student-designed materials. These come from the three research contexts, (1) Malaysia, (2) Nepal, and (3) Indonesia, and represent different approaches to creating multimodal texts. The analysis will focus exclusively on the student-generated texts and will exclude the pedagogical tasks that accompanied them because these reflected a teacher- and form-centered pedagogical approach that did not showcase learners' individuality.

Teaching Materials

Teaching Material 1: Making Belacan Fried Rice (Video)

It was evident that the video maker was well-versed in the characteristics/genre expectations of YouTube cooking videos and understood their intended effects as meaning-making tools. At the same time, the style of the video was highly reflective of her individual tastes and experiences. As she explains, the dish, *nasi goreng belacan*, is something that she makes regularly for herself at home. Hence, the video is designed to provide a valuable window into her daily interaction with local culture/cuisine. The multimodal text, therefore, was not created for the primary purpose of encouraging the viewer to make the dish themselves (unlike conventional cooking videos), but rather to share a small but significant aspect of her life and culture with other students. As such, it was expressive of her multicultural and multilingual ethnic identity as a Sarawakian/Malaysian.

The shots/images employed by the video could be examined both individually and in relationship to each other as sequenced shots/images. By careful design, the video evinced an overarching narrative structure with a

Multiliteracies and Student-Created Materials Design 51

beginning, middle, and end which was complemented with other multimodal elements (i.e., on-screen text, commentary/voiceover, and music). Each segment was presumably shot multiple times and carefully edited for pace and clarity. The video begins with a panning shot/moving image which introduces the finished dish and its personal importance. The camera movement ensured that the food didn't look static or uninteresting. It then cuts to a shot of the student/presenter in the background, introducing the different ingredients neatly arranged on plates and in bowls on a tabletop and placed prominently in the foreground. The composition of this shot demonstrated an awareness of the importance of introducing herself as a presenter but only in the larger context of a cooking video. Presenters must be engaging yet never overshadow the dish. The on-camera presentation was used exclusively at the beginning.

The next sequence of shots (the middle) covered the cooking process step by step. The point-of-view shot was employed consistently to place the viewer in her position as a chef, thereby inviting them to share in her experiences and see what she sees. Only the student's hands can be seen within the frame. Each shot provided a demonstration of each step while music and voiceover were used to enhance the experience by offering explicit instruction, clarifying details, and personal commentary. Time-consuming cooking steps were sped up to keep things fast and snappy. The video ends with a shot of the finished dish. The use of on-screen text naming the dish and oddly comical music made for an uncharacteristic conclusion. However, it was very much in keeping with her personal tastes, purposes, and choices. Putting potentially unfamiliar Malay words on screen aided cross-cultural communication. The music allowed for a light-hearted ending that was consistent with the casual nature of the dish.

In sum, the student was able to use/reproduce the appropriate characteristics of YouTube cooking videos with available resources (i.e., phone camera and editing software) for her own purposes without any explicit teacher guidance. The students showed a sophisticated understanding of her role as presenter, guide, and instructor. The video made an effective argument for her dish selection, its personal appeal, and its cultural significance.

Teaching Material 2: The Responsibility of Youth (Drawing)

This student-produced image/illustration from Nepal was designed as a prompt for writing and discussion tasks and assumed common understanding and acceptance of its central message about the overwhelming responsibilities that youths face today. A black-and-white pencil sketch (see Figure 2.1) appropriately bleak in tone shows a skeletal stick-like figure struggling to cross a high wire placed across a deep chasm. It is captioned, quite ironically: "The actual youth," given the highly stylized, surreal, and cynical representation of its ideas, which are more reflective of the individual's personal grievances than any universal truth. The illustration is however similar in quality to political cartoons, although its key characteristics do not conform to any recognizable multimodal text genre/culture in or out of school. The impossibly thin central

Figure 2.1 The responsibility of youth

figure may have taken inspiration from Tim Burton's Jack Skellington, but otherwise, the image's distorted and exaggerated style seems more strongly influenced by Japanese anime. The student's ultimate purpose, therefore, is self-expression through art, not cultural representation as there is little to tie it explicitly to any culture or convention.

The visual elements are meant to be allegorical and symbolic. The central figure is the very embodiment of suffering who is required to balance all manner of responsibilities on its thin frame. Upon its head is stacked a large pile of books on a mortar board. This appears to represent the burdens of academic life and learning. In one hand it holds a fishbowl labeled "emotions" from which water is seen to easily spill, indicating the challenge of keeping one's emotions in check. In its other hand is an open box/chest from which

Multiliteracies and Student-Created Materials Design 53

hand-like flames are escaping. This seems to warn of the dangers of temptation. An arrow pierces the figure's chest from behind; an act of betrayal (by adults?) perhaps that has not only gone through the heart but has pulled it clear out of the body. In place of a ribcage, we see the bars of a cage. Inside sits a bird, pointing to a lack of (and desire for) freedom. Finally, the high wire is not a straight line but a jagged one with many violent ups and downs, like an electrocardiogram (ECG) recording of intense stress and turmoil. The image speaks overwhelmingly of anger, frustration, and resentment.

The image goes against the grain of ELT material design which would depict student life in a more conventional, literal, and positive manner. This vision of student angst may or may not be the product of actual inner turmoil – at least, not to the degree depicted in the image. Regardless, by being subversive and speaking against adult authority and influence, the image makes a strong case for greater student agency, voice, and autonomy.

Teaching Material 3: Entertainment (Collage)

To facilitate a discussion of celebrity culture and influence, a group of Indonesian students created a collage of unlabeled/unidentified celebrity images taken from online sources that they assumed other students in the region would be familiar with. Interestingly, despite the global dominance of and their ready access to Western mass media and culture, all their chosen celebrities were of Asian or mixed Asian origin. Out of the nine chosen media personalities, four were Filipino or Filipino American, three were Indonesian, and two were Thai indicating an unmistakable preference for culturally and ethnically similar role models that they can identify with. The selection represented a mixture of mainstream (music) and social media personalities. One cannot help but notice the strong Filipino (as opposed to Indonesian) bias in the student's choices, but this may simply illustrate the rise of "P-pop" in Southeast Asia.

While the collage may or may not reflect the actual preferences and preoccupations of their regional peers, it nevertheless inscribes an intercultural and international space of shared values and understandings that is exclusive of the students' making. Their choices are not random but deliberate. Together, they establish new trends and patterns that define their tastes, attitudes, and identities that override any pre-existing regional, national, or cultural/subcultural distinctions. What is more, their choices are significant as they go against the very premise of ELT material design. Traditional ELT practices and materials, no matter how inclusive, still begin with Western values and ideas, although they may try to balance East and West in their representation of culture, life, and language use. However, based on what the students have generated, such "balanced" representations fall well short of acknowledging the students' local circumstances and global perspectives. Western celebrities were not included in the collage and may not even figure in their immediate worldview. Western-centric (hierarchical) and East-West (dichotomized) approaches to culture and

54   K. Mizusawa and T. Kiss

practice are unhelpful in ELT when students show the capacity to define their own popular cultural influences in more authentic, personal, pluralistic, and horizontal ways.

Discussion

When students use images rather than words as the dominant communicative mode, students can shift from being content consumers to providers/producers by finding their voices multimodally and exercising agency. The analyzed materials invite other students to actively explore their own and others' cultural identities and affiliations and forgo the constraints of standardized language learning.

Expression of Social/Cultural Identity

To reiterate, the success of student-created materials design can be measured by its ability to operate as a mode of self-expression. From the analysis of the sample materials, it was evident that the student-designers managed to take up a role and identity that was more authentic and meaningful than forcing themselves into prefabricated identity boxes. Through this, they were no longer marginal but central to the learning process (Kalantzis & Cope, 2008; Lim et al., 2021; Mizusawa & Kiss, 2020). In Material 1, the student presents her identity through her favorite dish. She tells us who she is and where she comes from. It also hints at (1) the sociocultural expectations of girls knowing how to cook and (2) her possible aspirations to be a YouTuber. Material 2 chose a harsh personal style and message; a stark contrast to colorful and nonconfrontational global textbooks. It defied convention by representing a struggling figure and subcultural identity, rather than a happy and successful learner. Material 3 shows learners expressing their worldview by choosing role models that resemble them, reflect regional/local tastes, and do not communicate predominantly in English, if at all. Indeed, choosing non-English speaking Asian celebrities is an attempt to give expression to a cultural identity that rejects standard British/American priorities/content. Through multimodal design work, students learned to take on the responsibility of showing who they are and who they can be (Lee, 2015; Metboki, 2018; Nguyen et al., 2021).

Utilizing and Challenging Communicative Conventions

As multimodal designers, students had the power to choose between convention or innovation, to follow standards or to forgo them, to reproduce and reimagine, or to create something new (Garcia et al., 2018). Material 1 opted to follow YouTube cooking videos, linguistically and visually, but they also highlighted their personal preferences and identity. Material 2 chose to challenge global textbook norms by initiating critical student dialogue on the negative impact of examination culture. Lastly, Material 3 chose to generate a celebrity collage of found images that helped inscribe a unique cultural space where new patterns and preoccupations could be discovered. It reflected a convergence culture, where meaning was generated from blending and borrowing (Jenkins, 2006; Mizusawa, 2021b).

The Pursuit of Social Justice

Students can become change agents when they are given new roles and responsibilities. However, survey data indicates that many teachers are still unwilling to let them even try. Their comments illustrate the preference for a functional classroom environment (Kalantzis & Cope, 2008; Mizusawa, 2021a) where learners are told to comply, not take control over their own learning (Joseph Jeyaraj & Harland, 2016; Vettorel, 2018). Clearly, teachers must allow their students to speak with their own voices, no matter how flawed and unconfident they may appear at first, instead of aiming for impossibly high benchmark standards which many will fail even with explicit teacher instruction (Glas et al., 2023; Takahashi, 2014; Thurairaj & Roy, 2012; Vettorel, 2018). This is a prerequisite for social justice in ELT.

The student-produced multimodal texts may be far from publication standards as they lack linguistic accuracy and/or substance. However, they are authentic and valuable cultural artifacts (Lee, 2015; Metboki, 2018; Nguyen et al., 2021); they evince cultural richness, communicative competence, and self-expression. What is more, these texts call for action and dialogue from other students in notable ways. The first material is an *invitation to participate* in the creation of a cultural dish. It is a cross-cultural action that bridges cultural divides. The second is an *invitation to interpret*, challenging viewers to make their own meanings from a symbolic image. As such, it functions as a transcultural provocation. The last material is an *invitation to endorse and affirm* a common (popular) intercultural space the students collectively defined.

Overall, these materials are facets of personal and cultural identity that would otherwise have remained invisible and unacknowledged in regular EL classrooms (Kiss & Rimbar, 2017). Student-created materials design thereby works to address the power imbalance between teacher-endorsed EL learning and student-voiced cultural expression. They point to the emancipatory potential of prioritizing authenticity over accuracy, the individual over standards, and digital culture over print culture in ELT classrooms.

Conclusion

Given the opportunity, students can design multimodal texts that could be used in ELT. By becoming cross-cultural material designers, they learn to take ownership of the learning process, develop their personal voices, and positively represent their social/cultural identities for the benefit of other young people in other similar, if not identical, learning contexts. It teaches them that their voices matter not only to their immediate community/peer group but

56 *K. Mizusawa and T. Kiss*

well beyond that. When language education encourages students "to become directly engaged with their own and other communities, to take what they learn in their classroom beyond the classroom walls, into the here and now" (Byram & Wagner, 2018, pp. 146–147), it will no longer be concerned with the accurate execution of language skills for assessment purposes. Only by challenging ELT conventions can social justice and student voices be legitimately advanced.

References

Ambele, E. A., & Boonsuk, Y. (2021). Voices of learners in Thai ELT classrooms: A wake up call towards teaching English as a lingua Franca. *Asian Englishes*, *23*(2), 201–217. https://doi.org/10.1080/13488678.2020.1759248

Aoyama, R., & Denton, L. (2022). Creating space for World Englishes perspectives in the ELT classroom: Voices of high school students in Japan. *TESL-EJ*, *26*(1), 1–21. https://doi.org/10.55593/ej.26101a5

Baker, W. (2012). From cultural awareness to intercultural awareness: Culture in ELT. *ELT Journal*, *66*(1), 62–70. https://doi.org/10.1093/elt/ccr017

Block, D. (2004). Globalization and language teaching. *ELT Journal*, *58*(1), 75–77. https://doi.org/10.1093/elt/58.1.75

Brown, C. A. (2022). Symbolic annihilation of social groups as hidden curriculum in Japanese ELT materials. *TESOL Quarterly*, *56*(2), 603–628. https://doi.org/10.1002/tesq.3073

Byram, M., & Wagner, M. (2018). Making a difference: Language teaching for intercultural and international dialogue. *Foreign Language Annals*, *51*(1), 140–151. https://doi.org/10.1111/flan.12319

Davis, A., Webb, S., Lackey, D., & DeVoss, D. N. (2010). Remix, play, and remediation: Undertheorized composing practices. In H. Urbanski (Ed.), *Writing and the digital generation: Essays on new media rhetoric* (pp. 186–197). McFarland & Company. https://doi.org/10.4324/9781315518497-2

Galloway, N., & Rose, H. (2018). Incorporating Global Englishes into the ELT classroom. *ELT Journal*, *72*(1), 3–14. https://doi.org/10.1093/elt/ccx010

Garcia, A., Luke, A., & Seglem, R. (2018). Looking at the next 20 years of multiliteracies: A discussion with Allan Luke. *Theory Into Practice*, *57*(1), 72–78. https://doi.org/10.1080/00405841.2017.1390330

Glas, K., Catalán, E., Donner, M., & Donoso, C. (2023). Designing and providing inclusive ELT materials in times of the global pandemic: A Chilean experience. *Innovation in Language Learning and Teaching*, *17*(1), 114–129. https://doi.org/10.1080/17501229.2021.1940187

Gregory, K., & Clarke, M. (2003). High-stakes assessment in England and Singapore. *Theory Into Practice*, *42*(1), 66–74. https://doi.org/10.1207/s15430421tip4201_9

Irham, Huda, M., Sari, R., & Rofiq, Z. (2022). ELF and multilingual justice in English language teaching practices: Voices from Indonesian English lecturers. *Asian Englishes*, *24*(3), 263–278. https://doi.org/10.1080/13488678.2021.1949779

Jenkins, H. (2006). *Convergence culture: Where old and new media collide*. New York University Press. https://doi.org/10.1177/0894439307306088

Jenkins, J. (2004). ELF at the gate: The position of English as a lingua franca. In *Proceedings of the 38th IATEFL International Conference* (pp. 33–42). IATEFL.

Joseph Jeyaraj, J., & Harland, T. (2016). Teaching with critical pedagogy in ELT: The problems of indoctrination and risk. *Pedagogy, Culture & Society*, *24*(4), 587–598. https://doi.org/10.1080/14681366.2016.1196722

Kalantzis, M., & Cope, B. (2008). Language education and multiliteracies. In S. May & N. H. Hornberger (Eds.), *Encyclopedia of language and education* (pp. 195–211). Springer. https://doi.org/10.1007/978-0-387-30424-3_15

Kapur, K. (2021). ELT and social justice in multicultural classrooms. *Babylonia, 1*, 24–29, https://doi.org/10.55393/babylonia.v1i.42

Kiss, T., & Mizusawa, K. (2018). Revisiting the pedagogy of multiliteracies: Writing instruction in a multicultural context. *Changing English, 25*(1), 59–68. https://doi.org/10.1080/1358684x.2017.1403283

Kiss, T., & Rimbar, H. (2017). Unity in diversity: How teachers address issues of culture in locally produced EFL material. *Folio, 18*, 4–11.

Kiss, T., & Rimbar, H. (2021). English language teacher agency in rural Sarawak: Exploiting teaching materials. *The English Teacher, 50*(2), 142–156. https://doi.org/10.52696/dcvu6828

Kiss, T., & Weninger, C. (2013). A semiotic exploration of cultural potential in EFL textbooks. *Malaysian Journal of ELT Research, 9*(1), 19–28.

Kress, G. (2003). *Literacy in the new media age*. Routledge. https://doi.org/10.4324/9780203299234

Leander, K., & Boldt, G. (2013). Rereading "A pedagogy of multiliteracies" bodies, texts, and emergence. *Journal of Literacy Research, 45*(1), 22–46. https://doi.org/10.1177/1086296x12468587

Lee, B. (2015). EFL learners' perspectives on ELT materials evaluation relative to learning styles. *RELC Journal, 46*(2), 147–163. https://doi.org/10.1177/0033688214564177

Lim, F. V., & Tan, J. M. (2021). Curriculum and assessment mismatch: Examining the role of images in literacy assessments. *The Australian Journal of Language and Literacy, 44*(3), 22–34. https://doi.org/10.1007/bf03652078

Lim, F. V., Toh, W., & Nguyen, T. T. H. (2022). Multimodality in the English language classroom: A systematic review of literature. *Linguistics and Education, 69*, 1–30, https://doi.org/10.1016/j.linged.2022.101048

Lim, F. V., Weninger, C., & Nguyen, T. T. H. (2021). "I expect boredom": Students' experiences and expectations of multiliteracies learning. *Literacy, 55*(2), 102–112. https://doi.org/10.1111/lit.12243

Metboki, Y. (2018). Problems hindering student teachers' ELT materials development: A study in the internship program in Eastern Indonesia. *English Review: Journal of English Education, 7*(1), 93–104. https://doi.org/10.25134/erjee.v7i1.1498

Mizusawa, K. (2018). *Mastering visual literacy: Interpreting and understanding visual media*. Star Publishing.

Mizusawa, K. (2021a). From functional literacy to multiliteracies: Understanding rich and visual texts in Singapore writing classrooms. *Asia Pacific Journal of Education, 41*(4), 727–739. https://doi.org/10.1080/02188791.2021.1997705

Mizusawa, K. (2021b). Remixing visual literacy for 21st-century adult education. In P. A. Robinson, K. V. Williams, & M. Stojanović (Eds.), *Global citizenship for adult education* (pp. 306–315). Routledge. https://doi.org/10.4324/9781003050421-39

Mizusawa, K., & Kiss, T. (2020). Connecting multiliteracies and writing pedagogy for 21st century English language classrooms: Key considerations for teacher education in Singapore and beyond. *Journal of Nusantara Studies (JONUS), 5*(2), 192–214. https://doi.org/10.24200/jonus.vol5iss2pp192-214

Nault, D. (2006). Going global: Rethinking culture teaching in ELT contexts. *Language, Culture and Curriculum, 19*(3), 314–328. https://doi.org/10.1080/07908310608668770

Nguyen, T. T. M., Marlina, R., & Cao, T. H. P. (2021). How well do ELT textbooks prepare students to use English in global contexts? An evaluation of the Vietnamese English textbooks from an English as an international language (EIL) perspective. *Asian Englishes, 23*(2), 184–200. https://doi.org/10.1080/13488678.2020.1717794

Pang, A. (2020). Multiliteracies in ELL curriculum implementation and pedagogy in multilingual classrooms of Southeast Asia. *English Teaching*, *75*(2), 149–166. https://doi.org/10.15858/engtea.75.2.202006.149

Puteh-Behak, F., Darmi, R., & Mohamed, Y. (2015). Implementation of a western-based multiliteracies pedagogy in Malaysia: A socio-cultural perspective. *GEMA Online Journal of Language Studies*, *15*(1), 1–24. https://doi.org/10.17576/gema-2015-1501-01

Rahman, M. A., Melliyani, M., Handrianto, C., Erma, E., & Rasool, S. (2022). Prospect and promise in integrating multiliteracy pedagogy in the English language classroom in Indonesia. *Eternal (English, Teaching, Learning, and Research Journal)*, *8*(1), 34–52. https://doi.org/10.24252/eternal.v81.2022.a3

Rogers, T. (2022). Youth activism through critical arts, transmedia, and multiliteracies. In B. Lingard, S. Sellar, S. Lewis, & G. W. Noblit (Eds.). *Oxford research encyclopedia of education*. Oxford University Press. https://doi.org/10.1093/acrefore/9780190264093.013.1783

Saldaña, J. (2021). *The coding manual for qualitative researchers*. Sage.

Sang, Y. (2017). Expanded territories of "literacy": New literacies and multiliteracies. *Journal of Education and Practice*, *8*(8), 16–19.

Sulistyowardani, M., Mambu, J. E., & Pattiwael, A. S. (2020). Indonesian EFL teachers' cognitions and practices related to social justice. *Indonesian Journal of Applied Linguistics*, *10*(2), 420–433. https://doi.org/10.17509/ijal.v10i2.28614

Takahashi, R. (2014). An analysis of ELF-oriented features in ELT coursebooks: Are attitudes towards non-native varieties changing in English language teaching policy and practice in Japan? *English Today*, *30*(1), 28–34. https://doi.org/10.1017/s0266078413000539

Tan, L., & Guo, L. (2014). Multiliteracies in an outcome-driven curriculum: Where is its fit? *The Asia-Pacific Education Researcher*, *23*(1), 29–36. https://doi.org/10.1007/s40299-013-0082-0

Thurairaj, S., & Roy, S. S. (2012). Teachers' emotions in ELT material design. *International Journal of Social Science and Humanity*, *2*(3), 232–236. https://doi.org/10.7763/ijssh.2012.v2.101

Vettorel, P. (2018). ELF and communication strategies: Are they taken into account in ELT materials? *RELC Journal*, *49*(1), 58–73. https://doi.org/10.1177/0033688217746204

Weninger, C. (2018). Introduction. In C. Weninger (Ed.), *From language skills to literacy: Broadening the scope of English language education through media literacy* (pp. 1–9). Routledge. https://doi.org/10.4324/9781315223100-1

Weninger, C., & Kiss, T. (2013). Culture in English as a foreign language (EFL) textbooks: A semiotic approach. *TESOL Quarterly*, *47*(4), 694–716. https://doi.org/10.1002/tesq.87

Part II

Multiliteracies Pedagogies for Inclusion in Diverse Communities

3 Multiliteracies for Social Inclusion and Plurilingual Identity Construction

Repositioning the Self in a Superdiverse Language Learning Environment

Barbara Spinelli

Introduction

The complexity of the multilingual and multicultural language learning communities has refocused language education toward issues of identity and subjectivity. Research in Applied Linguistics has shown the interconnections between globalization, multilingualism, and identity illustrating how individuals invest in language learning and socially construe their multiple identities (Davis & Norton, 2016; García, 2022; Pavlenko & Blackledge, 2003). These learning communities can locally reflect interaction patterns, conflictual forces, and power dynamics that characterize translocal communities. Learners bring their lifeworld differences that share with peers coming from diverse social, economic, and educational backgrounds. Such a sharing space may offer opportunities to cultivate an understanding of diversity and enhance civic engagement and community involvement by developing learners' self-expression and critical thinking (Cope & Kalantzis, 2024; Luke, 2018). However, "diversity" is not a neutral word recognized to appreciate the existence of a wide range of characteristics among human beings (Cope & Kalantzis, 2024). Diversity can imply differences in terms of access to educational tools and social resources according to social class, ethnic background, gender, and age. Such differences may include inequalities in participation in discursive practices due to different control and use of languages spoken and cultural representations (Kramsch, 2021). This latter aspect is particularly relevant in multilingual language learning environments because, as Baxter (2016) claims, languages are "the place where our sense of self and our identity or subjectivity is constructed and performed" (p. 36). Multilingual education, by valuing learners' plurilingual[1] capital, may challenge global and local language ideologies, which act as crucial mediating factors in identity construction. These ideologies can contribute to inequality and social hierarchization influencing how individuals are positioned by others and position themselves through discursive processes (Blackledge, 2000).

This chapter aims to explore the impact of an instructional intervention, specifically a recursive reflective itinerary, in a multilingual post-secondary

DOI: 10.4324/9781003438847-6

62   B. Spinelli

Italian language classroom. The focus is on how this intervention can foster the discursive practices and actively engage learners in developing their identity, while also cultivating an equal sense of belonging to their learning community through the recognition and respect of their lifeworld experiences and backgrounds. First, this chapter will describe how the educational objectives of this case study have been defined by drawing on multiliteracies and social justice beliefs and frameworks. Second, it will explore how a positioning-based reflective model designed to achieve those goals can impact the interplay of different and competing positions learners can take renegotiating their subjectivity through their *agency*. Finally, it will illustrate the outcomes of the qualitative data collected during this awareness-raising journey.

Becoming a Multiliterate Learner for Social Inclusion in a Multilingual World

According to Anstey and Bull, multiliterate individuals are those who "use literacy and literate practices with a range of texts and technologies; in socially responsible ways […] to fully participate in life as an […] informed citizen" (2007, p.55). Therefore, these multiliteracies skills (Cope & Kalantzis, 2000) play a pivotal role in fostering learning, facilitating social belonging, nurturing agency development, and enabling individuals to fully engage in society. In the last decade, scholars in the field of multiliteracies (Cope & Kalantzis, 2024; Luke, 2018) have emphasized the importance of these latter aspects by highlighting the need to teach critical and social literacies, which enable learners to explore underlying social values, attitudes, and promote social participation. Multiliteracies skills should not be taught as "neutral tools" (Luke, 2018, p. 302) but rather engaging learners in examining and constructing texts, identities, and forms of community actions through critical work, and lead to transformative knowledge and practices, which are essential components of a global citizenship education (UNESCO, 2015).

Languages and relations of power are always intertwined (Kramsch, 2021). Therefore, language learning communities can serve as spaces for reflecting on socio-cultural powers and dominant discourses that shape individuals' discursive practices and promote this transformative knowledge. Literate practices are, in fact, situated (Luke, 2018) through social contexts and activities and cannot be "addressed without attention to histories of power relations or group and individual struggle for identity" (Lewis et al., 2012, p. 3).

As previously stated, in a globalized world, multilingual language learning contexts can specifically question dominant ideologies such as the notion of one nation-one people-one language (Lo Bianco, 2004) that make multilingualism "invisible" or monolingual practices that raise questions of social justice by creating linguistic asymmetries and subordination. Researchers (Healy, 2008) have highlighted how literacy practices valued in education reflect the practices of dominant social groups. An illustration of this is labeling English as *a lingua franca* (Navarro et al., 2022). Such labeling can have

Multiliteracies for Social Inclusion and Plurilingual Identity Construction 63

detrimental effects on the academic, social, and emotional trajectories of plurilinguals. It may lead to misleading interpretations and create social exclusion when plurilingual speakers perceive English as a subtractive language within their linguistic repertoire.

By nurturing learners' critical awareness of dominant and alternative discourses, rather than simply acquiring them, we can promote "powerful literacy" (Gee, 1992, p. 25) essential for success in education and life, and for fostering social inclusion.

This agentive discourse plays a crucial role in the construction of plurilingual identities as it allows learners to become "active subjects" (Moje & Lewis, 2007, p. 19), enabling them to reconceptualize their skills and knowledge and to transform fixed discourses.

Therefore, the concept of "powerful literacy" in the current global society involves, but is not limited to, multimodal literacy—a combination of representational and communicational modes through images, speech, writing, and digital tools. In their revision of the multiliteracies framework, Cope and Kalantzis (2024) underscore the significance of broadening the interpretation of "multis." The emphasis on individual differences in utilizing multimodal representation and communication should be integrated with a deep understanding of the social diversity and complexity that characterize the multilayered global society, as shown in their new paradigm (Figure 3.1).

In this new paradigm, the concept of diversity is articulated and emphasized from a social perspective on the "multi-situational" side. This emphasis is crucial because social diversity is complex on both a global and local scale, such as within classroom communities. It plays a pivotal role in shaping individuals' identities, which constitutes the central focus explored in this chapter. Identity is a linguistically, individually, and socially mediated construct (Ayres-Bennett & Fisher, 2022; Forbes et al., 2021), and individuals can take and perform

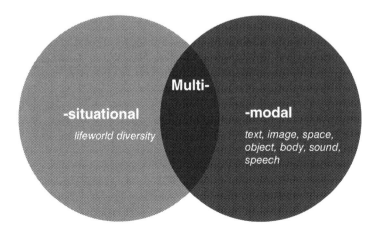

Figure 3.1 Multiliteracies new paradigm (Cope & Kalantzis, 2024)

64   *B. Spinelli*

different and sometimes conflictual positions in a particular *milieu* according to a combination of social, economic, and historical relations (Block, 2022).

This is why the Positioning Theory (PT) alongside a reflective approach proves to be a powerful framework for the case study presented in this chapter. Reflecting on individuals' lifeworld diversity and the process of identity formation is essential for developing social and critical literacies that promote values such as empathy, inclusiveness, and awareness of cross-cultural differences.

While the project described in this chapter involves both aspects of the new multiliteracies framework, the case study presented below will specifically focus on the "multi-situational" dimension of the language class as the subject of analysis, investigating possible consequences of the adopted methodological approach.

Designing Plurilingual Identity through Positioning and Reflexivity

Scholars on multilingualism agree that identity is not solely defined by psychological, social, economic, or geographical aspects, but rather, it is a contingent and "multidimensional phenomenon" (Block, 2022, p. 2). To capture this dynamic and multilayered nature of identity, PT, as defined by Harré and van Langenove (1999), explores individuals' capacity to actively alter their positions. Positions can encompass "social status, moral and personal attributes, characteristics, or abilities" and are "tied to social actions and accomplished in social practices" (Kayı-Aydar, 2019, p. 5). The PT, therefore, is crucial for learners and instructors to promote identity development (Kayı-Aydar & Miller, 2018) in multilingual learning communities. These educational settings can create space for enacting new identities by enabling "active position taking" (Luke, 2018, p. 239) and by acquiring and reframing skills and knowledge (Moje & Lewis, 2007).

Such a transformation may be possible when PT is embedded in and accompanied by analytical and reflective practices that may lead to a deeper understanding of identity (Block, 2022).

According to Harré and van Langenove (1999), the different positioning that individuals can take can be grouped into two macro-categories: Interactive and Reflexive positioning. The former refers to the process of positioning oneself in relation to others through social interactions, and the latter involves critically reflecting on how one is positioned within various social contexts and how these positions shape their behaviors and sense of self.

The reflective aspect of these positioning acts, carried out through discursive processes, is essential for "re-designing" identity. It encourages individuals to question and challenge societal norms, power structures, and the influence of social categorizations on their identity formation. The design metaphor, therefore, "is about creativity and agency" (Luke, 2018, p. 300) that can be shaped by positioning and offering opportunities for alternative paths of self-development.

Multiliteracies for Social Inclusion and Plurilingual Identity Construction 65

Scholars point out how identity-based education and interventions (Fisher et al., 2020; Forbes et al., 2021; Haukås et al., 2021) in multilingual language learning contexts are pivotal for such critical work. They emphasize that to be effective, any intervention must be *explicit* and *participatory*. This entails conscious engagement from learners as they consider their plurilingual identities, while also acknowledging the potential for change within these self-perceptions.

The instructional design model and pedagogical intervention of this case study are based on the insights provided by this conceptual framework.

Method

Setting and Participants

The participants of this case study were five students of the Italian Language Program, at a university in the U.S., who attended an Intermediate Italian language course aimed to promote oral skills at the B2 level of competence (Council of Europe, 2001). Despite the small class size, it encompassed a significant diversity in terms of students' ethnicity, education, and life experiences.[2] Their essential biographical profiles[3] are synthesized as follows.

- Jake is American with Greek roots and grew up in two different big capitals in Europe, speaking French, Greek (as a heritage language), and English. His linguistic repertoire also comprises Italian, Portuguese, Spanish, and Chinese.
- Nancy is from South America. Very early in her life, she migrated to the U.S. with her parents, who moved to North America in search of economic opportunities. Her linguistic repertoire includes Spanish as her mother tongue, English, and Italian as a heritage language.
- Lauren is from South America but from a different country than Nancy. Her grandfather moved to South America from Italy in the early 20th century for personal reasons. All her family and relatives in South America speak Italian and has strong links with her relatives in Italy. Lauren is bilingual, speaking Spanish and English. Her linguistic repertoire also includes Italian as a heritage language and French.
- Greta is of Italian American heritage from her mother's side. Her great-grandparents were from the South of Italy and migrated to the U.S. in search of a better quality of life and economic opportunities. Italian was not spoken in her family, and she has no connections with her Italian relatives in Italy. Her linguistic repertoire includes English, Italian as heritage language, Spanish, and Greek.
- Anna is American Jewish. She was born in the U.S. Her family moved to North America from Central Eastern Europe at the beginning of the 20th century due to discrimination motives. Her linguistic repertoire includes English as her mother tongue, Hebrew, Ancient Hebrew, Spanish, and Italian.

66 B. Spinelli

Instruction and Pedagogical Model

The instructional intervention described in this chapter took place during the 9th week of a 14-week semester of an Intermediate Italian language course. The main objective of the course was to cultivate learners' sensitivity and awareness toward diversity, analyzing it from various perspectives such as generational, historical, global, linguistic, socio-economic, and media representation.

The goal of the specific intervention was to examine this theme in connection with learners' own life experiences and the construction of their plurilingual identities. A pedagogical pathway was designed to guide learners in performing their identities "moment-to-moment," aiming to destabilize relations of power and develop agency by creating space for learners to position and reposition themselves and their discursive practices.

At the beginning of this journey, learners were asked to craft a digital plurilingual autobiography,[4] which they presented to their peers. During and after the presentations, peers were able to pose questions to explore further details. Narrative approaches and PT are interconnected in their focus on how individuals construct their identities, the role of language(s) and discourse, the importance of context, and the impact of social interactions (Block, 2022). Additionally, artifacts play a vital role in the process of meaning-making, as multiliteracies approaches suggest. Therefore, the use of an oral digital narrative text served as a significant organizing scheme for learners to describe their diverse life experiences and beliefs.

As Moje and Lewis argue, "autobiographies [...] are not just personal" (2007, p. 10) but socially situated. Both these aspects were involved in the reflexive process promoted by two follow-up activities. The second activity involved learners filling out a self-reflection questionnaire while watching their videotaped oral pluri-autobiographies. Through this process, they analyzed how they conveyed their "plurilingual selves" using linguistic devices, discourse markers, and metaphors, as well as their interaction with classmates.

The third activity consisted of an interview with the instructor[5] at the end of the semester, investigating deeper into some of the concepts that emerged during the self-reflection process.

The design of the reflective pathway allowed learners to engage with different levels of reflection, involving lower- to higher-order thinking processes.

The pedagogical model adopted for this pathway is summarized in Figure 3.2.

The creation of the digital plurilingual autobiography enabled what is defined as "prepositioning discourse" (Harré et al., 2009, p. 10), in which individuals use linguistic and discursive resources to establish roles within social contexts. This includes how they present themselves through character traits and biographical facts, how they use and compare languages they know,[6] how they talk about others, and how they position themselves in relation to various

Multiliteracies for Social Inclusion and Plurilingual Identity Construction 67

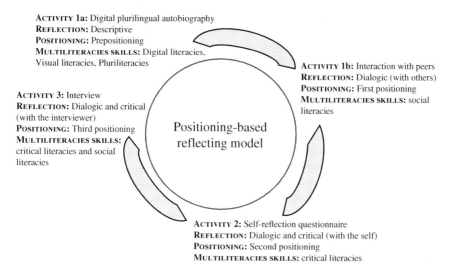

Figure 3.2 Position-based reflecting model

social categories. It is a significant positioning because it reflects how individuals actively participate in the social construction of reality and how language is used to influence and negotiate social meanings and relationships (Block, 2022). The reflective process activated in this step can be defined as "descriptive" (Hegarty, 2011, p. 10) since it allows learners to describe events and express feelings and emotions relating to them.

This activity was alternated with times when classmates could ask clarifying questions. In these moments, a first-order positioning occurred. According to Harré and van Langenove (1999), in first-order positioning, individuals position themselves and others in an ongoing interaction. This positioning involved a reflective process called "dialogic" (Hegarty, 2011, p. 10) that occurs when learners have opportunities to provide explanations or express judgment. However, it does not necessarily imply critical reflection (Hegarty, 2011, p. 10), which engages a higher order of thinking, such as self-awareness. As a matter of fact, most of the time, this initial positioning (Kayı-Aydar & Miller, 2018, p. 3) "is subconscious," and individuals "do not always intentionally position themselves or others in particular ways."

The second step of this reflective journey entailed learners individually watching the video of their presentation and answering some investigating questions. These purposefully crafted questions, designed by the instructor, aimed to foster learners' deeper reflection on the specific discursive practices and thoughts shared with their peers during the discussion. This phase enabled learners to take a second-order positioning. According to Harré and Van Langenove, a

68 B. Spinelli

second-order positioning occurs when "a first-order positioning is questioned or negotiated within an ongoing discussion" (1999, p. 21). The discussion, in this context, has to be interpreted as a conversation with the "self." Learners were encouraged to develop "critical reflection" (Hegarty, 2011, p. 10) by analyzing and questioning linguistic choices, ideas, and assumptions that emerged during the presentation and interaction in the classroom.

This self-conscious process culminated in the final step, in which the instructor had an individual face-to-face meeting with each learner during the last week of the semester. The scope of this meeting was to provide learners with opportunities to take a third order of positioning. As Block states, this positioning is "different from the previous two orders given its temporal, spatial (physical), social, and psychological separation from the original events" (2022, p. 86). The interview, based on *ad hoc* prompts provided by the instructor, accounted for one more chance for learners to rethink themselves by critically "re-reading" the previous experience of self-reflection, comparing and evaluating the different positions taken in that time frame. By revisiting that event, they were able to reflect upon what they learned from the experience and how this change would affect their future practices. These latter aspects are essential components of critical reflection that lead to transformative practices.

Data Analysis

The nature of this case study was relational and collaborative, as the researcher also served as the instructor, and therefore was part of the study, while learners by bringing their personal stories and beliefs played an active role in the research process. By adopting a qualitative approach, these data have been interpreted inductively. In facing the challenge of maintaining a balance between objectivity and subjectivity and being aware that it is not possible to entirely capture others' feelings and lives (Muramatsu, 2018), various research methods have been utilized.

A thick description method (Geertz, 1988), combined with the triangulation approach (Merriam & Tisdell, 2015), was employed through prolonged fieldwork and direct observation to gain a comprehensive understanding of learners' plurilingual identity negotiation. The thick description allowed for the exploration of deeper meanings and the identification of social and personal variables that influenced learners' beliefs and behaviors through the observation of their recursive reflective processes, classroom practices, and by means of field notes. This description was supported by a triangulation approach involving cross-referencing data collected from various resources, namely: (1) video recordings of learners' plurilingual autobiography; (2) self-awareness questionnaires designed based on the analysis of the video recordings; and (3) audio recordings of in-depth semi-structured final interviews, which were conducted based on an examination of those questionnaires.

Discussion

Given the limited space in this context, the data were analyzed by identifying the main themes and connections that emerged from the most significant research findings in the initial and final steps of the reflective journey.

Taking a Stance and Showing Insecurity

The sharing of plurilingual autobiographies in the social space was a crucial starting point to explore the social impact on learners' perception of self and how they positioned themselves in relation to the audience. An important aspect that surfaced in this time frame is that autobiographic telling has an impact on stories individuals tell themselves about themselves in the process of positioning (Harré et al., 2009). In this process, they are engaged in positioning moves using their own utterances and descriptive language to introduce themselves and their autobiographical events (Kayı-Aydar, 2019).

This became evident in their presentations as they agentively positioned themselves by taking a firm stand, as shown in the following extracts from their autobiographies:

Greta: I was born in [State of origin in the U.S.] … my Italian American family is a big family but *speaks English* not Italian *but* we have *Italian traditions* …I am *proud* to be Italian American […]

Nancy: My parents are from [State of origin in South America] … I moved with them to New York and I was [very little] … *speaking Spanish* and growing up in the [State of South America] *culture* was *beautiful* … *my people* are *fighters, hardworking, vibrant* and they *enjoy* their life […] I was *proud* to represent [her country] in the U.S. on the folk dance […]

Anna: To describe my plurilingual and pluricultural background I need to tell you the *story of my family* that is the *typical story of Ashkenazi Jews,* therefore this presentation will be *very Jewish* […]

In this discursive process of self-construction, words acquired significant meanings (e.g., adjectives, nouns, verbs learners used or what to tell and not to tell) (Deppermann, 2015). It is the symbolic power of language(s) that allows individuals "to construct social reality" (Kramsch, 2021, p. 5), a power "capable of maintaining or subverting the social order" (Bourdieu, 1991, p. 170). Through these discursive practices learners introduce themselves as an "Italian American girl," a "migrants' daughter" and a "Jewish girl." The repetitive use of the adjectives such as "proud" and the use of "very Jewish" denotes a strong position of alignment and a sense of belonging to a certain community. All three learners emphasized their cultural capital, an important insight that they will be able to further unfold along the reflexive process.

According to Kumaravadivelu (1999), sometimes individuals respond to dominant discourses by expanding their capital, and in Bourdieu's view

70   B. Spinelli

(1986), cultural capital is a form of power. Greta and Nancy's families kept their roots maintaining strong links with their home culture and Anna with her historical heritage.

Learners also recognized and claimed linguistic and identity vulnerability:

Greta: we have the accent of the Italian Americans from [State of origin in the U.S.] like "prociut" for "prosciutto" or "moz/mozzarell" for "mozzarella" *but* it is *bad*. [facial mimicry and gesture showing criticism]

Nancy: sometimes I feel *frustrated* [...]I have *liberal* and *progressive* ideas like in the U.S. *but* I am more *conservative* when I think about values related to the family or religion like in [State of origin in South America] [...] but growing in the U.S. was a *privilege* [...] I saw how *hardly* my parents worked and *sacrificed* everything for me [...] I learnt how to be *perseverant* [...]

Anna: *I do not know* where my family comes from [...] we think from [city of potential origin] [...] *I do not feel attached* to that area because when my family lived there it was a *difficult* time for *us*.

Greta pointed out her linguistic insecurity by defining her Italian American dialect as "bad" but the meaning of this adjective, accompanied by her gesture of disapproval and embarrassment, remained unspoken.

Nancy used words such as "sacrificed" and "frustrated" to highlight her socio-economic background and the conflicting and dichotomized nature of her multicultural identity.

Anna emphasized her sense of rootlessness, which could be implicitly interpreted as being influenced by discriminatory acts, with her statement, "It was a difficult time for us." These utterances triggered the positioning of the instructor and peers, who asked for further explanations during the question-focused class session and in the subsequent steps of the reflexive journey.

Perception of Individual Plurilingualism

In the phase of prepositioning, learners also revealed how they perceived the plurilingual nature of their linguistic repertoire and identity as emerged in the following excerpts:

Greta: I studied Spanish for two years *but* [...] I was *lonely* and *frustrated* ... *I did not want* to study Spanish... my peers spoke Spanish and I could not understand anything from their conversations ... but when I was a teenager, *I started to appreciate* this culture from Angie [her Hispanic friend]
Italian is the *language of my dreams* I studied Italian for three years in high school because *my identity is Italian*... I hope to study Italian in Italy [...] I hope to be a *citizen of the world* with Italian... I hope to

Multiliteracies for Social Inclusion and Plurilingual Identity Construction 71

have the *links* with Italy that my family does not have I hope I will be a more *confident* person.

Anna: *Modern Hebrew* is very important to me and to my culture and my family who lives in Israel ... is the language of the *rebirth* [...] in [the city in U.S. where she grew up] English but also Spanish are spoken that is the reason why I studied Spanish in high school [...]

Greta was forced to study Spanish because in the primary and lower secondary schools of her area, Italian was not taught. That caused her sense of exclusion in that learning community. This is an example of institutional language policies that might shape learners' perception of their plurilingual self. Greta's attitude, which she defines as a "defeatist attitude" in her self-reflection questionnaire, shows resistance to such dominant discourse and reclaims the right of appropriation of her heritage language, Italian, and Italian identity. As Kubota suggests, in this respect, the "decision of which language is to be taught is linked to [...] need-based arguments" (2005, p. 44) that may enforce positions of power and inequalities rather than the inclusivity promoted by language policies based on beliefs in multilingualism.

However, Greta also demonstrates that plurilingualism is dynamic and that events or encounters may lead to shifts in positioning, as shown by the relationship with her Hispanic friend. When Nancy asked her, during the interaction, "Now would you like to speak Spanish?," Greta responds with a prompt "yes, now, yes."

The emotional dimension is also highlighted by Anna when she reclaims her linguistic rights that are also human rights, defining Modern Hebrew as "the language of rebirth."

The sharing in the classroom of different life stories and backgrounds also highlighted diversity in terms of literate identities, practices, and personal pathways that might be affected by socio-economic factors.

This is the case of Jake and Lauren who, through their narratives, appear to identify themselves as "cosmopolitan" plurilingual speakers (Gunesch, 2008), as follows:

Jake: I was born in [city in the U.S.], I grew up in [city in Europe] and [another city in Europe] [...] I studied in *bilingual schools* [English and French] ever since I was born I have been exposed to 3 different languages [...] *Greek* is my *third language* because it is the language of my family [...] U.S. is the *opportunity* and *resourcefulness* [...]at university I studied Italian[...], Portuguese, and Spanish... I studied *Italian* because I am a huge fan of the *Italian culture*, I love to *travel* there, [...]

Lauren: I went to a *bilingual school, English and Spanish* [...] I studied *French* for 3 years [...] I *visited many different countries*, my parents love to travel, and *I was able to improve my languages...* I wanted to study *Italian* because of my family [...] Spanish is very important *but also*

72   B. Spinelli

> *English* now that I live in the U.S. … and it has helped me travel, *discover the world* and better understand where I would like to live in the *future*.

Cosmopolitan plurilinguals are generally considered privileged individuals who have access to extensive language education and international experiences, such as traveling, studying abroad, and receiving formal language training to develop plurilingual skills. Jake and Lauren highlighted their bilingual background and identified English as a key factor for success in life.

Ortega (2019) highlights the "elitist" nature of perceiving bilingualism "as a resource for developing economic prowess [...]" which "is encouraged while the bilingualism of migrants [...] is perceived and confronted as a problem" (p. 25). This ideology and emphasis on English can significantly influence parents' language policy (Skutnabb-Kangas et al., 2009) and impact how learners perceived their plurilingualism. It may lead to the establishment of hierarchies and power relations among the languages in their plurilingual repertoire, missing the focus of their interconnectedness. Often, this sense of inequality is closely associated with concepts such as class and race (Luke, 2018), as evidenced in the data below.

Classroom's Multilingual Identity(ies)

Plurilingual autobiographies, and peer questioning, facilitated the construction of a *classroom narrative* and empowered learners to recognize social cues, such as the power dynamics shaping social interactions, by directing their attention to features that influence how individuals are perceived and how they perceive themselves. These features may include language, ethnicity, race, and social class, as shown in the following data:

Instructor: Where did you hear this dialect … from your mother, your grand-mother …?
Greta: Um … it is more a mixed language… some words.
Instructor: Like "prosciut" …
Greta: Um… yea [gesture of disapproval]
Instructor: but you do not like it…
Greta: *No*
Instructor: Why?
Greta: Because when I say like *"ricot" my peers say* [...] [they make her feel uncomfortable]

By providing further explanations, Greta disclosed her sense of inadequacy and positioned herself as what Flores and Rosa define "racialized speaking subjects" (2015, p. 150), a term produced by racial ideologies. These ideologies reflect the tendency of society to marginalize those whose ethno-racial and sociolinguistic backgrounds deviate from the linguistic norm. Higher education, which mirrors broader society, embeds racialized speakers and raciolinguistic

Multiliteracies for Social Inclusion and Plurilingual Identity Construction   73

ideologies (Sekaja et al., 2022) that may cause bias and social hierarchies and have an impact on language use and perceptions. It is worth noting that in the post-instructional intervention, during the interview, the instructor will revisit this aspect by asking Greta: "Are you still using words like *prosciut* or *ricot*?" She will display resistance to this dominant discourse, repositioning herself with increased self-confidence as she responds, "Yes, absolutely, why not?" As Block points out, "communicative acts and events are saturated with power relationships" (2022, p. 92). This inequality can lead to "existential inequality" (Block, 2022, p. 55), which is shaped by various forms of social discrimination based on social categories, as is evident in the following exchange:

Lauren: How do you perceive your American-Jewish identity?
Anna: I feel like a Jewish-American *or* an American-Jew... I think *I am Jewish wherever I am*... and I am American, I like America [...]
Instructor: Is it conflictual or reconcilable?
Anna: *More reconcilable* then conflictual ... but *when something happens* like last week [act of Semitism] I recognize that *I am Jewish*... [hesitation] it's *complicated*.

Anna's responses highlighted the impact of events—such as instances of racism in this case—on positioning, revealing how these occurrences may force individuals to take binary or hierarchical positioning in plurilingual identity construction. This also emphasizes that human experiences are inherently situated within historically specific discourses, rather than being neutral (Baxter, 2016).

Second language education motivated by a pragmatic rationale may serve to maintain these unequal relations of power rather than promote equality and social inclusion as envisioned by multilingual education.

In this learning context, the development of a classroom collective history and the interpersonal and social exchange empowered learners to cultivate meaningful relationships through the promotion of empathy and an understanding of differences. Learners had the opportunity to delve into how their peers navigated plurilingual identity challenges, exploring diverse and complex experiences while also finding a bit of themselves within others' stories. In the examples above, for instance, both Anna and Greta revealed their discomfort with the difficulty or impossibility of expressing their "whole selves," including their cultures and languages. At the same time, learners also sought commonalities despite their different experiential and socio-economic backgrounds. For instance, during her presentation, Greta attempted to establish connections with Jake's story, emphasizing the significance of friendships in developing their plurilingual and pluricultural repertoire, as well as the cultural roots of their heritage languages. She stated:

[...] last summer we went to visit my best friend [who is Greek] Calliope's grandmother in Greece [...] the language and the culture, in my opinion, are so warm, are warm as in Naples [where her great-grandparents come from].

74   B. Spinelli

Greta provided examples of meaningful words in Greek and Neapolitan that conveyed this feeling, showing shared values between her and Jake's home country cultures. This is also an example of how individuals, in today's mobile society, function as "social chameleon constantly borrowing bits and pieces of identity from whatever source available" (Block, 2022, p. 11).

Kalantzis and Cope (2024) highlight the role of agency and participation in meaning-making processes by describing the process of "transposition" between the meaning individuals make for themselves, the meaning they communicate to others, and the meaning they make for themselves of others' communicated meanings. Within this learning environment, learners incorporate "a bit" of others' stories into their own narratives, thereby giving these stories a new interpretation.

During the second phase of the awareness-raising journey, learners engaged in an "intrapersonal conversation" and enhanced their critical literacies through a self-reflection questionnaire. This stage was underpinned by the belief that "individuals possess the capacity to actively... modify their positions" (Luke, 2018, p. 237). In this step, learners not only reaffirmed their initial stances but also questioned them, adopting an alternate perspective and reexamining their plurilingual identities, as Nancy stated: "[this questionnaire] helped me think about *what being multilingual and multicultural means to me*. I had not really sat down and thought about it before."

Designing Social Futures

The final step of this reflective journey, the follow-up interview, was designed to involve a "retrospective discussion of previous acts of positioning" (Deppermann, 2015, p. 373). It provided learners with the opportunity to revisit and elaborate on their previous storylines.

However, this phase wasn't limited to descriptive reflection alone; it also encompassed higher levels of reflection, such as critical reflection on what learners had gained from the entire pedagogical experience.

Learners, for instance, had opportunities to develop an awareness of how their family's language policy affected the development of their plurilingual selves, which triggered their agency, as shown in the following data:

Lauren: *English wasn't really an option for me.* My parents enrolled me [...] in a bilingual school [...] *Italian* on the other hand felt like my family's language [...] I think that it [pluri-biography] made me realize how much of an *influence my parents' decisions* for me when I was younger, *have had an impact on my multicultural and multilinguistic experience* [...] Maybe my mother did not speak *enough Italian* with me [...] because my *father did not speak it* but in the *future* [...] *I will speak in Italian and Spanish with my children*.

Multiliteracies for Social Inclusion and Plurilingual Identity Construction 75

Greta: I was *overwhelmingly* American [...] I've *only* been raised to understand *English* [...] my father has no sense of culture *but* my mother is *proud* of her Italian roots, and I want my connection with Italy for me and for my family.

This awareness encouraged learners to adopt a third-order positioning by considering their future agentic actions. These actions are purposive and situate individuals in relation to both their past and future (Richardson, 2015), bringing to the forefront the power to control their goals and future lives. Greta is reclaiming her Italian identity by positioning herself as a link between the past (a language/culture that was denied due to hegemonic discourse) and the future (asserting her role as a mediator). Lauren views this transformative experience as an opportunity to question her family's language policy.

Both learners analyzed the diverse factors that could influence various migration experiences, including historical, economic, socio-cultural, and political factors. These elements can shape distinct paths in life that impact positioning practices and identity construction, as Lauren and Greta pointed out:

Interviewer: Did the Italians who arrived in [her State in South America] at that time [when her grandfather migrated there] had to deal with prejudices and discrimination?

Lauren: *No*, they could *freely* speak their language and even if they spoke Italian, they *could integrate* ... there is a big Italian community... I was talking with Greta and her great-grandfathers did not allow her grandfathers to speak Italian... but my grandfather went to an *Italian school*, my mother went to an *Italian school* [...]

Greta: My great-grandfathers came from Naples ... but they did not speak ...

Interviewer: Why? Was it discriminatory?

Greta: Yes, but my grandfather *does not talk about it* ... it is *embarrassing*... it is *sad*... but when I told him that I was learning Italian he was *proud*...

Interviewer: Was he sad for not speaking his own language?

Greta: I do not know... I think when he was young that was *normal*... he *did not want a link* with Italy.

Interviewer: Why? Because your great-grand parents did not want him to have this link?

Greta: Yeah...but also because Americans called him wop [discriminatory attitude]

Interviewer: Wop?

Greta: Yes, *"without papers"* ... and when he was looking for a job, they treated him ...um

Interviewer: You mean mistreated him ...

Greta: *Yes* [...] it was *horrible* [...]

76   B. Spinelli

Greta has a history of migration characterized by what Weber (2009, p. 15) defines as "deliberate invisibilization." Her family chose to remain (linguistically/culturally) invisible to avoid being stigmatized as "different" or "others." This forced assimilation was the cost of achieving a better economic status in a diverse socio-cultural context (Skutnabb-Kangas et al., 2009). Greta identifies the discriminatory language used to stigmatize her family ("wop"), and she continues to display vulnerability due to this history of racial discrimination ("it is sad," "it was horrible," "it is embarrassing"). On the other hand, Lauren's family has a contrasting narrative of "visibility," where institutional language policy and language and culture maintenance played a crucial role.

Nancy provided another example of navigating migration processes. In her recent migration experience, her family's language policy challenged the assimilation phenomenon described above. She unpacked this concept by reflecting on and providing a deeper description of her dualistic perception of her multilingual identity:

Nancy: At home we *always* speak *Spanish* it is *forbidden* to speak *English*. My parents wanted our language/culture to *stay alive* [...] I use English only with my friends here and in academic contexts [...] I speak Italian just with my grandfather because he is the only one who speaks it.

However, she also underlined her agency:

Nancy: The separation [between Spanish and English] exists when I am frustrated [...] when I feel *disconnected* but I *learned to love both cultures*.

And she strongly asserted her agentic action in keeping the connections with her home culture by being an active and devoted spokeswoman and mediator:

Interviewer: You are doing an important job [volunteering in an association against domestic violence] ...
Nancy: ... yes, I want to *help*.
Interviewer: Are these women American women?
Nancy: No, *migrants* coming from different parts of South America
Interviewer: Is there a specific reason why you decided to do it?
Nancy: Yes, because they are migrants and I want *to help my people*... it is a *difficult* job... sometimes I feel bad, but it is *important*.

Pavlenko and Blackledge (2003) state that languages can be a site of solidarity and empowerment, and Nancy "performs" this positioning through the power of her actions.

Multiliteracies for Social Inclusion and Plurilingual Identity Construction   77

This final phase was also a further opportunity to rethink learners' plurilingual identity, as shown in the following data:

Anna: In the library we have a 15th century book [in Italian] and we also have the English translation, and *I was able to read the book in Italian* through this translation and to *compare the two languages* [...] It is important to read in the *original language* [...] this is why I am sorry for not including Italian in my pluri-biography [...] I was just thinking about the language of *my culture* [...] I do not have Italian roots [...] *but Italian* is part of *my mind* and *my culture.*

Anna reshapes her multilingual self by decategorizing multilingualism, questioning fixed relationships between language/ethnic group, language/religious group, and language/nationality, while recognizing its dynamic nature ("but Italian is part of my mind and my culture").

However, after a new discriminatory incident, she expressed her frustration with her multifaceted identity, stating, "It is difficult for an *American-Jew.*" She strongly identified with her Jewish community, expressing her discouragement with exclusion, and stating, "We are condemned to be the *others.*"

However, she also displays her investment for the future through agentic action:

Anna: At the university, the *best aspect of my life* is my political *organization...* my group aims to talk about Israel to let peers understand the situation [...]

She clearly positioned herself as an empowered speaker for disseminating knowledge of her language and culture.

These data show how the reflective and critical journey may serve as a pathway to guide learners in becoming "designers" of social futures. As Luke (2018) states, "designing [...] social futures" means engaging learners "in cultural and civic action and, indeed, identity [critical] work" (p. 300), fostering social change by learning how to live together within and across diversity and differences.

Conclusion

The instructional intervention and pedagogical model designed for this study facilitated an educational experience aimed at enhancing learners' awareness of the "coexistence of differences." Acanfora (2022) employs this definition to challenge the conventional understanding of inclusion. According to him, the term "inclusion" still implies imbalanced power dynamics between those who are expected to be inclusive and those who are expected to be included within a community.

The data collected in this case study showed that such differences involve "material differences" (e.g., differential access to social resources according to

78 B. Spinelli

social class), "embodied differences" (e.g., race and racism, age), and "symbolic differences" (e.g., language(s) spoken), which have a crucial impact on learners' plurilingual identity construction (Cope & Kalantzis, 2024).

The development of multiliteracies, including social literacies and critical literacies, which formed the foundation of the reflective process, enabled learners to familiarize themselves with and negotiate these differences through social participation and engagement with both lower and higher orders of thinking. This process also enabled a dynamic mode of positioning, through which learners were able to identify factors that influence their plurilingual identity construction. These factors encompassed family language policy, institutional language policy, life events, social status, social interactions, self-reflection, diverse migration experiences, and encounters.

They positioned and repositioned themselves along the reflective journey by challenging family ideologies and socially prescribed categories, and by questioning and reshaping their plurilingual selves.

The analysis of this data can offer valuable insights to language educators and researchers.

The outcomes of this case study may encourage instructors to shift their teaching emphasis toward representations and identity work, moving beyond mere language skills and competences. This implies the creation of an appropriate and comfortable ecological learning space wherein individuals' stories and multilingual backgrounds are not just understood but listened to, respected, and valued—a space "for learning in" and "learning from." As Moje and Lewis (2007) emphasize "learning is not only participation in discourse communities but also the process by which people become members of discourse communities" (p. 20). By understanding the locality of practices—the classroom as a microcosm of broader society and global flows—and by focusing on learning "community analysis" (Luke, 2018, p. 300), learners are enabled to develop global citizenship, as local literacies mirror global literacies.

Educational experiences of this kind can promote positive emotions (Forbes et al., 2021) and learners' well-being, as individuals in this fluid and mobile society seek "not instability […] but a more sense of stability" (Block, 2022, p. 12).

When considering researchers' work, two main aspects need to be taken into consideration. First, there is a need to avoid misleading descriptive categories, as the reality of learning communities can be more problematic and complex. This is especially crucial when labels are highly significant for representing multilingual contexts and analyzing identity construction.

For instance, the academic context described in this chapter might be perceived as "elitist" due to its international educational nature and the population's privileged access to various linguistic and technical resources (Barakos & Selleck, 2019). However, learners' narratives depicted a more complex portrait. The categorization of "elitism" may potentially oversimplify this complexity and ignore the multifaceted histories and life experiences of the learning community members, which can have significant implications for the on-the-ground research.

Multiliteracies for Social Inclusion and Plurilingual Identity Construction   79

Second, the outcomes of this case study underscore the importance of continuously exploring creative approaches to fostering participation, developing literacies such as social and critical literacies that generate new forms of knowledge, and encouraging collaboration. These include instructional interventions that can influence the construction of plurilingual and pluricultural identities, as described in recent research studies within the field of multilingual education (Ayres-Bennett & Fisher, 2022).

This case study has offered in-depth descriptions of the data, acknowledging the inherent limitations of all interpretative research and its inability to provide generalizations. Nevertheless, it is hoped that this research study contributes to the ongoing discourse mentioned above, which aims to foster the education of plurilingual and multiliterate learners, enabling them to become more responsible members of a global society.

Notes

1 In this chapter, the term "plurilingual" is used to describe the individual's linguistic repertoire, while "multilingual" to describe the existence of multiple languages within social contexts (Council of Europe, 2001).
2 This limited space represented a "superdiverse" learning environment. Superdiversity highlights a multi-dimensional perspective on diversity, moving beyond the ethnic group as "the sole unit of analysis" (Vertoc, 2007, p. 1025) and valuing the combination of factors that affect individuals' lives.
3 For ethical considerations, the following have been removed: (1) the real names of the participants (replaced by pseudonyms); (2) the students' countries of origin; (3) the university where the project took place; and (4) the year of the data collection.
4 This autobiography involved multiple modes of representation (i.e., texts such as songs, images, pictures, multilingual representations, metaphors) that engage various channels: audio, visual, and digital technologies such as PowerPoint, Story-Maps, Emaze, and ChatGPT DALL*E. This task, along with all reflective activities and interactions, was conducted in Italian with the possibility of code-switching into the languages of students' linguistic repertoire.
5 The instructor was also the researcher of this case study.
6 García et al. (2007) provide a plurilingual perspective on multiliteracies, defining pluriliteracies as the capacity of plurilingual speakers to draw on, combine, and switch between languages of their linguistic repertoire according to socio-cultural contest in which they interact.

References

Acanfora, F. (2022). *Di Pari Passo*. LUISS University Press.
Anstey, M., & Bull, G. (2007). *Teaching and learning in multiliteracies: Changing times, changing literacies*. International Reading Association.
Ayres-Bennett, W., & Fisher, L. (Eds.). (2022). *Multilingualism and identity*. Cambridge University Press.
Barakos, E., & Selleck, C. (2019). Elite multilingualism: Discourses, practices, and debates. *Journal of Multilingual and Multicultural Development, 40*(5), 1–14.
Baxter, J. (2016). Positioning language and identity. In S. Preece (Ed.), *The Routledge handbook of language and identity* (pp. 34–49). Routledge.

80   B. Spinelli

Blackledge, A. (2000). Monolingual ideologies in multilingual states: Language, hegemony and social justice in Western liberal democracies. *Estudios de Sociolingüística, 1(2)*, 25–45.

Block, D. (2022). *Innovations and challenges in identity research.* Routledge.

Bourdieu, P. (1986). The forms of capital. In J. Richardson (Ed.), *Handbook of theory and research for the sociology of education* (pp. 241–258). Greenwood.

Bourdieu, P. (1991). *Language and symbolic power.* Polity Press.

Cope, B., & Kalantzis, M. (Eds.). (2000). *Multiliteracies: Literacy learning and the design of social futures.* Routledge.

Cope, B., & Kalantzis, M. (2024). Towards education justice: The multiliteracies project revisited. In G. Zapata, M. Kalantzis, & B. Cope (Eds.), *Multiliteracies in international educational contexts.* Routledge.

Council of Europe (CEFR) (2001). *Common European framework of reference for languages: Learning, teaching, assessment.* Cambridge University Press.

Davis, R., & Norton, B. (2016). Investment and language learning in the 21st century. *Language et Société, 157(3)*, 19–38.

Deppermann, A. (2015). Positioning. In A. De Fina & A. Georgakopoulou (Eds.), *The handbook of narrative analysis* (pp. 369–387). John Wiley & Sons.

Fisher, L., Evans, M., Forbes, K., Gayton, A., & Liu, Y. (2020). Participative multilingual identity construction in the languages classroom: A multi-theoretical conceptualization. *International Journal of Multilingualism, 17(4)*, 448–466.

Flores, N., & Rosa, J. (2015). Undoing appropriateness: Raciolinguistic ideologies and language diversity in education. *Harvard Educational Review, 85(2)*, 149–171.

Forbes, K., Evans, M., Fisher, L., Gayton, A., Liu, Y., & Rutgers, D. (2021). Developing a multilingual identity in The languages classroom: The influence of an identity-based pedagogical intervention. *The Language Learning Journal, 49(4)*, 433–451.

García, O. (2022). Too much psychology? The role of the social in language learning motivation. In A. Al Hoorie (Ed.), *Language learning motivation: Concise accounts of key concepts* (pp. 27–36). Bloomsbury.

García, O., Bartlett, L., & Kleifjen, J. A. (2007). From biliteracy to pluriliteracies. In P. Auer & L. Wei (Eds.), *Handbook of multilingualism and multilingual communication* (pp. 207–228). Mouton de Gruyter.

Gee, J. P. (1992). *The social mind: Language, ideology, and social practice.* Bergin & Garvey.

Geertz, C. (1988). *Works and lives.* Standford University Press.

Gunesch, K. (2008). *Multilingualism and cosmopolitism.* Verlag Dr. Muller.

Harré, R., Moghaddam, F. M., Cairnie, T. P., Rothbart, D., & Sabat, S. R. (2009). Recent advances in positioning theory. *Theory & Phycology, 19(1)*, 5–31.

Harré, R., & van Langenove, L. (Eds.). (1999). *Positioning theory.* Blackwell.

Harré, R., Moghaddam, F. M., Cairnie, T. P., Rothbart, D. & Sabat, S. R. (2009). Recent advances in positioning theory. *Theory & Psychology, 19(5)*, 5–30.

Haukås, A., Storto, A., & Tiurikova, I. (2021). Developing and validating a questionnaire on young learners' multilingualism and multilingual identity. *The Language Learning Journal, 49(4)*, 404–419.

Healy, A. (2008). *Multiliteracies and diversity in education: New pedagogies for expanding landscapes.* Oxford University Press.

Hegarty, B. (2011). A Framework to guide professional learning and reflective practice. Doctor of Education thesis. Faculty of Education, University of Wollongong.

Kalantzis, M., & Cope, B. (2023). Multiliteracies: Life of an idea. *The International Journal of Literacies, 30(2)*, 17–89.

Kayı-Aydar, H. (2019). *Positioning theory in applied linguistics.* Palgrave Macmillan.

Kayı-Aydar, H., & Miller, E. R. (2018). Positioning in classroom discourse studies: A state-of-the-art review. *Classroom Discourse, 9(4)*, 1–16.

Kramsch, C. (2021). *Language as symbolic power*. Cambridge University Press.

Kubota, R. (2005). Second language teaching for multilingualism and multiculturalism: Politics, challenges, and possibilities. In Hoosain, R., & Salili, F. (Eds.), *Language and multicultural education* (pp. 31–55). Information Age Publishing.

Kumaravadivelu, B. (1999). Critical classroom discourse analysis. *TESOL Quarterly*, *33*(3), 453–484.

Lewis, C., Enciso, P., & Moje, E. B. (2007). *Reframing sociocultural research on literacy*. Routledge.

Lo Bianco, J. (2004). Invented languages and new worlds. *English Today*, *2*, 8–18.

Luke, A. (2018). *Critical literacy, schooling, and social justice*. Routledge.

Merriam, S. B., & Tisdell, E. J. (2015). *Qualitative research* (4th ed.). Jossey Bass.

Moje E. B., & Lewis, C. (2007). Examining opportunities to learn literacy: The role of critical sociocultural literacy research. In Lewis, C., Enciso, P., & Moje, E. B. (Eds.), *Reframing sociocultural research on literacy* (pp. 15–48). Routledge.

Muramatsu, C. (2018). *Portraits of second language learners*. Multilingual Matters.

Navarro, F., Lillis, T., Donahue, T., Curry, M.J., Ávila Reyes, N., Gustafsson, M., Zavala, V., Lauría, D., Lukin, A., McKinney, C., Feng, H., & Motta-Roth, D. (2022). Rethinking English as a lingua franca in scientific-academic contexts. A position statement. *Journal of English for Research Publication Purposes*, *3*(1), 143–153.

Ortega, L. (2019). SLA and the study of equitable multilingualism. *Modern Language Journal*, *103*, 23–38.

Pavlenko, A., & Blackledge, A. (2003). *Negotiation of identities in multilingual contexts*. Multilingual Matters Ltd.

Richardson, M. S. (2015). Agentic action in context. In R. A. Young, J. F. Domene, & L. Valach (Eds.), *Counseling and action: Toward life-enhancing work, relationships, and identity* (pp. 51–68). Springer Science, Business Media.

Sekaja, L., Adams, B. G., & Yağmur, K. (2022). Raciolinguistic ideologies as experienced by racialized academics in South Africa. *International Journal of Educational Research*, *116*, 2–14.

Skutnabb-Kangas, T., Phillipson, R., Mohanty, A. K., & Panda, M. (2009). *Social justice through multilingual education*. Multilingual Matters.

UNESCO (2015). *Global citizenship education*. Available from: https://unesdoc.unesco.org/ark:/48223/pf0000232993

Vertoc, S. (2007). Super-diversity and its implications. *Ethnic and Racial Studies*, *30*(6), 1024–1054.

Weber, J. J. (2009). *Multilingualism, education and change*. Peter Lang.

4 Drawing on Cope and Kalantzis' Transpositional Grammar to Explore L2 Identities through Multiliteracies

Susan M. Holloway

Introduction

This research explores the ways in which L2 (additional language) learners are better able to succeed in learning a new language when they feel emotionally and socially supported through literacy practices shaped by the principles articulated within a pedagogy of multiliteracies. In recent years in the Canadian context, which has high levels of immigration, there has been more attention paid to the pedagogy of L2 learners. This book chapter draws upon data from empirical research funded by the Social Sciences and Humanities Research Council (SSHRC) that in part explores the language learning experiences of L2 adolescent and adult learners through a multiliteracies lens. Using comparative case studies (Stake, 2005) and constructivist grounded theory (Charmaz, 2014) in this national study, high schools and government language learning councils as well as museums, art galleries, and other community-based organizations have also been included as sites to expand thinking about how multimodality (gestural, visual, audio, spatial, linguistic modes) can be incorporated to significantly increase L2 learners' abilities to engage in language learning.

The larger objectives of the SSHRC study informed by multiliteracies theory are to advance knowledge on teaching and learning literacy practices; enhance digital literacies amongst educators and learners; investigate teaching practices to support L2 learners; and identify creative teaching practices that are transferable between formal school classrooms and adult learning contexts. A subset of questions for this book chapter are as follows:

1 Does social justice play a role in the pedagogy of the research participants?
2 In what ways are L2 language learning, culture, and identity supported through transpositional grammar in a multiliteracies framework?

This book chapter will outline a literature review in the field of L2 learning from sociocultural perspectives and by drawing upon elements within Cope and Kalantzis' most contemporary writings in terms of how they conceptualize agency, participation, and design to contribute to a transpositional grammar of meaning-making. Subsequently, this chapter explains the research design, methodology, and

DOI: 10.4324/9781003438847-7

Drawing on Cope and Kalantzis' Transpositional Grammar   83

methods deployed in the study. The findings and discussion section examines ways in which a social justice perspective can ensure more equitable experiences and outcomes for L2 learners and greater shifts in perceptions of what is a plurilingual society. The themes discussed in this chapter are (1) The Transpositional Grammar of Agency; (2) Participation invites Social Justice Action; and (3) Learning by Design. Lastly, some concluding remarks will consider ways that teachers can adapt strategies used by participants in this study to inform their own L2 teaching.

Sociocultural Approaches to Additional Language Learning in Relation to Multiliteracies

It is only in recent years that the original New London Group's manifesto (NLG, 1996) that asserted cultural and linguistic diversity must be ubiquitous in everyday teaching has begun to evolve in new ways to explore the significance of L2 teaching and learning in particular ways (see introductory chapter). The New London Group (1996) recognized early on that:

> as soon as our sights are set on the objective of creating the learning conditions for full social participation, the issue of differences becomes critically important. How do we ensure that differences of culture, language, and gender are not barriers to educational success?
>
> (p. 1)

This is an important question to consider today as well. Multiliteracies draw attention to the need for sociocultural approaches to language learning, which have traditionally been focused almost exclusively on cognitive theory in what is called Second Language Acquisition (SLA) theory. While theories regarding SLA have value, as a richer alternative, scholars such as Cummins and Early (2015) have combined sociocultural approaches, multiliteracies, and cognitive theories, for instance, in their work on identity texts to affirm identities. For example, Cummins and Early (2015) documented through research three students of various ages and language abilities "sharing their experiences and language skills" in their creation of writing a personalized dual language book "both in Urdu and in English because their primary audience for the book consisted of younger students who were also from Urdu linguistic backgrounds" (p. 17).

In another study, Zapata and Ribota's (2021) mixed methods study explored the benefits of using Cope and Kalantzis' (2015) *Learning by Design* in teaching basic Spanish as an L2 at four different levels at a public university in the United States. They found that participants' levels of confidence in L2 speaking as well as their writing abilities improved. As Zapata and Ribota (2021) observed:

> the use of the L2 in the development of identity texts appeared to have helped students to move beyond constrained [Communicative Language Teaching] CLT-based contexts, and it developed other aspects of their

L2 performance, such as writing and reading (e.g., through their work with the sample texts used in [*Learning by Design*] *L-by-D's* experiencing and conceptualizing and the peer review activities).

(p. 12)

Zapata and Ribota (2021) pointed out that engaging in a scaffolded learning environment in which social and emotional needs were met, and in which learners' independent initiatives were also encouraged, interestingly played a role in success with the technical aspects of language learning. L2 language learning requires culturally responsive ways that embrace students' sociocultural backgrounds, experiences, and identities in projects that *also* give them significant direct instruction, practice, and feedback in the cognitive demands of acquiring a new language.

Various empirical multiliteracies studies have demonstrated a commitment to social justice teaching (Howell & Dyches, 2022; Turner, 2015). For example, Howell and Dyches (2022) researched racial literacies by combining multiliteracies, Critical Race Theory (CRT), and the writing process. They contended that a limitation of multiliteracies is that "even when educators value students' differences, they are still working within a system that is political, affected by systems of power" (p. 102). Working with 2 high school teachers and 24 student participants, this case study drew upon important elements of the New London Group's (2000) focus on multimodality and the Knowledge Processes such as overt instruction and critical framing to work through racial literacies with adolescents. While investigating important aspects of social justice using multiliteracies, the specifics of L2 language learning were not within the study's scope mandate. A fewer number of studies have also incorporated an explicit focus on the needs of L2 learning in relation to social justice perspectives (Ajayi, 2009; Holloway & Gouthro, 2020; Zaidi, 2020).

Woods et al. (2013) in the fourth year of a longitudinal research study in Australia that used multiliteracies pedagogy drew upon Nancy Fraser's definition of redistributive and recognitive social justice in which L2 learning was discussed. Recognitive social justice "insists that a variety of ways of knowing and of representing knowledge must be central within the curriculum" as well as ensuring cultural and linguistic diversity are made "visible in education" (p. 511). Redistributive social justice "is about the provision of funds, resources and supports to the education of traditionally marginalised cohorts of students" (p. 511). A key aspect of this research was to partner between researchers, teachers, and administrators. They invoked systemic change by enhancing

distributed leadership across the teaching staff in two ways: firstly, by providing opportunities for teachers to work with administration members to lead reform in particular areas and, secondly, to support all teachers as pedagogical leaders in their own classrooms through transparency in planning, pedagogy and assessment.

(p. 513)

Drawing on Cope and Kalantzis' Transpositional Grammar   85

Luke, an original member of the New London Group, and one of the researchers in this study, has always advocated for the importance of schools connecting to home cultures, providing a curriculum that speaks to current, relevant issues in society, and insisting on intellectually demanding expectations for historically marginalized learners. These representative studies reflect some of the ways that social justice issues have been taken up within multiliteracies L2 pedagogy through empirical research.

Social Justice Orientations in L2 Learning that Utilize Multiliteracies Theory

Multiliteracies provides an important theoretical framework to better explain why and how a social justice orientation toward L2 learning requires taking into account sociocultural perspectives. In *Making Sense* (2020) and *Adding Sense* (2020), Cope and Kalantzis develop a grammar of multimodal meaning to deepen our understanding of the breadth of communication. While they acknowledge these books are broadly theoretical, and do not address social justice issues in direct ways, they nevertheless claim, "our profession is education, where the greatest challenges of our time are inequality of outcomes, learner diversity, and the transformative potential of new technologies" (2020, p. 5). The broader theory they articulate has important implications for how we conceptualize the analytical language of multiliteracies theory. In this transpositional grammar, for example, Cope and Kalantzis (2020) discuss the meaning and "sense-making potentials" (p. 11) as follows:

> From one meaning form to another, the potentials for meaning are different in some significant ways. These differences are also the reason why we often overlay and juxtapose forms, for instance image with text, because the two can reinforce each other to make a shared message, each contributing something that complements the other in the combined effort.
>
> (p. 12)

Multimodality always has significant cultural implications (Jewitt, 2009; Kress, 2010). Furthermore, in L2 learning, expansive forms of communication matter, not only in terms of general communication but also the ability to shift between modes in ways that stretch and capture meanings that draw upon the strengths of multiple modes employed for specific purposes. According to Cope and Kalantzis (2020), language learning effectively involves becoming cognizant of the potentials of meaning-making by harnessing a wide range of modes and understanding the nuances of expression they offer.

Kalantzis and Cope (2020) theorize the term agency. Agency connotes a sense of hope and is a part of the emancipatory discourse that comes out of Paulo Freire's (1992/2021) *Pedagogy of Hope*. Freire (1992/2021) argues for hope while fully acknowledging systemic barriers, Freire perceives hope to give individuals a sense of agentic power through their imaginations and engagement

86 *S. M. Holloway*

in civic actions for a more just society. Cope and Kalantzis (2020) maintain that "agency is a process of causing" (p. 175). Rather than thinking of "agency" in a more traditional sense of people acting of their own volition to bring about change, Cope and Kalantzis (2020) and Kalantzis and Cope (2020) theorize about agency as *always relational* to structures and events that shape those actions. Thus, like Freire, Cope and Kalantzis believe that being an agent of change is more than individual willpower as it is always contextualized by larger societal occurrences. We will return to this argument in the findings and discussion to explore agency as well as the concepts of participation and design in more depth.

Research Design, Methodology, and Methods

Research Study

This study explored multiliteracies in a variety of adolescent and adult settings in the Canadian context. The research was funded through a Social Sciences Humanities and Research Council (SSHRC) Insight grant. I, Susan Holloway, as the Principal Investigator at the University of Windsor, Ontario worked with my Co-Investigator, Dr. Patricia Gouthro, at Mount Saint Vincent University, Nova Scotia. We worked with two collaborators, respectively, from the government and the secondary school systems, and a research team of graduate students.

Participants

There were 41 participants in total in the study which included adult educators, adult learners, high school teachers, high school students, provincial policy makers as well as administrators in schools and community-based organizations.

Recruitment

Recruitment was done through access to Listservs via our collaborators using a short email and poster to invite participants. For community-based organizations that had their contact information available in the public realm, we contacted them directly via email. And for adult learners and high school students, their teachers (who were themselves participants) invited learners to participate in the research if they wished to do so. Purposive sampling ensured participants came from urban and rural environments as well as a range of subject disciplines.

Research Sites

Research was conducted in Windsor and Essex County in the province of Ontario and in Halifax and the Halifax Regional Municipality in the province of Nova Scotia, Canada.

Drawing on Cope and Kalantzis' Transpositional Grammar   87

Ethics

This study received full ethics clearance from the universities and school board. Participants had the option to make their identities public or kept confidential. The school board policies requested confidentiality of high school participants for publications. Member checking was used.

Methods

Participants had options. They could be interviewed for 1 hour in a face-to-face interview. They could allow us to come into their classrooms or learning spaces to do observations. These observations involved pen-to-paper notes (later typed and uploaded to our secure database) that were usually done for 3–4 hours approximately four to five times over the course of several months. Document analysis was another method that involved educators sharing their lesson or unit plans, assessment and evaluation pieces, or exemplars.

Secondary Data

Participants also had the option for us to come into their learning space to film one class. For the original film footage, media release forms were used. Anyone who chose to be outside of the camera's view could do so. The media release forms gave the option of checking secondary data usage, which then went through the Review Ethics Board for clearance. Some of these film excerpts appear on a web platform called The Multiliteracies Project (MLP)[1] we created to see teaching, hear educators in short interviews, and showcase teaching materials to better explain multiliteracies in practice.

Data Analysis

We used multiple case studies (Stake, 2005) to compare the teaching and learning practices in various adult community-based settings as well as adolescents in high schools. As Stake (2005) notes, "naturalistic, ethnographic, phenomenological caseworkers also seek what is *ordinary* in happenings, in settings, in expression of value" (p. 453). We wanted to investigate everyday pedagogy to consider ways in which social justice perspectives might undergird the learning experience. In the selection of cases, we also purposefully chose sites that may not normally be thought of as traditional classrooms such as a dance center or an art gallery to broaden thinking around multimodal teaching and learning.

The methodology we drew upon was constructivist grounded theory as developed by Charmaz (2005) who explains "grounded theory methods consist of simultaneous data collection and analysis, with each informing and focusing the other throughout the research process" (p. 508). Following constructivist grounded theory (Charmaz, 2014), our research utilized what Charmaz names as *coding, focused codes,* and *memo writing* to draw out

88   *S. M. Holloway*

emerging themes. As a part of this dynamic methodology, our research team reviewed the coding to discuss, compare, and contrast our perspectives. Furthermore, Charmaz (2005) reflects on the value of constructivist grounded theory to better understand a social justice outlook: "researchers can give their data multiple readings and renderings. Interests in social justice, for example, would lead a researcher to note points of struggle and conflict and to look for how participants defined and acted in such moments" (p. 517). This methodology is named as constructivist because it takes into account the researcher's positionality and biases (Charmaz, 2014). For example, I (Susan) am a white, straight, and middle-class woman; my experiences in life shape the way I interpret research. No research is bias-free.

Findings and Discussion

Three themes that emerged from the data are: (1) The Transpositional Grammar of Agency; (2) Participation invites Social Justice Action; (3) Learning by Design. Cope and Kalantzis' (2020) and Kalantzis and Cope's (2020) theoretical propositions regarding agency, participation, and design are used to provide insight into social justice perspectives in L2 learning.

The Transpositional Grammar of Agency

Cope and Kalantzis (2020) and Kalantzis and Cope (2020) draw upon linguistics, philosophy, fine art, and history to formulate an integrated approach to transpositional grammar that in part ascribes new ways of thinking about agency. In defining agency, Cope and Kalantzis (2020) note "in every act of meaning we establish roles: speaker/listener, writer/reader, designer/user, maker/consumer, gesturer/observer, and soundmaker/hearer" (p. 45). Our agency can be thought of as fluidly engaging in these distinct roles to analyze complex problems using the best resources possible.

Educators can promote agency. Anh Nguyen, a participant in our study and the Artistic Director of HNM Dance, uniquely brought together adult community members and professional dancers to work creatively through dance. In interview, Anh recalled working with the local art gallery. They offered a yoga class based on responding to art in the gallery:

> Art yoga. So, yoga among art and, of course, our yoga classes are very dance integrated. You know, movement-based responding to paintings on the wall, responding to sculptures and the shape of them and we would make it into ourselves.

Adult learners were asked to feel and engage in movement based on the relationship between the visuals of art, the spatial dimensions of the room, and their own embodied expression (also in relation to the other dancers). Anh explained, "Maybe change facing and then we would see something else, maybe a colour or something and just a little bit of a relationship with the space." By "change facing" Anh referred to dancers literally turning their bodies to aspects of the art and the space to experience a new viewpoint and relationship with the space. To recall what Cope and Kalantzis propose, the dancers expanded their roles to simultaneously engage as "gesturer/observer" and "designer/user." Cope and Kalantzis (2020) elaborate: "Agency is always there, in and through meanings made in text, image, space, objects, body, sound, and speech … we can experience different sense orientations" (p. 175). By consciously widening the dancers' engagement with their surroundings, their agency was also being developed, creating new orientations through relations. Socially, we see transpositional grammar also integrates socially situated practice with a range of modes. To illustrate this point, one of the *focused codes* in our data for Barb Robinson, a participant and one of the HNM dancers, stated: "Barb illustrates some excellent examples of showcasing cultural diversity through dance, as well as how history and cultural are brought to life through art."

The agency of the art gallery's audience is also invited as they are drawn into joining the dancers, even if only for a brief time. Anh noted:

And again with art, instead of doing whatever the class it is, it does not matter where we are, we just completely let that space inform how the class is going to respond to it. And we also have people walking around looking at art at the same time as we are doing this. And they would look at us too as we were installation art. So, someone would sit and join in for a little bit and then leave.

The audience members joined in the performance and, moreover, helped to influence it. This alludes to Augusto Boal's Theatre of the Oppressed, which brings together community-based members onto the stage to actively participate in the shaping of the drama. The spectators also participate as actors in this art gallery forum. Boal's work was inspired by Freire's articulation of power relationships that recognize the oppressive forces but also foregrounded the importance of individuals effectively having agency and engaging in problem-posing.

Liesel Deppe, another study participant and a musician in 4th Wall Music, also recognized the value of breaking down the fourth wall between musicians and audience members as seen in this original film footage under the excerpt "Teaching about the Flute" on the MLP web platform.[2] Audience members were invited to physically work through their breath to experience how a flute is played. Liesel in interview reflected on how she demonstrated how to make a sound on the flute: "You can link it to something they [audience members] already know … like blowing across the top of a pop bottle … is usually the closest thing [to] something people know." In coding the research data, we draw from the *memo writing* for Liesel's interview to elaborate on her point: "Metaphorically transforming professional and abstract instrument playing

90   S. M. Holloway

techniques into the easy-to-understand daily routine not only solves audiences' confusion but also builds a vivid learning atmosphere." L2 language teaching can similarly draw upon music, dance, spatial relations, and interactive roles of "speaker/listener, writer/reader, designer/user, maker/consumer, gesturer/observer, and soundmaker/hearer" (p. 45) to innovatively cultivate L2 learners' agency.

In their examination of a historical painting by Turner, Cope and Kalantzis (2020) emphasize that distinct modes create meaning in distinct ways. They posit that "temporal order" is necessary to talk about the painting, and by contrast, "spatial order" is required to view the painting. Or, as they put it, "speech affords agency to the listener to configure space in their mind's eye. Image affords agency to the listener to configure time in their mind's eye" (p. 177). Furthermore, they contend that "to supplement or break free from the affordances of speech, we juxtapose pictures" (p. 179).

Karolina Gombos, a study participant who taught lower intermediate English classes at the Multicultural Council of Windsor and Essex County promoted her adult learners' agency by giving them the opportunity to juxtapose various modalities to best represent their families. Karolina asked students to do a mini presentation using simple sentence structures in their L2 that are based on the 5Ws (who, what, when, where, and why). Using a family photo that is projected onto the big screen, each adult learner used gestures such as pointing, imitating certain movements such as "hugging," or for instance, a surprised facial expression to convey their meaning adjacent to the enlarged family photo (Holloway, 2023). These learners experience agency in the sense that they command the usage of multimodality and its various affordances and constraints to express their thoughts in their L2. Transpositional grammar thus also helps to share aspects of their cultural identities in affirming ways. The Multicultural Council afforded institutional support for this type of learning.

Participation Invites Social Justice Action

Cope and Kalantzis claim in *Making Sense* (2020) and *Adding Sense* (Kalantzis & Cope, 2020) that *representation, communication,* and *interpretation* are the dimensions that allow for participation. *Representation* is the inner talk and mind's eye ability to visualize an image or plan: "how I might navigate a space" (2020, p. 50). *Communication* "is manifestly social: to encounter a meaning that has been made by another" (Kalantzis & Cope, 2020, p. 49), through any mode drawing upon material resources (be it a pen, paintbrush, or physical gesture). *Interpretation* is the analysis by the audience that follows from the communication. Participation and civic engagement are always touted as fundamental to social justice change.

Participation theorized in this way helps us to make sense of the social justice meanings found in this research study. One of our research sites, Mount Saint Vincent University Art Gallery in Nova Scotia, worked in partnership

Drawing on Cope and Kalantzis' Transpositional Grammar   91

with Eyelevel Gallery to present a traveling exhibition organized and circulated by Truck Contemporary Art, Calgary, entitled "Taskoch pipon kona kah nipa muskoseya, nepin pesim eti pimachihew/Like the Winter Snow Kills the Grass, the Summer Sun Revives." This exhibition of artistic works by seven Indigenous artists from across Canada aimed "to address and initiate a discussion on how Indigenous languages intertwine with Indigenous epistemologies and how the dormancy and extinction of Indigenous languages leads to a hindrance of culture and knowledge"[3]. We used document analysis to capture aspects of this traveling exhibition. Joi T. Arcand (2019), as one of the artists, created the artwork *Wayfinding*, which is a series of four neon signs in Plains Cree syllabics, which are then translated by Arcand into Plains Cree. Wayfinding is a traditional form of navigation in Indigenous cultures, and it also references graphic meaning-making. As provided in the information card beside the artwork:

> Wayfinding also describes Arcand's own path towards language reclamation. The phrases were translated by Darryl Chamakese, a fluent nehiyawewin speaker from Chitek Lake, Saskatchewan. Wayfinding uses diary-entry style statements while gesturing towards the work of language revitalization experts such as the late Ida McLeod and Freda Ahenakew.

> Arcand's dreams, ambitions, and frustrations are illuminated by the four phrases:

> 1 (blue sign) I want to speak cree, (but)
> 2 (white sign) I don't have my words.

> and the response:

> 3 (pink sign) don't be shy!
> 4 (yellow sign) (kiyäm) never mind!

There is grieving of languages and culture loss: "I want to speak cree, (but)/I don't have my words" alongside tongue-in-cheek humor: "don't be shy!/never mind!" juxtaposed in the illuminated neon Cree signs, which make up this art installation. Only "pink sign" was displayed at this travelling exhibition.

Canada has a long history of colonization of Indigenous people and their lands, for example, in the genocide of Indigenous people through the residential school system that forcibly removed children from their families and cultures. Calls to Action from the Truth and Reconciliation Commission of Canada are only starting to be addressed by the government and the people of Canada. Arcand's (2019) artwork integrates digital literacy into traditional Indigenous languages, reflecting that these languages are dynamic and continue to adapt to a changing world.

92 S. M. Holloway

In terms of cultural epistemology, Kalantzis and Cope (2020) note that representation is "grounded in our life-specific and materially grounded experiences of speech, sight, embodiment, and space" (p. 50). Hence, for Arcand through this artwork, her art acknowledges the loss of her native tongue, and the long-term implications of this loss of a way to express oneself by being immersed in the language/culture of an Indigenous person's heritage, which is also a call for recognitive social justice. The MSVU Art Gallery curator and a participant, Laura Ritchie, said in interview:

> All but one of the artists in the show... do not speak those languages. The languages that are represented in their works are Indigenous languages that they have had to learn. They could not actually speak them because they have been removed from them, and that part of the story is something that you would not really know unless you engage in the work.

Reclaiming language, it could be argued, is meaning-making "based on our social-historical experiences of meaning" (Kalantzis & Cope, 2020, p. 50). Wayfinding is an apt metaphor to represent and communicate the rich histories of Indigenous cultures tied to the land and full of wisdom while simultaneously acknowledging the need to reconcile a history steeped in discrimination and marginalization.

If social justice is about better equitable outcomes for socially and historically marginalized populations, art may invite new dialogue that addresses recognitive and redistributive justice. Kalantzis and Cope (2020) point out that "a grammatical transposition" using the "word 'grammar' in its narrower sense, as the syntax of speech, or in the broader sense of patterns in meaning" (p. 51) is necessary as we move between *representation*, *communication*, and *interpretation*. L2 learning is more than just the parsing of basic grammatical structures assigned to standardized forms of language. In this art exhibition, participation as a visitor to the art gallery entails perhaps a level of discomfort in that many of the artworks used various Indigenous languages (spoken or written) with no translation provided in English. In this way, the dominance of English as a colonial language is challenged. The power dynamics of negotiating language are defamiliarized when translation is not automatically available. The visitor's participation in the exhibition is further extended to seek out meaning using multimodality layered with the linguistic mode.

In thinking through culturally responsive pedagogy, which aligns in many ways with multiliteracies pedagogy in being attuned to students' backgrounds, one policy maker in our study reflected on a story shared by an elementary teacher trying to ensure Indigenous students felt they could participate fully in a mathematics class because their culture was being affirmed:

> So, they [the teacher] say, "OK, you have five birds sitting on a branch. You're trying to hunt them, you take a shot, you hit one of the birds, how many birds are left?" And so everyone, of course, is saying 4,

but the First Nations child is saying, "None! Obviously, when you shoot the gun, they're all going fly away, right?" So … in terms of being culturally responsive … that's something we have to learn. Like we have to pay attention. We have to ask those questions.

Social justice is in part figuring out how to create a safe and welcoming ambience in which difficult conversations about relevant topics can be pursued in a classroom wherein students come from many diverse cultural and linguistic backgrounds. Like the visual representation of the Cultural Iceberg image,[4] more superficial aspects of culture tend to get celebrated in educational spaces. Yet, there needs to be a dialogue about the invisible parts of the iceberg below the surface – concepts of time, attitudes toward elders, beauty ideals – those aspects of deep culture that can at times cause friction or misunderstandings between individuals or groups often because of miscues and misreadings of cultural mores. This policy maker was willing to consider that an open mindset, humble disposition, and willingness to learn about other cultures, languages, and histories were a first step toward greater educational equity.

Equity requires leadership. Karin Falconer taught English to Canadian newcomers at the Multicultural Council to intermediate adult learners. As observed in our field notes, Karin explicitly set out expectations for how students would treat one another both inside and outside of her classroom during everyday conversations with her students:

- Culture and integration: Karin encourages and introduces topics such as the LGBTQ+ community and resources in conversation with the class. Karin makes sure to note that opinions on any topic are valid, but students must all respect each other and members of their larger communities. Respect means respecting oneself and others' opinions.
- Karin: "Respect is mandatory in the classroom and out" (Fieldnotes, January 30, 2020).

Karin was proactive in creating a safe environment for all learners knowing that participation needed ground rules and that a leadership vacuum did not equate with neutral values. Prejudice and discrimination could seep into any learning space. In interview, Karin explained she showed students their interests mattered to her: "I ask the students on a needs assessment at the beginning, what is it you want to learn this semester?" In this way, she modeled reciprocal respect for the learners.

Learning by Design

Without explicitly saying so, Cope and Kalantzis appear to further evolve one of their key theoretical concepts, *Learning by Design* (see the introductory chapter of the book). They posit (2020) that "there are three parts to the

94 *S. M. Holloway*

process of design," which are design, designing, and designed, that are comparable to "processes of transposition in all meaning" (p. 71). They conceptualized as follows:

> Design (patterns): Patterns of meaning in found objects (human and natural) and lived experience .... Designing (actions): The mental and physical work of meaning in the amalgam of ideas and materialized action (praxis) .... Designed (artifacts): Something made, a trace of the thinking and bodily efforts put into meaning.
>
> (p. 71)

Cope and Kalantzis (2020) emphasize the greatest value of this theoretical proposition is that "in parsing a designed artifact we have a theory that accounts both for congruence (the patterns replicated), and incongruences (the impossibility of faithful replication, and the patterns of divergence)" (p. 71). This ability to reconcile "divergence" is what allows for a more coherent rationale of patterns of meaning that always have differences.

Cope and Kalantzis' (2020,) and Kalantzis and Cope's (2020) evolving theoretical framing of *Learning by Design* has value for how we might read Towela Okwudire's experiences in designing a series of lessons. Towela was a participant in our study and Director of French Lit., an organization that taught French to adults. She also worked in a school for gifted adolescents in the United States. She asked these latter students to learn French by studying the French Revolution and wanted them to create their own ballet in French since, as Towela pointed out in interview ballet was "invented in the court of Louis XIV." In having the class collaborate with a dance teacher, she wanted them "to see the connection between body movement and language." Towela commented:

> So they were learning verbs, like verbs of movement and just trying to take it more than "je vais" and "je marche", right, "I go" and "I walk." And using words like "crawl" and "climb" and "expand and contract."

Design is evident. Towela designed a lesson that drew on her students' prior knowledge such as French, movement, and dance to learn ballet. This prior knowledge gives "'rules' of meaning" to draw upon for "partial replication" (2020, p.71).

When choosing from an infinite number of choices, *designing* is shaped "in terms of our identities, and our identities in terms of the unique history of living experience in each of us" (2020, p. 71). Towela reflected that when she taught this unit, several students hated it. They and their parents complained to the school director, who nevertheless supported Towela's pedagogical choices. It was five years later when Towela was talking to these same students about this L2 dance project, who now surprisingly claimed "they thought it was great" that she had an epiphany about her own teaching. Towela recounted

Drawing on Cope and Kalantzis' Transpositional Grammar 95

that she realized one of the students, who identified as non-binary (but had not yet articulated this aspect of their identity as a younger person),

> he did not like the way people described his masculinity. So he did not like how when they did the dance project, the girls went…he wanted to join a group with more girls because many of them were his friends. He did not want to join the boys because they were not very nice to him. And so he did not like the project simply because of that…At the end, he found a way to make the project work for him. He wrote an original choreography. It was brilliant!

Designing needs to be a negotiation between the teacher and students. Towela retrospectively came to realize that this student's dislike of the project was not about learning French through bloody revolutionary history or even being asked to choreograph and dance ballet. Their concerns, which completely affected their disposition to participate in the project, related to gender identity.

Towela connected this student's experience to her own identity as a Black woman born in Zambia, raised in the United States, and then immigrated to Canada at the end of high school. She found people wanted to know her "European, colonial language," but as Towela put it, "I learned that anybody who is going to encounter me just has to sit through my story of language." She recognized in this student something she herself had experienced – that identity is complex and cannot always be easily unpacked in relation to curriculum, despite her well-planned "objectives and goals and rubrics" for this series of lessons.

Thus, in the *designed*, "we can track the bending of these patterns in the process of designing" (p. 71). It is not so much a revised lesson plan inasmuch as the architecture of lesson planning had now shifted for Towela based on her philosophical process in which she more fully recognized identity as foundational to teaching and learning. This process of *design, designing*, and *designed* provides a new template that Cope and Kalantzis (2020) name "the wellsprings of personal voice, creativity, and human identities" (p. 71). Creativity, intellectual curiosity, and compassion are important qualities in the endeavor to push forward with a social justice mandate in education, which starts with the recognition of agency and plurality of identities including plurilingualism.

Concluding Remarks

In Cope and Kalantzis' (2020) and Kalantzis and Cope's 2020) most recent work, they delve deeper into literacies by contextualizing many concepts such as multimodality in terms of their historic roots of literacy, philosophy, and educational theories. Teachers can empower their L2 students through activities that utilize transpositional grammar in a way that is similar to the ones used by the participants discussed in this chapter. A teacher can model transposition – "reframing of meaning in one form, then another, or several together at the same time" (Cope & Kalantzis, 2020, p. 1) through activities that transpose the narrative in new modes. For example, like Karolina, educators can ask students to tell a story that starts with a personal photograph and is reframed into an oral presentation supported through gestural and facial expressions. The student can then transpose the presentation into a written dialogue or a diorama.

Transpositional grammar is reframing in a social sense as well as considering modality. It is social in that students are reframing when they bridge between their lives in school and outside of school, which in turn gives greater coherence to their L2 language learning experiences. Karin, for instance, establishes a welcoming ambience with her students by allowing them to draw upon cultural and linguistic experiences from their home country to inform their thinking in their new L2 about new experiences. Teachers can emulate Karin's explicit instruction around what it means to be respectful on potentially controversial issues to create an inclusive classroom. Like Anh or Towela, teachers can consider how dance be integrated into classroom practice. One way to incorporate dance would be for students to record themselves dancing, which is then paired with a written reflection in their L2 to create a narrative. In our document analysis of Arcand's digital artwork written in her Indigenous language, we see that teachers could similarly ask students to pair digital literacies with traditional aspects of a student's home language to explore social justice issues. For example, they could combine using multimodal digital storytelling software such as ACMI Generator with cultural concepts they wish to compare between their homeland and the new country as a way to consider redistributive and recognitive social justice as well.

Kalantzis et al. (2016) claim that for L2s, "local diversity and global connectedness" mean that the most important skill for students to learn "is to negotiate differences in social languages, dialects, code-switching and hybrid cross-cultural discourse" (p. 51). Transpositional grammar gives us a critical way to create, identify, develop, and critique L2 teaching and learning practices. Multiliteracies can help forge a strong pedagogical approach to additional language learning that places equity and inclusion squarely at the center of its mandate.

Acknowledgments

This research is supported by Holloway and Gouthro's (2018–2024) Social Sciences and Humanities Research Council of Canada (SSHRC) Insight grant # 435-2018-070.

Notes

1 www.multiliteraciesproject.com
2 https://multiliteraciesproject.com/adult-education/4th-wall-music/

3 https://www.msvuart.ca/exhibition/pipon-kona-nepin-pesim/
4 https://www.researchgate.net/publication/361162662_Multilingualism_and_Intercultural_Competence/figures?lo=1

References

Ajayi, L. (2009). English as a second language learners' exploration of multimodal texts in a junior high school. *Journal of Adolescent & Adult Literacy, 52*(7), 585–595. https://doi.org/10.1598/JAAL.52.7.4

Arcand, J. T. (2019). *Wayfinding, Ēkāwiya nēpēwisi (don't be shy)* (2nd ed.). [Neon Channel Sign]. Courtesy of the Saskatchewan Art Board. Travelling Exhibition at Mount Saint Vincent Art Gallery, Halifax, Nova Scotia, Canada.

Charmaz, K. (2005). Grounded theory in the 21st century: Applications for advancing social justice. In N. K. Denzin & Y. S. Lincoln (Eds.), *The Sage handbook of qualitative research* (3rd ed., pp. 507–535). Sage.

Charmaz, K. (2014). *Constructing ground theory* (2nd ed.). Sage.

Cope, B., & Kalantzis, M. (2015). The things you do to know: An introduction to the pedagogy of multiliteracies. In B. Cope & M. Kalantzis (Eds.). *A pedagogy of multiliteracies: Learning by design* (pp. 1–36). Palgrave Macmillan.

Cope, B., & Kalantzis, M. (2020). *Making sense: Reference, agency, and structure in a grammar of multimodal meaning.* Cambridge UP.

Cummins, J., & Early, M. (2015). *Big ideas for expanding minds: Teaching English language learners across the curriculum.* Pearson.

Freire, P. (2021). *Pedagogy of hope: Reliving pedagogy of the oppressed* (R. R. Barr, Trans.). Bloomsbury. (Original work published in 1992)

Holloway, S. M. (2023). *Canadian educators using multiliteracies pedagogies to teach L2 adult learner immigrants.* International Associate of Teachers as a Foreign Language (IATEFL) English to Speakers of Other Languages (ESOL) *ESOL Matters* Newsletter, 1, 4–8.

Holloway, S. M., & Gouthro, P. A. (2020). Using a multiliteracies approach to foster critical and creative pedagogies for adult learners. *Journal of Adult and Continuing Education, 26*(2), 203–220.

Howell, E., & Dyches, J. (2022). Sharpening students' racial literacies through multimodal subversion. *Journal of Adolescent and Adult Literacy, 66*(2), 100–110.

Jewitt, C. (2009). *The Routledge handbook of multimodal analysis.* Routledge.

Kalantzis, M., & Cope, B. (2020). *Adding sense: Context and interest in a grammar of multimodal meaning.* Cambridge UP.

Kalantzis, M., Cope, B., Chan, E., & Dalley-Trim, L. (2016). *Literacies* (2nd ed.). Cambridge UP.

Kress, G. (2010). *Multimodality: A social semiotic approach to contemporary communication.* Routledge.

New London Group. (1996). A pedagogy of multiliteracies: Designing social futures. *Harvard Educational Review, 66*(1), 60–92.

New London Group. *Multiliteracies: Literacy learning and the design of social futures* (B. Cope & M. Kalantzis, Eds.). Routledge.

Stake, R. E. (2005). Qualitative case studies. In N. K. Denzin & Y. S. Lincoln (Eds.), *The Sage handbook of qualitative research* (3rd ed., pp. 433–466). Sage.

Turner, S. (2015). Transforming locked doors: Using multiliteracies to recontextualize identities and learning for youth living on the margins. In F. B. Boyd & C. H. Brock (Eds.), *Social diversity with multiliteracies: Complexity in teaching and learning* (pp. 168–185). Routledge.

98   *S. M. Holloway*

Woods, A., Dooley, K., Luke, A., & Exley, B. (2013). School leadership, literacy and social justice: The place of local school curriculum planning and reform. In I. Bogotch &
C. M Shields (Eds.), *International handbook of educational leadership and social (in)
justice* (pp. 509–520). Springer. https://doi.org/10.1007/978-94-007-6555-9_28
Zaidi, R. (2020). Dual-language books: Enhancing engagement and language awareness. *Journal of Literacy Research, 52*(3), 269–292.
Zapata, G. C., & Ribota, A. (2021). The instructional benefits of identity texts and
learning by design for learner motivation in required second language classes. *Pedagogies: An International Journal, 16*(1), 1–18. https://doi.org/10.1080/15544
80X.2020.1738937

Part III

Critical Literacies Development through Linguistic Landscapes

5 Reading Japanese Linguistic Landscapes for Critical Multiliteracies

Nurturing Agency and Criticality for Social Justice

Yuri Kumagai

Introduction

In 1996, New London Group (hereafter NLG) published a manifest that proposed a pedagogy of multiliteracies, a framework that envisioned new approaches that would prepare students for the world with "the multiplicity of communications channels and media, and increased saliency of cultural and linguistic diversity" (New London Group [NLG], 1996, p. 63). Almost 30 years later, their visions for "designing social futures" are still, or even more, relevant today. Communication landscapes have become even more complex with new tools and platforms, inundating us with news and information: some reliable, some questionable. Furthermore, increased cultural and linguistic diversity has become the norm, which has created unwarranted tensions and divisions in many parts of the world, often leading to violence and discrimination targeted against those who are minoritized.

To prepare students to navigate and assess the credibility and legitimacy of information, and to encourage them to imagine and pursue societies that are safe and more just, it is important for us, language teachers, to put nurturing students' agency and criticality at the foundation of our language teaching practices. Here, "criticality" refers to one's capacity to pay attention and understand the way in which reality is mediated by language and the way in which speakers and writers use language to construct the texts that represent their versions of reality (Janks, 2010). Additionally, it encourages one to take action to positively impact the society. While it is still a dominant practice in many additional language classrooms, teaching "mere literacy" (NLG, 1996, p. 64) that focuses on decoding and encoding just "language" (usually a singular national language) is not enough to guide students to become critical participants in today's multilingual and multicultural textual world.

With that in mind, in 2018, I designed a linguistic landscape project for my Japanese language course at a liberal arts college in the United States. By taking advantage of linguistic landscapes as sociocultural, multimodal texts that are imbued with and reflect values, assumptions, attitudes, etc. of a given community, the project aims to develop students' criticality by having them

DOI: 10.4324/9781003438847-9

102   *Y. Kumagai*

analyze various aspects of signs, all the while drawing on principles outlined by the pedagogy of multiliteracies.

In what follows, I first briefly describe the fundamental tenets of the pedagogy of multiliteracies, followed by a summary of studies that took advantage of linguistic landscapes as learning resources in additional language education. Next, I introduce my own linguistic landscape project and use one group of students' project as a case study to demonstrate their processes of knowledge construction. I conclude with the potential that linguistic landscapes offer in designing critical language teaching practices.

Pedagogy of Multiliteracies

To articulate their vision of the pedagogy, the NLG used a metalanguage based on the concept of "design" and proposed that "any semiotic activity, including using language to produce or consume texts" should be treated "as a matter of Design" (NLG, 2000, p. 20). The NLG also proposed the four pedagogical components in the pedagogy of multiliteracies—*Situated Practice, Overt Instruction, Critical Framing*, and *Transformed Practice*—which were later reformulated by Kalantzis and Cope (2012) to four knowledge processes, or "foundational types of [students'] thinking in action" (p. 356): *Experiencing, Conceptualizing, Analyzing*, and *Applying* (see pp. 2–3 introductory chapter). Each knowledge process includes two elements. *Experiencing* involves immersion and the use of *Available Designs*, both from the students' "lifeworlds" (*Experiencing the Known*) and from different, unfamiliar contexts (*Experiencing the New*). *Conceptualizing* seeks to supplement immersion by developing students' systematic, analytical, and conscious understanding (*Conceptualizing by Naming*) by making tacit knowledge explicit and generalizing from particular encounters (*Conceptualizing with Theory*). *Analyzing* aims to develop students' skills in analytical thinking, that is to be able to reason, draw inferential and deductive conclusions (*Analyzing Functionally*), as well as to critically reflect and evaluate their own and other people's perspectives, interests, and motives implicated in texts (*Analyzing Critically*). Finally, *Applying* entails "re-creating a discourse by engaging in it for our real purposes" (NLG, 2000, p. 36), which is accomplished by implementing and testing the validity of what was previously learned (*Applying Appropriately*) and by making an attempt to intervene in the world with innovative and creative application (*Applying Creatively*).

Since its initial proposal in the context of L1 education, the pedagogy of multiliteracies (or somewhat different iterations) has been taken up by various scholars in the field of additional language education. Many collegiate language programs face the two-tier system problem—that is, there is a gap between lower language levels, emphasizing oral, transactional communication, and upper language levels, emphasizing text-based, literal analysis. The pedagogy of multiliteracies is seen as one way of creating coherent curricula by addressing this discrepancy (Paesani et al., 2015; Swaffar & Arens, 2005).

Reading Japanese Linguistic Landscapes for Critical Multiliteracies 103

In addition, the pedagogy of multiliteracies provides insights into the design of multimodal curricular projects that aim to provide students with the opportunity to engage in various authentic language practices that go beyond the classroom practices (see Kumagai et al., 2015). Finally, the benefits of designing content-based instruction (CBI) (Turpin, 2021) and content and language integrated learning (CLIL) (Dupuy, 2011) with multiliteracies approaches have been observed, as has using the notion of genre as an organizing principle to design multiliteracies informed curricula (e.g., Kumagai & Iwasaki, 2015; López-Sánchez, 2015; Warren & Winkler, 2015). Linguistic landscapes with rich employment of multilingual and multimodal resources have gained popularity as learning resources for cultivating students' multiliteracies in additional language classrooms, which I will turn to next.

Linguistic Landscapes

As linguistic landscape directly deals with languages in public spaces, it has been used as a resource in the field of second language acquisition and additional language education (see also Chapter 6 of this volume). Studies that used linguistic landscape for the purpose of additional language learning discuss a variety of educational benefits from linguistic competence (i.e., writing systems, vocabulary, expression, grammar) (e.g., Rowland, 2013; Sayer, 2009) and pragmatic competence (Cenoz & Gorter, 2008; Rowland, 2013) to critical language awareness (Cadi et al., 2023) and multimodal and multilingual communication—i.e., multiliteracies (Cenoz & Gorter, 2008; Malinowski, 2009; Shohamy & Gorter, 2009). All of these studies highlight that the use of linguistic landscape in additional language education offers a learning space beyond the classroom for students to critically engage with texts.

Some studies specifically draw on the pedagogy of multiliteracies as a framework for designing their instructional projects. For example, Lozano et al. (2020), using the lens of *knowledge processes*, argue that the student-centered, inquiry-based LL projects in elementary-level college Spanish courses in New York City provided students with opportunities to reflect upon the construction of identities and socioeconomic and political conditions of Hispanic/Latino/a/x communities in the city as embedded in signage and other public art and spaces. Likewise, drawing upon the NLG's four pedagogical components with "critical action" as an added element, Akimenko (2021) proposed an instructional project with the goal of encouraging students to develop their plurilingual competence by "tak[ing] an activism stance and becom[ing] critical researchers who work toward changing unequal power relations in the society" (p. 280).

As living texts that constitute and are constituted by historical, political, and sociocultural spaces with various languages and multimodality, linguistic landscapes offer valuable resources for students to develop and cultivate multiliteracies. While some projects conducted as a part of "language learning" aim for students to arrive at the "right" interpretation of signs (as "native

104   *Y. Kumagai*

speakers" would do) and consider that as evidence for their skills with the target language, the current project appreciates that different interpretations of signs by the students are invaluable for all the participants (including the instructor), who can then recognize that meaning-making is the product of socioculturally informed norms and assumptions, diverse viewpoints, and personal experiences. Discussing issues such as why we arrive at different interpretations, what causes such different interpretations, whether one interpretation could be more valid than others, and why it is so, offers eye-opening experiences for us to reflect and rethink our unconscious, implicit biases. The current study aims at opening up a dialogical space for us to engage in such discussions, which would nurture the students' criticality preparing them to become empowered translingual and transcultural citizens in today's superdiverse world.

The Project: "Cities in Japan; Linguistic Landscape Project"

The Setting

The college I teach at is in a small New England town in the United States. It is a women's liberal arts college with about 2,500 students. The college has an open curriculum and is known for its progressive, feminist-oriented education. The "Cities in Japan: Linguistic Landscape Project" (the LL Project hereafter) has been a part of my second-year (fourth semester) Japanese language course curriculum since the Spring of 2018. The course meets five days a week for 50 minutes per class. The course curriculum is built around a textbook called Tobira (Oka et al., 2009), which is a topic-based, reading-emphasized textbook for intermediate learners of Japanese. The LL project was added to the curriculum but progressed independently from classroom instructions throughout the semester. Unlike large American cities such as New York City or Los Angeles, the town where my college is located has no area where students can experience "Japan/Japanese language." I thus decided to use Google Street View as a tool for students to virtually walk down the streets in Japanese cities of their choice.

The LL project is a student-led, inquiry-based, collaborative project that takes advantage of linguistic landscapes for the purpose of learning about the Japanese language, cultures, and society. It takes an approach that encourages students to connect language/culture learning with other subject matters, their lived experiences, and their expertise. It also takes the translingual approach that urges students to draw on various languages and other knowledge as resources for carrying out the project. By capitalizing on linguistic landscapes as authentic sociocultural texts, the LL project aims at providing students with an experience that allows them to examine issues such as what languages and other semiotic systems are used on signs, what those signs suggest about the makeup of the community or official language policies, and what power relationships among different languages can be extrapolated from

Reading Japanese Linguistic Landscapes for Critical Multiliteracies 105

the signs. The LL project is not focused on reading "Japanese language" on signage to develop linguistic knowledge *per se,* although the students are certainly expected to expand their language capacities via analysis of the signs and the presentation of their findings in oral and written forms. More importantly, the LL project aims to develop the students' "critical language awareness" (Fairclough, 2013), metalinguistic knowledge, and awareness of social, political, and ideological aspects of language and discourse. To borrow Paulo Freire's famous words about what literacy entails, the students engage in "reading words to read worlds" (Freire & Macedo, 1987).

Characteristics of Japanese Language Literacy

The Japanese language has three distinctive orthographies: *hiragana, katakana,* and *kanji.* These systems (along with the Roman alphabet, called *romaji*) are all used in typical Japanese texts. *Hiragana* and *katakana* are sound-based, phonetic scripts called syllabaries, and both have 46 symbols. Some of the symbols are manipulated to represent other sounds by adding one of two small diacritics at the top right corner. The other system, *kanji* (Chinese characters), is a meaning-based script where each character represents a concept. There are approximately 10,000 *kanji* in use (Taylor & Taylor, 2014); however, the government's current script policy (updated in 2010) lists 2,136 *kanji* as "*joyo kanji,*" or commonly used *kanji.* In practice, 3,000–3,500 *kanji* are needed to read texts such as newspapers, and novels and to function as a literate member of Japanese society (Seeley, 2000).

Each writing system has some normative rules: *kanji* is used for content words, *hiragana* primarily for function words (i.e., case markers and verbal/adjectival suffixes), and *katakana* mainly for foreign-origin words. Nevertheless, a writer has some freedom in their choice of orthography. For example, *manga* (Japanese comic books) can be written in *hiragana* (まんが), *katakana* (マンガ), *kanji* (漫画), or even *romaji* (Manga), and each choice evokes different images and effects (Robertson, 2020).[1]

In analyzing Japanese advertising design, Bartal (2013) contends that "Japanese writing is first and foremost visual" (p. 66), and that the choice of writing system and typography "is not just a decorative, but a meaningful tool that builds the visual shape of the language and influences the textual content, just as much as the words themselves" (p. 57). This characteristic of "text as image" in Japanese writing is particularly relevant in analyzing linguistic landscapes and developing multiliteracies in the Japanese language.

The Project Procedure

The general procedure of the project is as follows:

1 Introduction of the LL Project
2 Google Map/Street View Workshop

106 *Y. Kumagai*

3 Choose a city to explore and select ten signs that capture your interest:

   a Include both public and private signs.

   b Include at least three for which you do not know what the sign means/ is for.

   c Consider the following aspects when capturing the image of signs:

      • Use of multiple languages?

      • Use of multiple writing systems?

      • Use of multimodality?

4 Engage in analysis of the signs on four levels based on the guiding questions (see Appendix).

   a Analysis 1: Describing/Decoding—Experiencing

   b Analysis 2: Meaning-Making—Conceptualizing

   c Analysis 3: Analyzing/Critiquing—Analyzing

   d Analysis 4: Transforming—Applying

5 Share analysis on Analysis 1 (Google Slides presentation) in class.
6 Share analysis on Analyses 2 and 3 (Google Slides presentation) in class.
7 Select four signs (from the initial ten signs) that will be the subject of a group-written analytical and reflective essay and write an essay using Google Docs (based on the rubric).
8 Meet with the instructor as a group (consultation sessions) regarding the feedback received on the essay and for further exchanges of ideas.
9 Revise the analytical and reflective essay.
10 Create a multimodal text on the WordPress site by uploading the revised essay along with selected images (multiple revisions based on the rubric).
11 Present the project in class as a group at the end of the semester.
12 Submit reflections (self-evaluation) on the LL Project's process and final product via Google Forms.

The four-level, multiple layers of analysis with guiding questions (#4) was inspired by the four knowledge processes of Multiliteracies and Learning by Design (Cope & Kalantzis, 2009; NLG, 1996/2000) as well as the four resources model of critical literacy (Luke & Freebody, 1999), with modifications to accommodate the goals of the LL project. Analysis 1 asks students to observe, describe, and decode the selected signs and their locations. It allows students to immerse themselves in a (virtual) area/street that is new and unfamiliar and allows them to gather information for further analysis (*experiencing the new*). Analysis 2 requires students to be "active concept and theory-makers" (Cope & Kalantzis, 2009, p. 18). The students are asked to consider the purpose/function of the signs and their target viewers, as well as to pay attention to the sign's design elements (multimodality) and to deduce meaning by "weaving" between experiential and conceptual knowledge. In Analysis 3, students critically analyze the effect and effectiveness of the signs in relation to the presumed intention and implicit meanings that the signs communicate with various viewers. The students are instructed to pay attention not only to what is present but also to what is missing from the signs. Analysis 4 asks students to redesign one of the public signs to make it more inclusive, offering greater access to people with diverse backgrounds. That is, by transforming the sign, students make "the world anew with fresh and creative forms of action and perception" (Cope & Kalantzis, 2015, p. 22).

The sharing sessions (#3, 4, and 9) and meeting with the instructor (#6) serve as spaces for promoting dialogical processes among all the participants (including the instructor). The students are instructed to design the final multimodal text on WordPress (#8) for those Japanese language/culture learners who are not familiar with the linguistic landscapes in Japan. With a clear audience in mind, students designed their texts drawing on diverse genres of their choice (e.g., travel guides, investigated pieces, and social critiques).

Students' Learning from the LL Project

I have written elsewhere about the LL projects from a variety of theoretical perspectives. I have discussed the project's design and the students' products in the context of a virtual ethnographic investigation during the COVID-19 pandemic (Kumagai, 2022). I also highlighted the LL project can challenge students' stereotypical images of Japan/Japanese language (Kumagai, 2023, forthcoming) and can encourage them to critique the government's language policy (Kumagai & Takahashi, 2023). Furthermore, I have used the notions of "incompetence" (Kumagai, 2024) and "diversity and inclusion" (Doerr & Kumagai, 2022) as a framework to analyze students' learning from the LL project.

In this chapter, I use one group of students' work as a case study and discuss it from the view of *knowledge processes* of multiliteracies. I will also highlight how the LL project nurtured students' agency and criticality pertaining to a social justice issue. The case discussed in this chapter is from a project that was conducted by two students—Mei and Qingxia[2]—during the Spring 2019 semester.

Mei and Qingxia: "Sleepless Town, Hiding Town"

Mei and Qingxia were both international students from China. Mei was a first-year student who was double-majoring in history and art history, whereas Qingxia was a third-year student whose major was psychology. Mei and Qingxia chose, as their site of exploration, two areas in Shinjuku, Tokyo: Kabuki-chō and Shinjuku Ni-chōme. Kabuki-chō is one of the most famous entertainment districts in Japan, and the area has many restaurants, bars, hostess/host clubs,[3] and nightclubs. Shinjuku Ni-chōme is known as Tokyo's hub of gay subculture, housing the world's highest concentration of gay bars (McLelland et al., 2007).

Kabuki-chō is marked by a huge, red neon gate sign that says "Kabuki-chō Ichiban-gai (Kabuki-chō, the First Street)." Both Mei and Qingxia had previously visited Tokyo and seen the famous sign. They also knew of the area from dramas and movies that are popular in China. As for the Ni-chōme, Mei had been unfamiliar with the area until Qingxia told her that it is famous as "an LGBTQ town." Qingxia knew of the area from a song she liked but had never seen the area before. During the post-project interview, Qingxia explained that they chose these two neighboring areas in Shinjuku because both areas are famous entertainment districts in Tokyo but cater to different populations. Thus, they wanted to compare how their linguistic landscapes may or may not be similar. Prior to exploring the area via Google Street View, Qingxia expected the Ni-chōme to be "a place like a rainbow street in San Francisco," but it turned out that "it was completely different from what I imagined." She explained that this surprise was the impetus for her and Mei to investigate the Ni-chōme in greater depth.

Mei and Qingxia titled their WordPress post "眠らない街・隠している街 (Sleepless Town, Hiding Town)," with a featured image of the Kabuki-chō Ichiban-gai sign. In their post, they selected and analyzed four signs: (1) the sign for Kabuki-chō, Ichiban-gai (Figure 5.1); (2) the advertisement sign for a hostess club, "*Deai kafe Kirari* (Encounter Café Twinkle)"; (3) the street sign for the Ni-chōme entrance (Figure 5.2); and (4) the sign for a gay bar, "酒吧 0 & 1 (Bar [in Chinese language] 0 & 1)" (Figure 5.3).[4]

In their opening paragraph, Mei and Qingxia observed that there were notable differences in the types of signs that exist in Kabuki-chō and No-chōme,

Figure 5.1 Kabuki-chō Ichiban-gai sign at night
Source: https://commons.wikimedia.org/w/index.php?curid=52578985

Reading Japanese Linguistic Landscapes for Critical Multiliteracies 109

Figure 5.2 Shinjuku Ni-chōme (North) sign next to a traffic light
Source: ©2023 Google

Figure 5.3 Name display sign on a window for a gay bar "酒吧 0 & 1"
Source: ©2023 Google

as well as differences in the ways that bars and clubs advertise their presence. In particular, the students noticed that the Kabuki-chō signs are much more visible and showier than the Ni-chōme signs. Based on this observation, they posed a question: "Does Ni-chōme want to become a world-famous entertainment attraction like Kabuki-chō?" They wrote that they would use their experience and knowledge of world culture and history to investigate this question.

110   *Y. Kumagai*

Mei and Qingxia's post regarding the Kabuki-chō, Ichiban-gai sign is presented below in only English translation[5] for the interest of space:

> Talking about Kabuki-chō, we cannot forget this sign. [...] In 1969, the Shinjuku ward installed this sign as a part of the city planning. [...] We feel that the purpose of the sign is not just to inform, but also to advertise. For many foreigners, Kabuki-chō and this sign are one of the most famous spots to visit in Tokyo. The reason for choosing the red color illumination may be because it corresponds to the meaning of "red light" as in "red light district." At night, this sign brilliantly stands out. Even though it is written only in *kanji*, we think that it is a sign that is easily recognizable.

In the first paragraph, Mei and Qingxia highlight the significance of this sign ("cannot forget") and describe the sign in a historical context ("the Shinjuku ward installed," "in 1969," "a part of the city planning") in order to situate the sign in a broader social context. They then explained that the sign's function is "not just to inform" but "also to advertise." They paid particular attention to various design elements: the choice of writing system ("*kanji*") and the use of color ("red"). They associated red with the idea of a "red light district" and argued that its purpose is to "stand out." After their analysis of the two Kabuki-chō signs, Mei and Qingxia asked their readers to consider: "Are the signs in Ni-chōme, the entertainment district for LGBTQ people, the same as those in Kabuki-chō? Please look at the next signs with this question in mind."

Mei and Qingxia wrote the following about the sign for the Ni-chōme entrance:

> This sign, too, was installed by the Shinjuku ward. It is here to inform people of the location of the Ni-chōme. [...] This simple sign is composed in Japanese, *kanji* and *rōmaji*. The design of the white background with blue letters is simple but stands out. Yet, in comparison to the red and gaudy sign in Kabuki-chō, the sign for Ni-chōme is a normal sign. The reason may be that the shops in Ni-chōme do not want to widely advertise, unlike those in Kabuki-chō. [...] Because LGBTQ in East Asia is a taboo topic, [...] LGBTQ people may need a safe space.

Here, Mei and Qingxia compare the "red and gaudy" Kabuki-chō sign to the "simple" and "normal" Ni-chōme sign—both public signs installed by the Shinjuku ward—and highlight the significant stylistic differences between the two. They also noted their interpretations of the different functions that each sign plays (i.e., "inform" and "advertise" for Kabuki-chō, and "inform" and "guide" for Ni-chōme), deducing meaning from their different styles. We can see here that the students are actively engaging with the texts (i.e., signs) by "conceptualizing and theory-making," using their powers of observations, world knowledge, and experiences of issues pertaining to LGBTQ people in East Asian societies. Through such thinking processes, they came to conclude that Ni-chōme may serve as a "safe space" for the LGBTQ community.

Reading Japanese Linguistic Landscapes for Critical Multiliteracies   111

As if to prove their theory, they selected a gay bar's sign (Figure 5.3) as the topic of their final analysis.

They wrote:

> It is interesting that the sign uses Chinese language instead of Japanese *kanji*. Why is there a sign with only Chinese in Shinjuku, Japan? First, this red Chinese word means "bar" in Japanese. […] What is interesting about this sign is the use of numbers "0 & 1" in white color. This "0 & 1" is not for "0 & 1" in computer programming but rather represents the "roles" for Chinese homosexual men when dating. […] In China, LG-BTQ people are not socially accepted, like in Japan. […] And so, many terms were invented on the Internet that other people would not understand. […] Because we are Chinese, when we saw this sign, we immediately understood that "Ah, this is a shop for homosexual men." But for people who do not know the Chinese language and who are not familiar with the LGBTQ culture in China, this sign is not easily understandable.

For this segment, the students first highlighted the unusualness of the sign that only uses the Chinese language even though it is in Japan. By taking advantage of their language resource of Chinese, they explain to their readers that the Chinese word means "bar." They then drew on their knowledge of secret/coded terms in the Chinese LGBTQ community to explain the meaning of "0 & 1," after which they describe the marginalized status and negative treatments that LGBTQ people face in Chinese society ("like in Japan").

In the next paragraph, the students argue that the general characteristics of the signs in Ni-chōme are difficult to understand for those who are not already familiar with the area/community. They further emphasized the societal pressures that LGBTQ people feel due to the fact that most East Asian countries exhibit a societal preference for heteronormativity ("Because most societies in East Asia are heteronormative, we think that LBGTQ people feel the pressure to hide their identity.").

During their post-project, individual interview, both Mei and Qingxia stated that the advertisements for Kabuki-chō's bars and clubs are gaudy and that the intentions of the signs are clear: to attract new customers. In comparison, they elaborated on the inaccessible characters on shop signs in Ni-chōme: "If you don't know the name and location of the bar, you cannot find it by just walking on the street" (Mei); "I was only able to find a lesbian bar my friend told me about only after I put the address on the Google Map" (Qingxia). After their experience of virtually exploring these streets, the students began to think about the meaning of "hidden" in Ni-chōme. They expressed their thoughts in the concluding paragraph of their WordPress essay:

> […] In the old days, since discrimination was much more severe, we believe that Ni-chōme was even more hidden. But recently, as in the case of the sign for the "Bar 0 & 1," there exist some signs that are

112 *Y. Kumagai*

understandable only by the people who belong to the community. [...] Such signs partially hide and partially express identity to those who understand [the meaning of sign]. The safe space that allows "partially hiding and partially expressing" would not let/allow Ni-chōme to become a tourist stop like Kabuki-chō.

Here, Mei and Qingxia referred to historical changes by comparing the "old days" and "recent" sociocultural conditions regarding the LGBTQ community in Japan and noted the different degrees of being "hidden": in the past, the shop/bar might have been more "hidden" because discrimination was much more severe, whereas now it is only partially hidden to those who do not belong to the community. The students' use of a negative causative structure (二丁目を歌舞伎町のような観光地にさせない; "would not let/allow Ni-chōme to become a tourist spot like Kabuki-chō") communicates a strong acknowledgment of the will by the member of the LGBTQ community.

The last phase of the LL project instructed the students to redesign one of the public signs (Analysis 4). However, Mei and Qingxia decided not to do this task. During their interviews, they gave two reasons for their decision. First, because neither student is a member of the LGBTQ community, they felt that it was not their place to question the decisions made by the sign-makers. Qingxia said, "I don't want to make a decision for them. I want to respect their choice"; likewise, Mei said, "If you change the style of a sign, I felt like it's making a joke. I think it is their choice." Second, and more importantly, they wanted to respect the community's (possible) need to have a "safe space" by Ni-chōme being hidden. Thus, instead of redesigning the sign, Mei and Qingxia creatively designed their multimodal post with an image that moves from sign 1 to sign 3 (and vice versa), by using the Image Juxtaposition tool of H5P.[6] With that, readers can see a "sharp, direct comparison" (Qingxia) between the two signs. This demonstrates that the students exercised their agency based on their independent thinking and beliefs.

Through their comparative investigation of the signs in Kabuki-chō and Ni-chōme, Mei and Qingxia seem to have gained some understanding of the situations faced by sexual minorities in Tokyo. Qingxia noted in the post-project questionnaire that "I gained a brief understanding about the attitude Japanese society holds toward LGBTQ—not openly against, yet not welcome."

Discussion

What thinking processes did Mei and Qingxia go through to understand and create knowledge in the LL project? Figure 5.4 describes the knowledge construction processes that were facilitated through the inquiry-based, collaborative nature of the LL project. Throughout the semester, Mei and Qingxia engaged in discussion among themselves as a team, brought their ideas to class to share them with their peers and instructor, and actively took part in a consultation session where they exchanged ideas with the instructor.

Reading Japanese Linguistic Landscapes for Critical Multiliteracies 113

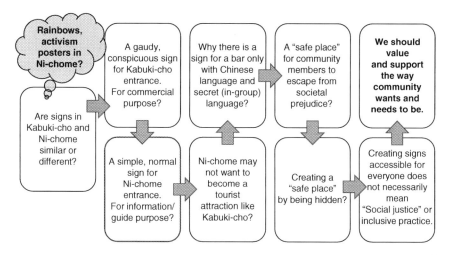

Figure 5.4 Mei and Qingxia's knowledge processes

Their exploration began with simple questions motivated by their curiosity: "Are signs in Kabuki-chō and Ni-chōme similar or different? Is Ni-chōme like a rainbow street in San Francisco?" In order to address their questions, they first engaged in *experiencing* signs in two areas by paying attention to various design elements. They then worked on *conceptualizing* the explicit and implicit meanings of the signs in their social context, *analyzing* signs to construct their own theories, and, finally, *applying appropriately* by NOT redesigning the existing sign and *applying creatively* by designing their multimodal text using the image juxtaposition tool to appeal to their readers. In the process, they raised a series of complex questions: Which situation is preferable: a tourist attraction such as a well-established rainbow street in San Francisco, or a quieter community such as Ni-chōme, which allows for its members to safely gather? Who decides which is preferable? And for whom would it be preferable?

The LL project allowed students to connect and apply their rich knowledge when making sense of the new phenomena that they encountered. During her interviews, Mei said, "I was able to combine all of my knowledge in this project." Likewise, Qingxia said:

This project allowed me to connect everything I knew from the past into one. …Also, because I did not know a lot of vocabulary I did a lot of translation, and it was really great that I finally had a chance to connect three languages together. Before I only had a chance to connect Chinese and English, or Chinese and Japanese, but the link between English and Japanese was broken, or a little link. Because of this project, I found a stable triangle for my three languages.

114 *Y. Kumagai*

Both students stated that they took advantage of all their knowledge, skills, and experiences to engage with and complete the project. They used knowledge gained from college courses such as history, politics, and literatures of Japan and East Asia, as well as their personal experiential knowledge of socio-political conditions pertaining to sexual minorities in both their home country (China) and the United States.

The knowledge that they produced was significant not only for Mei and Qingxia themselves but also for the other participants in the project—i.e., their peers and instructor. Mei and Qingxia's project helped others to reconsider what is meant by "inclusion," which is one of the key concepts of "Diversity, Equity, and Inclusion (DEI)" initiatives that have been hailed as an essential component of social justice. When discussing what types of signs in public spaces may be considered inclusive, we normally think of those that are accessible to as many people as possible by using multiple languages, integrating symbols or illustrations, or, in the case of Japanese, using *yasashī nihongo* (plain/easy/simplified/gentle Japanese).[7] However, Mei and Qingxia's project has demonstrated that sometimes it may be desirable for an area to be made inaccessible to the larger public. This allows for marginalized people to find a "safe space" that acts as "a refuge from daily life," providing with them a sense of "inclusion." As Mei said in her interview, "Unless the society or government policy changes, I want this place to be their shelter, a place to be who they are." The argument presented by Mei and Qingxia reminds us that practices of "inclusion" and "exclusion" are not clear-cut, but the differences between them may sometimes just be a thin line. Such a realization is of critical importance if we are to obtain a nuanced understanding of social justice issues, view situations from the perspectives of those who are affected by these issues, and become their allies. Mei and Qingxia's project provided all of us with an invaluable opportunity to see the possible dangers and inequity inherent in equating "inclusion" with giving the same information to everyone.

Conclusions

The LL project was based on the principles of Pedagogy of Multiliteracies, with a particular emphasis on nurturing students' agency and criticality. Although this chapter only discussed one pair of students' knowledge construction processes, other groups of students also created significant knowledge for envisioning societies that are more socially just. For example, some students recognized that the use of the Korean language in a Korean town wasn't necessarily meant to value the language of Korean residents in Japan; rather, it could be part of a "commercial" strategy or could be a means for evoking an "exotic" feeling (see Kumagai & Takahashi, 2023). One group of students argued that the overwhelming dominance of English usage on signs was indicative of a disregard for the needs of "foreign" residents from neighboring East and Southeast Asian countries (who outnumber native English speakers), while another group critiqued a paternalistic approach toward visually impaired people that

Reading Japanese Linguistic Landscapes for Critical Multiliteracies   115

was evident in public announcement posters at train stations in Tokyo. All of these students took the social issues seriously, reflected on their own lifeworlds, and redesigned the signs so as to assert and achieve their own visions of equity.

The LL project uses students' questions and curiosities as a starting point, values their own various language and cultural resources, and trusts and acknowledges their agency to set and move forward with their own agendas and goals, while providing ample opportunities and spaces to engage in dialogues with other people. The LL project offers invaluable educational spaces where diverse interpretations and sociopolitical views are negotiated, leading all of us to critically reflect and rethink our assumptions or "commonsense" that we take for granted. Unlike activities in many additional language classrooms where the teacher (often a "native speaker") enjoys the ultimate authority with "correct" answers, spaces afforded by the LL project destabilize and shift the dichotomous power relationships between teacher and students, native and non-native speakers, and those who possess specific knowledge and those without, since signs' "intentions" are not always explicit (Doerr & Kumagai, 2022).

We now live in an uncertain time, facing numerous unprecedented problems of enormous degrees from threats to democracy (which is often promoted by the spread of disinformation), environmental/climate calamities, and violence against minoritized groups of people, to an unknown future with Artificial Intelligence, and restrictions posed by some local governments on what can be taught in schools (e.g., Florida). What we need—now more than ever—are language teaching practices that move away from the monolingual approach and shift toward *trans*lingual practices. We need to value all language resources (including multimodality), encourage students to employ all types of experiences and knowledge for meaning-making practices, emphasize the centrality of agency and criticality in order to prepare them to become critical readers of linguistic and social texts with their own agendas, and inspire them to become language users and creators who can and are willing to positively impact the world around them. It is my hope that the LL project introduced here, even in a small way, may contribute to such educational endeavors.

Acknowledgment

This chapter is based on a presentation at the 2019 Princeton Japanese Pedagogy Forum delivered by Ms. Yuko Takahashi and myself. I acknowledge and appreciate her insights while preparing for our presentation. The writing and any shortcomings of this chapter are solely my responsibility.

Notes

1 For example, reading experiments conducted by Ukita et al. (1996) revealed that when Japanese readers see the *kanji* word for *isu*, chair (椅子), an image of an old-fashioned, strongly build chair is usually generated, while the *katakana* (イス) generates an image of a modern, elegant chair, and the *hiragana* (いす) is associated with a simple wooden chair (in Iwahara et al., 2003, p. 393).

116 Y. Kumagai

2 All names are pseudonyms.
3 A hostess club is a type of nightclub where female staff cater to men seeking drinks and attentive conversation, whereas a host club is an establishment where young male staff attend to women.
4 The screenshots from Google Street View that the students used on their post on the College's WordPress site (not open to the public) have been replaced by license-free images of the same locations.
5 Translations of the students' essays are done by the author.
6 Image Juxtaposition of H5P allows one to compare two images interactively by moving a slider between the images.
7 "*Yasashī nihongo*" denotes a variety of Japanese language modified for those who are not proficient in Japanese (Ito & Tokarev, 2021). The idea and the term were originally proposed by Sato (1996) as a response to 1995's Great Hanshin-Awaji earthquake, when crucial disaster-related information failed to reach people who didn't speak English or Japanese. Since then, the use of *yasashī nihongo* has been extended in non-disaster situations and is often recommended for communication in public sites such as regional government offices and tourism (Iori, 2016). However, various critiques have arisen, as the use of *yasashī nihongo* can perpetuate the power hierarchy between Japanese and non-Japanese speakers.

References

Akimenko, O. (2021). "Activizing" the pedagogy of multiliteracies: The dynamic, action-oriented turn with languacultural landscape studies. *Cahiers De L'ilob/OLBI Journal, 11*, 259–286.

Bartal, O. (2013). Text as image in Japanese advertising typography design. *Design Issues, 29*(1), 51–66.

Cadi, S., Latisha, M., Siemushyna, M., & Young, A. S. (2023). Empowering students and raising critical language awareness through a collaborative multidisciplinary project. In S. Melo-Pfeifer (Ed.), *Linguistic landscapes in language and teacher education, multilingual teaching and learning inside and beyond the classroom* (pp. 57–73). Springer International Publishing.

Cenoz, J., & Gorter, D. (2008). The linguistic landscape as an additional source of input in second language acquisition. *International Review of Applied Linguistics in Language Teaching, 46*, 267–287.4.

Cope, B., & Kalantzis, M. (2009). Multiliteracies: New literacies, new learning. *Pedagogies: An International Journal, 43*(3), 164–195.

Cope, B., & Kalantzis, M. (2015). The things you do to know: An introduction to the pedagogy of multiliteracies. In B. Cope & M. Kalantzis (Eds.), *A pedagogy of multiliteracies: Learning by design* (pp. 1–36). Palgrave Macmillan.

Doerr, N. M., & Kumagai, Y. (2022). Flickers of difference: Living and learning with others through inclusive classroom projects. In N. J. Gozik & H. B. Hamir (Eds.), *A house where all belong: Redesigning education abroad for inclusive excellence abroad* (pp. 203–224). The Forum on Education Abroad.

Dupuy, B. (2011). CLIL: Achieving its goals through a multiliteracies framework. *Latin American Journal of Content & Language Integrated Learning, 4*(2), 21–32.

Fairclough, N. (2013). *Critical language awareness.* Routledge.

Freire, P., & Macedo, D. (1987). *Literacy: Reading the word and the world.* Bergin & Garvey.

Iori, I. (2016). The enterprise of Yasashii Nihongo: For a sustainable multicultural society in Japan. *Jinbun-Shizen Kenkyu, 10*, 4–19.

Ito, H., & Tokarev, A. (2021). From Yasashii Nihongo in non-disaster times towards a plurilingual language education approach: An outlook from the perspective of "reasonable accommodation". *F1000Research, 10*, 1–16.

Reading Japanese Linguistic Landscapes for Critical Multiliteracies 117

Iwahara, A., Hatta, T., & Maehara, A. (2003). The effects of a sense of compatibility between type of script and word in written Japanese. *Reading and Writing, 16*, 377–397.

Janks, H. (2010). Language, power and pedagogies. *Sociolinguistics and Language Education, 1*(3), 40–61.

Kalantzis, M., & Cope, B. (2012). New learning: A charter for change in education. *Critical Studies in Education, 53*(1), 83–94.

Kumagai, Y. (forthcoming). Challenging the ideas of "Japan" and "Japanese language" in foreign language education: Linguistic landscapes project. In I. Gaitanidis & G. Poole (Eds.), *Teaching Japan: A handbook*. Amsterdam University Press.

Kumagai, Y. (2022). Google Street View ni yoru online field work [Online fieldwork using Google Street View]. In A. Murata, A. Minoo, & S. Shinji (Eds.), *Learning fieldwork: From collaboration with international students to online data collection* (pp. 128–135). Nakanishi-ya Shuppan.

Kumagai, Y. (2023). Critical literacies in East Asian languages: Examples from Japanese in foreign language education. In R. Tierney, F. Rizv, E. Kadriye, & G. Smith (Eds.), *International encyclopedia of education (4e)* (pp. 112–122). Elsevier.

Kumagai, Y. (2024). "Incompetence" as a productive force for making the invisible visible: Reading linguistic landscapes as a dialogic space for knowledge creation for all. In N. M. Doerr (Ed.), *Politics of "Incompetence": Learning language, relations of power, and daily resistance* (pp. 77–99). Lexington Books.

Kumagai, Y., & Iwasaki, N. (2015). Reading words to read worlds: A Genre-based critical multiliteracies curriculum in Intermediate/Advanced Japanese language education. In Y. Kumagai, A. Lopez-Sanchez, & S. Wu (Eds.), *Multiliteracies in world language education* (pp. 107–131). Routledge.

Kumagai, Y., & Takahashi, Y. (2023). "Of course just in Japanese! Why would the government do anything else? This is Japan!": Developing critical literacy through a linguistic landscape project in a Japanese language classroom. In K. F. Davidson, S. M. Johnson, & L. J. Randolph Jr. (Eds.), *How we take action: Social justice in PK-16 language classrooms* (pp. 335–347). Information Age Publishing.

Kumagai, Y., Lopez-Sanchez, A., & Wu, S. (Eds.). (2015). *Multiliteracies in world language education*. Routledge.

López-Sánchez, A. (2015). Redesigning the intermediate level of the Spanish curriculum through a multiliteracies lens. In Y. Kumagai, A. López-Sánchez, & S. Wu (Eds.), *Multiliteracies in world language education* (pp. 58–80). Routledge.

Lozano, M. E., Jiménez-Caicedo, J. P., & Abraham, L. B. (2020). Linguistic landscape projects in language teaching: Opportunities for critical language learning beyond the classroom. In D. Malinowski, H. H. Maxim, & S. Dubreil (Eds.), *Language teaching in the linguistic landscape: Mobilizing pedagogy in public space* (pp. 17–42). Springer.

Luke, A., & Freebody, P. (1999). A map of possible practices: Further notes on the four resources model. *Practically Primary, 4*(2), 5–8.

Malinowski, D. (2009). Authorship in the linguistic landscape. A multimodal performative view. In E. Shohamy & D. Gorter (Eds.), *Linguistic landscape expanding the scenery* (pp. 107–125). Routledge.

McLelland, M., Suganuma, K., & Welker, J. (Eds.). (2007). *Queer voices from Japan: First person narratives from Japan's sexual minorities*. Lexington Books.

New London Group (NLG). (1996). A pedagogy of multiliteracies: Designing social futures. *Harvard Educational Review, 66*(1), 60–92.

New London Group (NLG). (2000). A pedagogy of multiliteracies: Designing social futures. In B. Cope & M. Kalantzis (Eds.), *Multiliteracies: Literacy learning and the design of social futures* (pp. 9–37). Routledge.

Oka, M., Tsutsui, M., Kondo, J., Emori, S., Hanai, Y., & Ishikawa, S. (2009). *Tobira: Gateway to advanced Japanese*. Kuroshio Publishers.

118 *Y. Kumagai*

Paesani, K. W., Allen, H. W., Dupuy, B., Liskin-Gasparro, J. E., & Lacorte, M. E. (2015). *A multiliteracies framework for collegiate foreign language teaching.* Pearson.

Robertson, W. C. (2020). *Scripting Japan: Orthography, variation, and the creation of meaning in written Japanese.* Routledge.

Rowland, L. (2013). The pedagogical benefits of a linguistic landscape project in Japan. *International Journal of Bilingual Education and Bilingualism, 16*(4), 494–505.

Sato, K. (1996). Gaikokujin no tame no saigaiji no kotoba [language for disaster time for foreigners]. *Gakken Gengo, 25*(2), 94–101.

Sayer, P. (2009). Using the linguistic landscape as a pedagogical resource. *ELT Journal, 64*(2), 143–154.

Seeley, C. (2000). *A history of writing in Japan.* University of Hawaii Press.

Shohamy, E., & Gorter, D. (Eds.). (2009). *Linguistic landscape: Expanding the scenery.* Routledge.

Swaffar, J. K., & Arens, K. (2005). *Remapping the foreign language curriculum: An approach through multiple literacies.* Modern Language Association.

Taylor, M. M., & Taylor, I. (2014). *Writing and literacy in Chinese, Korean and Japanese.* John Benjamins Publishing Company.

Turpin, K. M. (2021). Multiliteracies pedagogy: Theory to practice for scaffolding sustainability literacies. In J. J. De La Fuente (Ed.), *Education for sustainable development in foreign language learning* (pp. 34–49). Routledge.

Ukita, J., Sugishima, I., Minagawa, N., Inoue M. & Kasyu, K. (1996). Psychological research for written forms of Japanese words. Japanese Psychological Monograph, No. 25, Japanese Psychological Association.

Warren, M., & Winkler, C. (2015). Developing multiliteracies through genre in the beginner German classroom. In Y. Kumagai, A. Lopez-Sanchez, & S. Wu (Eds.), *Multiliteracies in world language education* (pp. 29–57). Routledge.

Appendix: Analysis Guiding Questions

Analysis 1 (Experiencing)

- Where the sign was located?
- What language(s) is used?
- What writing systems are used for Japanese words? (i.e., *Hiragana, Katakana, Kanji,* and *Rōmaji*)
- What other modes are used (alone or together with written language)? (e.g., pictures/illustrations, figures, symbols, maps, use of colors, layout, and typography)
- What does the sign say?
- Are all languages used to communicate the same meaning or different meanings?

Analysis 2 (Conceptualizing)

- Who created the sign? Is it public or private? How do you know?
- Why do you think the sign was located where you found it?
- What is the purpose of the sign? (e.g., informing, warning, and advertising)
- Who is the intended audience? How do you know?

Reading Japanese Linguistic Landscapes for Critical Multiliteracies 119

- Why do you think particular writing systems are used? Why do you think particular language(s) are used?
- How do different modes help to communicate the meaning? Are they helping/contradicting each other?

Analysis 3 (Analyzing)

- Do you think the sign is communicating its intention well?
- Is it easy for everyone to understand? If not, who may have difficulty understanding?
- Why do you think certain language(s) are used but not others?
- What does the sign tell you about the area? (e.g., who lives and who regularly visits the area)
- What does the sign tell you about the relationship between different language groups living there?
- What is your reaction to the sign? How do you feel about the sign?

Analysis 4 (Applying)

- What suggestions can you make to the creator of the sign to make it communicate better?
- How can you change the sign to be more helpful for everyone?
- Design your own signs.

6 L2 Learners Engaging with Linguistic Landscapes in the Classroom

Developing Criticality and Inspiring Agency

Mónica Lourenço and Sílvia Melo-Pfeifer

Introduction

Linguistic landscapes (LLs), the interwoven interplay of multisemiotic and multisensorial meaning containers in public and private spaces, provide an arena for investigating agency as related to (multi)literacy(ies), language rights, and identity. As a complex ensemble of different languages, semiotic signs, and other sense makers and sense containers (Jaworski & Thurlow, 2010; Pennycook, 2019; see also Kumagai, in this volume), LLs can be used to develop multiliteracies. Following the introduction to this volume, we see multiliteracies as the sum of knowledge and abilities necessary to read, interpret, and act upon the world, which is made of concurrent and intertwined semiotic clues. Multiliteracies encompass not only linguistic competences in a variety of languages but also visual literacy, critical literacy, and cultural literacy. Communication and meaning-making in the LL thus occur through diverse modes, including text, images, sound and smell, and digital media. In order to understand an LL holistically, multiliteracies are thus fundamental. In the school context, reflecting on the LL has been claimed to help students unveil situations of linguistic (in)equity and exert their agency as micro-policy actors in their own communities (Brinkmann et al., 2022; Shohamy & Pennycook, 2022).

In this contribution, we claim that LLs offer a practical and visible entry point to explore multiliteracies in the classroom, by examining the ways in which languages, modes of communication, and cultural identities intersect in public spaces (see also Kumagai, in this volume). LLs in education, we will show, further have the potential to enhance students' criticality and agency, by allowing them to express their linguistic identities and reinforce their perspectives on linguistic rights, power dynamics among different communities, and how public spaces should be shaped.

The research question underlying this chapter is "how do L2 learners develop criticality and agency through the exploration of LLs in the classroom?". Through the presentation of two case studies with young learners in Germany, we analyze interaction dynamics in the classroom that have the

DOI: 10.4324/9781003438847-10

L2 *Learners Engaging with Linguistic Landscapes in the Classroom*   121

potential to validate and celebrate students' linguistic identities, while at the same time enacting their criticality, agency, and multiliteracies. The chapter is organized as follows. In the first part, we summarize how LLs have been used in education, focusing on the language classroom and on young learners, as this is the context covered by our empirical study. Secondly, we present the design of the empirical study, describing the contexts and participants of the two case studies, the data collected, and the methodology used for data analysis. Following this presentation, we will carry out a micro-analysis of pedagogical interaction taking place inside and outside the classroom, in order to answer our research question. The discussion of the findings and the conclusion will critically address the concept of "agency", which will be reassessed in terms of pedagogical practices.

Theoretical Background

Linguistic Landscapes in Education and the Pedagogy of Multiliteracies

The field of second language (L2) learning has developed incrementally in the past decades to embrace not only new methods but also new goals and principles. While developing learners' spoken and written communication skills is still of relevance today, in order to help learners strive in complex, uncertain, and multicultural societies, teachers need to activate their prior knowledge, connect to their real lives, draw upon their linguistic and cultural repertoires, provide them with opportunities to use language through multiple modalities, and inspire them to build more inclusive and just societies.

As proposed in the introduction to this volume, a pedagogy of multiliteracies seems fit for this endeavor as it views learners' diverse languages, cultures, identities, and lived experiences as intrinsic parts of their learning (Cope & Kalantzis, 2015; New London Group, 1996). The term "multiliteracies" was first introduced in the late 1990s to encapsulate "the multiplicity of communications channels and media, and the increasing salience of cultural and linguistic diversity" (New London Group, 1996, p. 62) in rapidly evolving, globalized contexts. The framework for enacting a multiliteracies pedagogy consists of four instructional components: (1) *situated practice*, which involves building on the lived experiences, interests, needs, and identities of learners; (2) *overt instruction*, which focuses on providing intentional and direct instruction to scaffold learning; (3) *critical framing*, in which learners critically read "texts" they encounter in relation to their political, sociocultural, historical, and ideological contexts and social practices; and (4) *transformed practice*, which involves learners creatively applying what they have learned to transform or design texts which incorporate multiple modes (linguistic, visual, audio, gestural, spatial, and multimodal).

Multiliteracies activities allow L2 learners to draw upon their diverse, rich, and dynamic funds of knowledge through both linguistic and non-linguistic modes of communication, providing them with opportunities to make sense of their learning experiences (which take place both inside and outside the classroom) using multiple modalities, instead of relying solely on the target language. As a result, learners expand their linguistic and semiotic repertoire, leveraging different modes of expression, develop critical literacy, and affirm their own identities (Rajendram et al., 2022).

Consistent with multiliteracies pedagogies, activities that promote active exploration of the LL can contribute to learners becoming more attentive to language practices, varieties, and modalities in their multilingual communities and spaces, and developing a critical awareness of what lies beneath particular language choices. As LLs reflect the complex linguistic and cultural makeup of society, they can provide insights into the presence, usage, and power dynamics of languages within a specific community or geographical area. Hence, LL activities can promote social justice by directing learners' attention to the visibility of languages in varying modes in particular locations and sites, and by encouraging them to consider their role and agency in "rewriting" the LL to make it more inclusive and attractive.

The contribution of LL to (language) education is evidenced in the burgeoning literature in the field (e.g., Krompák et al., 2022; Malinowski et al., 2020; Melo-Pfeifer, 2023; Solmaz & Przymus, 2021). Overall, two complementary trends can be identified in the study of LLs in education (Gorter & Cenoz, 2021): the first trend focuses on the analysis of the "schoolscape" (i.e., the signage on display inside an educational institution); the second trend addresses the potential of LL as pedagogical resources. This latter trend may involve the exploration of the LL outside the school walls. In this context, learners engage with tangible examples of language diversity in public spaces (usually by taking photographs, conducting interviews, and/or making notes) and examine how languages function in different contexts. Past and current research on LL (Cenoz & Gorter, 2008; De Wilde et al., 2021) suggests that involving students in fieldwork, as ethnographers or sociolinguists who photograph and analyze the LL, can be a valuable and engaging learning experience, contributing to incidental language learning, to the development of pragmatic competence, and to supporting critical literacy skills.

However, as cautioned by Chern and Dooley (2014), learning about languages and diversity while walking down the street does not come automatically; learners have to be made aware and learn how to critically examine the signs they see. This is particularly relevant when we want learners to reflect upon issues of power and inequality in the LL, which requires them to move past what they observe to critically examine language choices, power dynamics, and respective social implications (Shohamy & Waksman, 2009). This attests to the relevance of looking at the way the LL is used in the classroom to promote critical language awareness, develop (multi)literacies, help learners (re) construct their identity, and foster their agency. We dedicate the next section to exploring this issue, focusing on studies that specifically address "young learners" (as defined by Nunan, 2011) in L2 or multilingual classrooms, given their relevance to our own research.

Exploring Linguistic Landscapes in the Language Classroom with Young Learners

The potential of the LL as a pedagogical tool for meaningful language learning is not limited to one target group. As evidenced by extensive research, learners of all ages, from very young children to university students, can be involved in exploring and learning from the signage present in their surroundings (e.g., Krompák et al., 2022). In this section, we highlight studies conducted with primary and lower secondary school children, here understood as encompassing learners from 6 to 14 years old. In doing so, we draw on Brinkmann et al. (2022) and Melo-Pfeifer and Silva (2021) who distinguish between three linguistic foci in the use of LLs in the classroom: a *multilingual focus*, which attempts to raise learners' awareness of the linguistic and cultural diversity in their environment; a *monolingual focus*, which engages learners in analyzing the presence of a specific language in the LL; and a *mixed focus*, which sees the LL as a pedagogical tool that serves the two previous foci.

A seminal example of the multilingual focus is a longitudinal study developed by Dagenais et al. (2009) in Montréal and Vancouver with 10- and 11-year-old children who were invited to imagine the language of their neighborhoods and construct their identities in relation to them. Through exploring the LL, children became more attentive to the non-neutrality of written communication, developing critical awareness of language, diversity, and power dynamics (see also Tjandra, 2021, in the Canadian context). Along the same lines, Clemente et al. (2012) used language awareness activities to develop six-year-old children's ability to read, understand, and question the LL. They introduced the children to six endangered languages through books, videos, and songs and led discussions about language rights. The children's interactions showed that exposure to unfamiliar languages enhanced their ability to "read the world" in a critical way, as well as their willingness to preserve languages, particularly in their written form. The focus on learners' engagement and agency is also evident in Sullivan et al.'s (2021) study of Year 6 students in a linguistically diverse municipality in Sweden. The students took photos of the LL in their school and lifeworlds and discussed the presence or absence of specific languages and their impact on democratic participation. They also engaged in "participatory linguistic landscaping", considering ways to make their school more welcoming for students with languages other than Swedish.

Despite their disparate foci, current studies attest to the central role of the classroom as the space where (language) learners become more aware of the LL (Gorter et al., 2021; Roos & Nicholas, 2019; Tjandra, 2021). Furthermore, they underscore the pedagogical potential of LLs to develop young learners' critical awareness of language and linguistic diversity, their competences in the target language, as well as their engagement in imagining more inclusive and democratic communities.

The Present Study

Addressing this background, we developed a multiple case study that aimed to investigate how L2 learners develop their criticality and agency through the exploration of LLs in the classroom. Two separate school settings in Germany were analyzed – a highly linguistically diverse urban primary bilingual school and a more homogeneous peri-urban lower secondary school. Data were collected in the context of student practicum by two pre-service teachers of Spanish as an L2, who separately transcribed the data for their respective master's thesis (Cordero, 2020; Von Holt, 2022).

Data Collection

Our empirical study can be described as a multiple case study. A case is "an instance, incident, or unit of something, and can be anything – a person, an organization, an event, a decision, an action, a location" (Schwandt & Gates, 2017, p. 341). Our study involves studying and analyzing two individual cases to gain a comprehensive insight into the phenomenon of the pedagogical use of LLs in education and to provide a deeper understanding of our research question. We selected two cases that share certain characteristics or are relevant to the research topic. Firstly, the two cases involve two schools in the north of Germany that participated in the LoCALL project. LoCALL, which stands for "LOcal Linguistic Landscapes for global language education in the school context", was a collaborative European project developed between 2019 and 2022, which was coordinated by the University of Hamburg (in Germany) in conjunction with the participants from France, the Netherlands, Portugal, and Spain. In the scope of the project, pedagogical resources were created, implemented, and evaluated by teachers and students in the partner schools. Secondly, in both schools, the teachers were simultaneously researchers interested in the outcomes of the pedagogical introduction of LLs as a resource and as a learning object. Despite these commonalities, the two studies differ in multiple ways, as highlighted in the following section. Table 6.1 presents both settings. In the next two sections, we present the settings in more detail, focusing on the activities carried out in each classroom.

Table 6.1 The two settings

Setting	Location	School context	School subject	Number of students	Ages
Setting 1	Urban context (Hamburg)	Primary school	Across the curriculum	11	8 and 9 years old
Setting 2	Peri-urban context (Lower Saxony)	Lower secondary school	Spanish classroom	29	12–14 years old

L2 Learners Engaging with Linguistic Landscapes in the Classroom   125

Setting 1: Primary School

The introduction of LLs occurred in the third school year, in 2021, amidst the COVID-19 pandemic. Considering that the school has a high number of plurilingual students with a migrant background (around 50 percent of the school population) and the class had a very high percentage of students in that situation (80 percent of students with a knowledge of 18 different languages in total), the teacher, who had himself a migrant background, designed the tasks around the critical discovery of students' plurilingualism and of the multilingualism of the city, contrasting both. To pursue these aims, the teacher developed a pedagogical sequence with four phases, which corresponded to four sessions, following a multilingual orientation (Table 6.2).

During the task completion, the teacher, who identifies himself as plurilingual, collected 11 linguistic biographies, 11 envisioned LLs, around 4 hours of recorded interactions, and individual interviews with the students.

Setting 2: Lower Secondary School

Multilingualism and interculturality are very present in the course, as evidenced by the 15 different languages identified in the students' language biographies. The teacher developed a pedagogical unit for the Spanish class based on the exploration of the LL of their town and the subsequent creation of a quiz for the LoCALL app (see Marques et al., 2023, for a presentation of this app). This meant that the students had to take photos outside the classroom, bring them to class, and select those that presented linguistic and semiotic elements deemed salient for questioning. This is due to the fact that, when working with the LoCALL app, students have to select images, create questions, think of answers in a multiple-choice format, and write targeted

Table 6.2 Tasks developed in Setting 1

Phase	Tasks	Aims	Duration
Phase 1	Drawing linguistic portraits (the linguistic silhouette)	Students discover, share, and reflect on their linguistic portraits and those of the other students.	60 min
Phase 2	Discovering the LL	Students discover the linguistic diversity in their environment.	60 min
Phase 3	Drawing and presenting an envisioned LL	Students represent the LL they would like to see around them.	60 min
Phase 4	Interviewing students	Students reflect on the added value of reflecting on individual and societal multilingualism.	around 20 min (per student)

Source: Adapted from Cordero (2020).

126   *M. Lourenço and S. Melo-Pfeifer*

Table 6.3 Tasks developed in Setting 2

Phase	Tasks	Aims	Duration
Phase 1	Drawing linguistic portraits (the linguistic silhouette)	Students discover, share, and reflect on their linguistic portraits, understand the concept of LL, and discover the features of the LoCALL app.	90 min
Phase 2	Planning the games for the App (group work)	Students explore the resources they will be working on during the photo safari.	90 min
Phase 3	Taking photos (photo safari)	Students discover together and in groups the LL of their town.	90 min
Phase 4	Creating questions for the LoCALL app	Students select photos for the game (two per group) and think of questions, answers, and feedback for the game.	90 min
Phase 5	Adding questions to the LoCALL app platform	Students learn how to use the LoCALL app dashboard.	90 min
Phase 6	Adding questions to the LoCALL app platform, playing the game in the app, and providing feedback	Students experiment with the game they created and assess the added value of the pedagogical unit on LL.	90 min

Source: Adapted from Von Holt (2022).

user feedback. Table 6.3 presents the different phases of the pedagogical unit. Even though the teacher designed a unit that had a monolingual focus in mind (added attention should be given to Spanish), the other languages of the town were also expected to be explored.

During Phase 3, students carried a voice recorder with them and recorded their interactions during the photo safari. The teacher noticed that the students were very motivated by the idea of discovering "linguistic treasures". In the original draft of the pedagogical unit, the extension of the photo safari to free time was not planned, but the students showed a lively interest in continuing the search for language finds to complete the data bank they had constructed during Phase 3.

Data Analysis

In our multiple case study, a range of materials was collected, including drawings made by the students, photos, presentations prepared by the teachers, students' individual reflections, and audio-recorded interactions taking place inside and outside the school. In the scope of this chapter, we will focus on the analysis of episodes of interaction, resorting to heuristic instruments of conversation and discourse analysis (Toerien, 2014; Willig, 2014). By following

L2 Learners Engaging with Linguistic Landscapes in the Classroom   127

this method, we aim to capture context-specific details on the use of LLs in education (in primary and lower secondary education) and generate nuanced and contextually rich findings in both contexts to develop theory around the concept of agency and to address the practical implications of "agency-oriented pedagogies".

For this study, we selected four interactional episodes, based mainly on the criteria of significance and richness regarding the treatment of the research question. The four episodes, which occurred in German and were translated by the authors, bring a diversity of perspectives and new insights. Therefore, the aim was not to conduct a comparative study but rather to compile information from two different settings to complexify the answer to our guiding question.

Findings

Setting One: Primary School

In Setting 1, during the second day of the work with LL (Phase 2), the teacher brought a video with visual and audible landscapes. The students had to identify the languages, guess the meanings of words and sentences, and discuss the linguistic choices. Excerpt 1 of the interactions took place during the discussion of the soundscape recorded in the metro. Students' names are signaled by the abbreviations KV, KE, KBO, and KRE.

Excerpt 1

Teacher (T) – A woman was speaking. What languages did you hear?
KV – English and German
T – And can you say which came first? (…)
KE – In German and then in English: "S1, S3…"
KBO – I wanted to say that.
T – She was talking about the metro, wasn't she?
KE – Yes, in German the first time, and then you can understand: "S3 and the ferry".
T – And do you think she repeated the same thing or said different things?
KBO – She repeated the same thing, only in a different language. Firstly, she said it in German and then in English. Maybe some of them can speak English and understand it.
T – She also spoke a little English. And can you imagine why she spoke in German first and then in English?
KRE – Because there are more Germans on the train than foreig … other people?

Students and teachers reflect together about the presence of different languages in the soundscape of the metro. The reflection is prompted by direct

128   *M. Lourenço and S. Melo-Pfeifer*

questions from the teacher, who scaffolds the discussion to guide the students in the (re)construction of knowledge (e.g., "What languages did you hear?", "Can you say which came first?"). He directs the students to reflect on language presence, language hierarchies, and the functions of repeating the same information in different languages. Therefore, in the first moment, the teacher scaffolds the analysis of the LL, and then he moves to elicit an interpretation from the students ("Can you imagine why she spoke in German first and then in English?"). The students always answer the direct questions promptly using their declarative knowledge, by naming the languages they have heard, for instance, and advance an interpretation for the observed linguistic dispositions ("there are more Gerssmans on the train"). By doing so, they connect the visibility of the languages to the sociolinguistic reality, in general, and to the demographic presence of speakers, more specifically.

After discussing the LL the teacher encounters in his daily life, he pushes the discussion forward toward the interpretation of the linguistic diversity identified in the photos and audio documents (Phase 2). The prompt to initiate the discussion is "Is there a reason why so many languages are spoken here in X [name of the neighborhood the students live in]?" (Excerpt 2).

Excerpt 2

T – I wanted to ask you something else. Is there a reason why so many languages are spoken here in X?

KA – Because people who have moved to another country or here speak their language, of course, because they can't learn it [German] straight away.

T – There are many people, yes?

KV – Well, there are people from other countries who travel here and, for example, from America, they come here and speak English and then they also learn German and so on.

KRE – Many people speak a different language, and they can't learn the language from Germany or German so quickly.

KMA – If you are born in another country and then fly to another country and want to live there, then, of course, you must learn the language, but, of course, you forget the other languages. So, the other languages, they know them too and they speak them with their families.

(…)

KRE – Something very important. Some people come from other countries and then they come here and when they go shopping or something and if they don't know what something means, then they can ask the staff because they can sometimes speak different languages (…).

From the moment the teacher prompts the discussion, he leaves space for the students to advance their own interpretations regarding multilingualism in their neighborhood. The students associate the presence of different languages in the LL with migration and displacement ("people who have moved to another

L2 Learners Engaging with Linguistic Landscapes in the Classroom 129

country", "people from other countries", "born in another country" or "who come from another country"). Languages are therefore conceptualized in terms of their spatialization and connection to countries. In a second move, multilingualism in the LL is associated with the impossibility of learning the new languages immediately ("they can't learn it straight away", "they can't learn the language from Germany or German so quickly"). By reflecting on why some people speak different languages, the students inadvertently reproduce the ideology that integration depends on the command of the majority language ("if you (…) want to live there, of course you have to learn the language") and the ideology "one language-one country" ("the language from Germany" is equalized to "German" by the use of "or", which makes both synonyms). This excerpt illustrates how students make sense of migration and displacement: they articulate the need to learn the new language (a process that is perceived as taking time) as being associated with the need to maintain their home languages ("the other languages, they know them too and they speak these with their families"). It is plausible to assume that by articulating these discourses and ideologies, they are reflecting on and making sense of their own situations, in a mirror effect, as the class has 80 percent of students with a migrant background.

Students display understanding towards people who cannot learn the language immediately and show difficulties in their everyday interactions ("when they go shopping or something and if they don't know what something means, then they can ask the staff"). These reflections show instances of what we could call "language solidarity", in which more proficient speakers of the majority language are constructed as "people who can help". The last utterance in this excerpt reveals a different level of reflection and interpretation: the connection between being multilingual to "staff" in the supermarkets, which are usually underpaid jobs, left to workers considered to be less qualified ("then they can ask the staff, because they can sometimes speak different languages"). Being multilingual, in this assumption, is a proxy of socioeconomic status, even if the students do not openly claim it.

Taken as a whole, the repetition of formulas such as "of course" and "because" lets us perceive what students consider to be the "linguistic normality" around them and thus how they internalize this normality. Finally, this excerpt is important to signal the involvement of the students in the interpretation of their linguistic surroundings, which is observed in the way they display agentivity: they voluntarily take the floor through self-selection and see their contributions as important to the ongoing discussion ("something very important").

Setting Two: Lower Secondary School

To illustrate Setting 2, we chose two sequences recorded by the students themselves, outside the classroom. The interactions are nevertheless pedagogical, as students permanently recall the learning contract (tasks and aims). One group of students is exploring the town on their own during the photo safari

130   *M. Lourenço and S. Melo-Pfeifer*

(Phase 3). They carry a voice recorder and are negotiating the spaces they should visit. The transcript of the interaction (Excerpt 3) does not allow us to identify the students speaking but it gives us a vivid account of the interaction dynamics they engage in during their walk.

Excerpt 3

– Shall we go back to an ice cream store or something now?
– Yes, we can just photograph this frozen yogurt ice cream if they have it there.
– But then we could also just photograph our clothes.
– Then we can go directly to DM [German store for cosmetics] and take any products.
– Let it! Just pick up something… whatever we can find here so publicly…
– Yes, I do not pay attention to it when I go shopping, whether that is in different languages.
– Yes, when you come from abroad then I look at it but…
– DM, I actually thought it would be a good idea.
(…)
– Les Ombres, this is, uhm, this is Spanish.
– Yes, that's good.
– Yes, if this is [actually] Spanish…
– So, perfect.
– Les Ombres, is there anything else Spanish out here?
– We can take other languages as well.
– Excellent?
– More hair stuff?
– This is 100 percent not German here, but what is it?
– This looks a bit like French here.
– It is Italian.
– Coloration, this is English, not Spanish.
– Yes, take a picture, please.
– It doesn't matter now because we don't need [to photograph] only Spanish stuff ….

The students doing their ethnographic walk recall a place where they had already spotted different languages ("an ice cream store") and are now hunting for other languages in their immediate surroundings. They start brainstorming about other languages and artifacts they could take a picture of, coming up with ideas such as clothes or stores with international products. This moment is important to notice how students gain a growing awareness of languages around them, including not just storefronts and signage on the street but also their own clothing and the products inside stores. They also start reflecting on the limited attention they usually pay to languages around them ("I do not pay attention to it when I go shopping") or how they do pay

L2 Learners Engaging with Linguistic Landscapes in the Classroom   131

attention to languages when someone "comes from abroad". This sentence shows that displaying certain languages in clothes is a proxy of otherness and that students perceive it as distinctive ("when you come from abroad then I look at it"). What remains to be answered is how and why students come to recognize someone "from abroad", making them pay attention to some people and not to others.

From what seems to be an interaction inside the DM store, the students start, as in Excerpt 1, by trying to identify the languages they encounter. They discuss the languages they can associate with "les ombres", "excellent", and "coloration". It is interesting to analyze how "les ombres" ("the shadows", in French) is mistakenly taken as Spanish, probably because of the similarity to "los hombres" ("the men", in English). Despite the skepticism of one student ("if this is [actually] Spanish..."), the other students assume that that is indeed Spanish ("is there anything else Spanish out here?") and seem to be happy to abide by the task provided by the teacher (i.e., looking for Spanish as a priority). This seems to show how students, despite the freedom granted to them, still worry about the framework of the school task, what frames the limits of their agency outside school ("Yes, take a picture, please"). Interestingly, the students also recall the teacher opening up spaces to hunt for multilingualism ("We can take other languages as well" and "we don't need only Spanish stuff"). These instances of negotiation are important to understand how students cope with the dilemma of being in the Spanish classroom (even if transported beyond the school walls) and concomitantly being confronted with other languages. Eventually, the students end up combining the monolingual and the multilingual foci on the exploration and description of the LL.

In Excerpt 4 (Phase 4), another group of students is exploring the linguistic environment, selecting the photos, and thinking together about explanations about why they chose a specific one. The interaction, which is recorded by the students themselves, is very humorous, interspersed with pseudo-rhymes in French and name associations. The excerpt starts with students recalling the pedagogical contract prompting a set of interpretations.

Excerpt 4

– We now have to ask two questions about each picture and always think of four possible answers.
– We always have to say why we find it so exciting.
– Okay, who wants to write it down?
– I'm writing it down, dude.
– Because the fonts are so different. And because the fireman has such a stupid nose.
– The recording. Try to keep it down. (…)
– Okay, because it looks very funny. And because it's very colorful. It stands out.
– Because it's funny and creative with the colors.

132   *M. Lourenço and S. Melo-Pfeifer*

– Write it down like this.
– Yes, that's the beak somehow. And the fire can walk and has arms and a face.
– The bottom one is so elegant, it's like Paris. It's a more expensive street. You're standing with a baguette like this ….
– Brigitte.
– And then Brigitte walks behind you like this … (laughter)
– When you laugh, I have to laugh too, because your laugh is so funny.
– Brigitte, the Fitte one. What's that laugh of yours … Kettle. Like a kettle. I don't know, she's got this ….
– OK, why did you choose Brigitte?
– Because I know at least what language that is.
– French. Bonjour, bonjour Baguette.
(…)
– That looks really elegant.
– We chose the picture, didn't we?
– We chose the picture because we are very interested in what language it is and - because it looks very Parisian.
– It looks so expensive. Because it looked creative and funny.

In this sequence, the students try to find valid arguments to choose a specific photo, which displays the name of a jewelry shop ("Bijou Brigitte"). The first explanations are not related to the language of the sign, but rather to the semiotic environment: the fonts are different, it is colorful, and the images are funny. These three elements, one student wraps up, make the store "stand out". They decide collaboratively on a tentative argument "Because it's funny and creative with the colors" (followed by the approval "write it down like this"). They continue interpreting the semiotics of the store and come to a second category of arguments: the store looks "elegant, it's like Paris. It's a more expensive street. You're standing with a baguette like this…". By verbalizing this sequence of utterances, they bring the lifestyle, the spatiality, and the socioeconomic status together, which they end up connecting to French, a language they identify easily ("I know at least what language that is"). Interestingly, this identification prompts the group to playfully mock the language, through the playful mimicry of greetings in French ("Bonjour, bonjour Baguette").

After a moment of funny repetition of jokes, they came across on TikTok around the use of foreign names; they return to the task and acknowledge that the visuals accompanying the store are elegant ("That looks really elegant"), again formulating an idea attached to French culture: "It looks very Parisian". In this sequence, Paris is immediately associated with being elegant and expensive, two assumptions that go undisputed by the other members of the group. The group finally agrees on the two justifications: "We chose the picture because we are very interested in what language it is and – because it looks very Parisian" and "It looks so expensive. Because it looked creative and funny".

Discussion

Our findings show that students were able to discuss their and others' plurilingual repertoires and identities, to unveil situations of sociolinguistic (in)equity, as well as possibilities to exert their agency. We could see that students in both settings were able to observe, describe, and interpret the LL they encountered, through guided scaffolding from the teacher (in Setting 1) or through the completion of research-based tasks in (guided) autonomy (in Setting 2). In both settings, students bring funds of knowledge (languages they know and identify, for example), lived experiences in their communities, and spaces of socialization (observations in the supermarket, ideologies related to lifestyles, etc.) to co-construct knowledge and make sense of what they see and hear around them. We can therefore relate the analysis of the pedagogical interactions about the LL to the framework of multiliteracies (New London Group, 1996) in several ways:

- Situated practice: talking about and walking around the LL involves the recalling of students' and teachers' lived experiences and are therefore pedagogical activities based on their identities. From this perspective, the pedagogical work with LL in the classroom is a form of identity work.
- Overt instruction: teachers play a major role in designing instruction and scaffolding learning, by asking questions that trigger students' involvement and support their maximal identity investment. In Setting 1, the teacher formulates questions that are increasingly complex, moving from observation to interpretation. In Setting 2, even though the analyzed sequences focus on group work outside the classroom, we can observe how the pedagogical contract is always recalled. This means that, even when the teacher is absent, students know that their work is embedded in a pedagogical framework. In both cases, through different means, teachers orchestrate and mediate the pedagogical tasks and their outcomes.
- Critical framing: through the exploration of the LL, either through multimodal transposition to the classroom in Setting 1 (using the videos and photos brought by the teacher) or *in loco* in Setting 2 (through students' ethnographic walks), students are able to critically read the "texts" they encounter, meaning not just identifying and counting languages but interpreting their presence, their functions, and the ideologies standing behind their choice. We could see that reading the LL is not reduced to the reading of linguistic features but combines the reading of fonts, colors, and photos, in a multisemiotic and multimodal reading process. Furthermore, students connect the texts and situations they encounter to social practices (such as the one we described in terms of linguistic solidarity).
- Transformed practice: although this dimension was not fully covered by the interactional sequences highlighted in the analysis, we can nevertheless see instances of transfer of arguments being brought to the discussion to explain other situations (Excerpt 1) and students engaging in playful and creative interactions to explore the LL (Excerpt 4).

134 M. Lourenço and S. Melo-Pfeifer

Answering our research question, "how do L2 learners develop their own criticality and agency through the exploration of LL in the classroom?", we could observe a growing agency and involvement (both cognitive and emotional) in task completion. Students take the floor to participate in the discussions; they consider their work and contributions to be meaningful; they recall their lived experiences to interpret complex sociolinguistic situations; they engage in negotiation sequences about places to visit, photos to be taken, and justifications to be provided. Such signs of criticality and agency are not dependent on the physical presence of the teacher (as seen in Setting 2). Indeed, what seems paramount in enhancing criticality and agency is the pedagogical scaffolding of the teacher, which can occur synchronously or asynchronously, through task design.

Based on the findings and their discussion, we problematize the notion of student agency and the practices and limitations around its development in classroom settings. Indeed, students' agency does not seem to be either independent from teachers' guided and designed instruction or fully purposive and conscious (Scollon & Scollon, 2003, p. 15). Having said this, we prefer to describe the observed practices and outcomes in terms of "agency-oriented pedagogy", which, in our study, is developed around the principles of action research, participation, positionality, and criticality. These principles apply to students and teachers alike; as both teachers and students in the two settings engage in action research to prepare and/or accomplish the tasks, they all take part in the research being co-developed (meaning they are all co-ethnographers of their multisemiotic and multimodal surroundings); they bring their own formal and informal experiences with languages and migration to co-construct the meaning of what they observe and uncover collaboratively; and they take a personal critical stance to complex sociolinguistic realities. Despite our analysis being inconclusive on how students could use the critical reflections initiated in the classroom to act upon the LL, perhaps because of students' cognitive and moral maturity development (Sullivan et al., 2021), we can nevertheless claim that the tasks designed and even co-performed by the teachers constitute a starting point for transformational practices with and for young learners.

Conclusion

This study reveals how exploring LLs in the classroom is a complex pedagogical matter, although very engaging for both students and teachers. As highlighted by Roos and Nicholas (2019, p. 93), "it presents challenging choices and offers intriguing opportunities for both teachers and learners in working out how to go beyond and beneath the surface of language". Taken together, both our literature review and our multiple case study show that working with the LL provides opportunities for young language learners to develop awareness of language and linguistic diversity and to gain new, deeper, and critical insights into social, cultural, political, and economic values attached to the presence of languages in the LL.

L2 Learners Engaging with Linguistic Landscapes in the Classroom 135

Furthermore, the literature review and the case study underscore the potential of LLs to give a voice to young learners regarding them as meaning makers and social actors who have a say in expressing their own identities and their understandings of social life. Hence, the LL should not be regarded only as a resource for documentation and inquiry but as an instructive, (re)constructive, and powerful pedagogical tool that can be successfully and effectively used early on to develop critical language awareness, critical multiliteracies, agency, and social activism (Shohamy & Waksman, 2009).

References

Brinkmann, L. M., Duarte, J., & Melo-Pfeifer, S. (2022). Promoting plurilingualism through linguistic landscapes: A multi-method and multi-site study in Germany and the Netherlands. *TESL Canada Journal, 38*(2), 88–112.

Cenoz, J., & Gorter, D. (2008). The linguistic landscape as an additional source of input in second language acquisition. *IRAL – International Review of Applied Linguistics in Language Teaching, 46*(3), 267–287. https://doi.org/10.1515/IRAL.2008.012

Chern, C.-I., & Dooley, K. (2014). Learning English by walking down the street. *ELT Journal, 68*(2), 113–123. https://doi.org/10.1093/elt/cct067

Clemente, M., Andrade, A. I., & Martins, F. (2012). Learning to read the world, learning to look at the linguistic landscape: A study in the first years of formal education. In C. Hélot, M. Barni, R. Janssens, & C. Bagna (Eds.), *Linguistic landscapes, multilingualism and social change* (pp. 267–285). Peter Lang.

Cope, B., & Kalantzis, M. (Eds.). (2015). *Multiliteracies: Literacy learning and the design of social futures.* Routledge.

Cordero, F. (2020). *El paisaje lingüístico como recurso pedagógico para el desarrollo de la consciencia lingüística del alumnado plurilingüe: un estudio de caso en la escuela de Educación Primaria en Hamburgo* [MA thesis, University of Hamburg].

Dagenais, D., Moore, D., Sabatier, C., Lamarre, P., & Armand, F. (2009). Linguistic landscape and language awareness. In E. Shohamy & D. Gorter (Eds.), *Linguistic landscape: Expanding the scenery* (pp. 253–269). Routledge.

De Wilde, J., Verhoene, J., Tondeur, J., & Van Praet, E. (2021). 'Go in practice': Linguistic landscape and outdoor learning. In E. Krompák, V. Fernández-Mallat, & S. Meyer (Eds.), *Linguistic landscape and educational spaces* (pp. 214–231). Multilingual Matters.

Gorter, D., & Cenoz, J. (2021). Linguistic landscapes in educational contexts: An afterword. In E. Krompák, V. Fernández-Mallat, & S. Meyer (Eds.), *Linguistic landscape and educational spaces* (pp. 277–290). Multilingual Matters.

Gorter, D., Cenoz, J., & Van der Worp, K. (2021). The linguistic landscape as a resource for language learning and raising language awareness. *Journal of Spanish Language Teaching, 8*(2), 161–181. https://doi.org/10.1080/23247797.2021.2014029

Jaworski, A., & Thurlow, C. (Eds.). (2010). *Semiotic landscapes: Language, image, space.* Continuum.

Krompák, E., Fernández-Mallat, V., & Meyer, S. (Eds.). (2022). *Linguistic landscape and educational spaces.* Multilingual Matters.

136 M. Lourenço and S. Melo-Pfeifer

Kumagai, Y. (2024). Reading Japanese Linguistic landscapes for critical multiliteracies: Nurturing agency and criticality for social justice. In V. Tavares (Ed.), *Social justice through pedagogy of multiliteracies*. Routledge.

Malinowski, D., Maxim, H., & Dubreil, S. (Eds.). (2020). *Language teaching in the linguistic landscape. Mobilizing pedagogy in public space*. Springer.

Marques, M., Lourenço, M., Pombo, L., Neves, A., Laranjeiro, D., & Martins, F. (2023). The LoCALL app: A mobile tool to promote learning from and about linguistic landscapes. In S. Melo-Pfeifer (Ed.), *Linguistic landscapes in language and teacher education* (pp. 139–162). Springer.

Melo-Pfeifer, S. (Ed.). (2023). *Linguistic landscapes in language and teacher education*. Springer.

Melo-Pfeifer, S., & Silva, F. (2021). Potencial didático da paisagem linguística no ensino-aprendizagem do português: um estudo da paisagem linguística do "Portugiesenviertel" de Hamburgo. In N. Dominique & M. Souza Neto (Eds.), *Microgeopolítica da língua portuguesa: ações, desafios e perspectivas* (pp. 85–107). Boavista Press.

New London Group. (1996). A pedagogy of multiliteracies: Designing social futures. *Harvard Educational Review*, 66(1), 60–92. https://doi.org/10.17763/haer.66.1.17370n67v22j160u

Nunan, D. (2011). *Teaching English to young learners*. Anaheim University Press.

Pennycook, A. (2019). Linguistic landscapes and semiotic assemblages. In M. Pütz & N. Mundt (Eds.), *Expanding the linguistic landscape* (pp. 75–88). Multilingual Matters.

Rajendram, S., Burton, J., & Wong, W. (2022). Online translanguaging and multiliteracies strategies to support K–12 multilingual learners: Identity texts, linguistic landscapes, and photovoice. *TESOL Journal, 13*, e685, 1–19. https://doi.org/10.1002/tesj.685

Roos, J., & Nicholas, H. (2019). Using young learners' language environments for EFL learning, *AILA Review, 32*, 91–111. https://doi.org/10.1075/aila.00022.roo

Schwandt, T. A., & Gates, E. F. (2017). Case study methodology. In N. K. Denzin & Y. S. Lincoln (Eds.), *The SAGE handbook of qualitative research* (5 ed., pp. 341–358). Sage.

Scollon, R., & Scollon, S. W. (2003). *Discourses in place: Language in the material world*. Routledge.

Shohamy, E., & Pennycook, A. (2022). Language, pedagogy, and active participant engagement gaze in the multilingual landscape. In R. Blackwood & U. Røyneland (Eds.), *Spaces of multilingualism* (pp. 31–47). Routledge.

Shohamy, E., & Waksman, S. (2009). Linguistic landscape as an ecological arena: Modalities, meanings, negotiations, education. In E. Shohamy & D. Gorter (Eds.), *Linguistic landscape: Expanding the scenery* (pp. 313–331). Routledge.

Solmaz, O., & Przymus, S. (Eds.). (2021). *Linguistic landscapes in English language teaching: A pedagogical guidebook*. Dicle University, Turkey & Forth Worth: Texas Christian University, US. https://repository.tcu.edu/handle/116099117/45344

Sullivan, K. P. H., Waldmann, C., & Wiklund, M. (2021). Using participatory linguistic landscapes as pedagogy for democracy: A didactic study in a primary school classroom. In E. Krompák, V. Fernández-Mallat, & S. Meyer (Eds.), *Linguistic landscape and educational spaces* (pp. 193–213). Multilingual Matters.

Tjandra, C. (2021). Supporting newcomer children's language awareness, incidental language learning, and identity negotiation through the multilingual linguistic landscape: An exploratory case study. *The Canadian Modern Language Review/ La revue canadienne des langues vivantes, 77*(1), 1–22. https://doi.org/10.3138/cmlr-2019-0060

Toerien, M. (2014). Conversations and conversation analysis. In U. Flick (Ed.), *The SAGE handbook of qualitative data analysis* (pp. 327–340). Sage.

Von Holt, R. (2022). *Wie wirkt sich die Arbeit mit* Linguistic Landscapes *auf die* Language Awareness *von SchülerInnen aus?* [MA thesis, University of Hamburg].

Willig, C. (2014). Discourses and discourse analysis. In U. Flick (Ed.), *The SAGE handbook of qualitative data analysis* (pp. 341–353). Sage.

Part IV

Multiliteracies for Social Justice in Teacher Education Contexts

7 Building Deaf Agency through the Teaching and Learning of 'English Grammar Games'

Jenny Webster, Ulrike Zeshan, Nirav Pal, and Deepu Manavalamamuni

Introduction

Despite decades of research into deaf community sign languages, there is still a global context of limited recognition of sign languages and poor educational opportunities for deaf children (Wang & Andrews, 2020). The traditional approaches to deaf people's education often fail to value and utilize the skills that they bring into the educational setting, such as fluency in sign language. In contrast to these deficit models, the multiliteracies approach (Cope & Kalantzis, 2000; New London Group, 1996) highlights the importance of deaf students' semiotic repertoire (Kusters et al., 2017), which includes signing, writing, fingerspelling, and drawing, among others. The 'multi' dimension in multiliteracies involves the use and recognition of multiple languages and socially and culturally appropriate forms of language, including non-standard and popular language varieties, as well as the central role of multiple modes, including visual and gestural, in communication (Cope & Kalantzis, 2009).

A common approach for teaching English to deaf signers is to explain the 'rules' of English in sign language (Randhawa, 2005; Tang, 2017). But an intelligible medium of instruction such as a sign language is not enough. Interventions must also be based on a linguistic rationale, and English Grammar Games (EGGs) may facilitate this in a way that also builds agency. Each game starts with a 'real-life English' (RLE) text, and players must find parts of the text that match abstract grammatical structures given as prompts. The prompts combine grammatical frames with semantic expressions in square brackets, highlighting local structures embedded in authentic texts. Players then write and share their own examples using the same structures (see Figure 7.1).

This chapter examines data from training sessions on how to create EGGs and use them with deaf learners. These sessions were delivered in November and December 2021 by 2 deaf instructors (Pal and Manavalamamuni) to 12 deaf trainee tutors in India, as a follow-up to the 'Peer-to-Peer Deaf Multiliteracies' project (2017–2020, Webster & Zeshan, 2021a, 2021b). This was the second in a series of three successive international projects led by the

DOI: 10.4324/9781003438847-12

142   *J. Webster et al.*

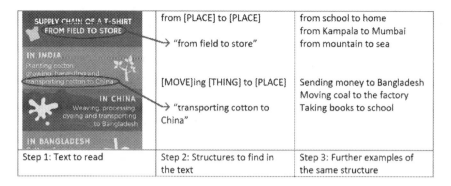

Figure 7.1 The grammar game process (Papen & Zeshan, 2021)

International Institute for Sign Languages and Deaf Studies (iSLanDS) at the University of Central Lancashire in collaboration with partner organizations in the UK, South Asia, and sub-Saharan Africa. All three projects were funded by the UK's Economic and Social Research Council (ESRC) and the Foreign, Commonwealth & Development Office (FCDO), through their joint scheme 'Raising Learning Outcomes in Education Systems'. The projects involved working with young deaf people in India, Ghana, and Uganda to facilitate their acquisition of reading, writing, and multiliteracies skills through sign languages in programs led by deaf peer tutors. They followed a learner-centered approach, aiming to use deaf communities' own resources and making full use of accessible communication in a deaf-friendly environment. Rather than implementing individual interventions, the research team sought to establish new ecosystems of learning where different elements of the learning situation come together and support each other in novel ways (Fan, 2018). The immediate goal was to increase deaf learners' access to literacy and multiliteracies learning, but capacity building was also a central focus, and the research team trained a group of young deaf professionals including the two master trainers whose work is explored in this chapter. The chapter looks at the extent to which these master trainers were able to teach their trainees to identify texts and create EGGs on their own, how the trainees used multiliteracies skills to extract grammatical structures from the texts and generate their own phrases, and how the use of EGGs may relate to social justice for deaf signers.

The next section provides a review of the literature on EGGs and their development for use with deaf learners in particular. In the third section, the files from the training are discussed, and then the fourth section presents the scholar-practitioners' reflections on the training they delivered, with particular reference to the contribution that EGGs may make toward deaf teachers' professionalization and social justice. A conclusion is offered in the final section.

Games as a Bridge between Real-Life English Texts and Grammar Learning

'Real-life English' resources for language learning have been used since the 1970s, when Phillips and Shettlesworth (1978), for instance, highlighted the practical and pedagogical benefits of exploiting them in course design, albeit for non-deaf learners. These kinds of materials are more associated with the communicative framework of language teaching than with structuralism (Mestari & Malabar, 2016), and they have also been referred to as 'realia' and 'authentic tasks' (Richards & Rodgers, 2014, p. 189). Examples of realia are said to include newspaper ads, television weather reports, and the websites of online booksellers. Such resources can be harnessed in tasks such as using a weather report to create a map with weather symbols or producing a comparative analysis of book prices and delivery times (Richards & Rodgers, 2014).

The idea of authentic or RLE texts was central to the Peer-to-Peer Deaf Multiliteracies project and the starting point for experimentation with the game methodology to provide a more accessible alternative for deaf learners (Papen & Zeshan, 2021). The use of such texts, including adverts, recipes, application forms, information posters, film subtitles, cartoons, poems, websites, and social media posts, makes communication and everyday uses of English central to the learning process. It may also maximize opportunities for deaf learners to have agency over their own learning by selecting sample texts themselves that interest and motivate them.

Theoretically, RLE-based tasks can be seen as activating and validating the 'literacy identities' of learners (see introduction by Tavares, this volume), which in the case of deaf signers has often been shaped by the experience of being discouraged or even prohibited from using the only language that is fully accessible to them, and seeing it castigated as deviant and worthless (see Macedo & Bartolomé, 2014). A deaf learner's agency and identity are likely to be strengthened by engaging in tasks that are meaningful to them and discussed in sign language.

Using data from Gallaudet University's Science of Learning Center on Visual Language and Visual Learning (VL2), Stone and colleagues (2015) found support for the notion that fingerspelling and reading reinforce each other due to requiring similar foundational skills in deciphering and recognizing words. This implies that for deaf learners, English literacy may be bolstered through multiliteracies-based teaching that connects signing, fingerspelling, and orthographic decoding.

Papen and Tusting (2020) found that deaf peer tutors were able to use RLE texts in a teaching approach that harnessed Indian Sign Language (ISL), shared online materials, and peer learning. This means of delivery, particularly the use of ISL, differs from what is typically available to deaf learners in India and many other countries, where teachers of the deaf are often hearing people who lack proficiency in sign language and have not received the training necessary to communicate with their learners effectively and understand their needs

144   *J. Webster et al.*

(see Kelly et al., 2020, on South Africa). However, Papen and Tusting (2020) remarked that the deaf peer tutors often perceived these RLE texts as complex and experienced considerable difficulty in connecting them to grammar lessons. Similarly, the students who participated in the study by Papen and Gillen (2022) said they felt too much time was spent on discussing authentic texts and not enough time was dedicated to grammar.

These experiences suggest that the 'real literacies' concept is not straightforward to apply to classroom pedagogy (Papen & Tusting, 2020). In particular, a bridge is needed between the samples of language that deaf learners are confronted with in RLE texts and their understanding of the English grammar that is manifested in these sample texts. As explained in Papen and Zeshan (2021), one way to make this easier is by using the EGG approach. EGGs draw on analogy to support learners' understanding of contextually bounded grammatical structures so that learners are not immediately confronted with generic grammatical meta-language such as *adjectives, possessives, predicates,* and the like.

In a non-deaf context, Lawrence and Lawrence (2013) studied the attitudes of student teachers in India toward using grammar games to teach English. They found that the majority had a favorable attitude toward using these games, particularly females and undergraduates (versus postgraduates). Likewise, in their work with deaf learners in India, Papen and Zeshan (2021) concluded that the EGG method was well received and showed promise, but they also outlined some ideas for making it target the needs of this group more closely. One of these was to add more types of group interactions, including some competitive features, to the games, in accordance with feedback from deaf tutors and learners. For example, players might be divided into two teams and compete to produce the most correct examples, or there could be a timed race to identify an abstract pattern in the sample text. Another development path they highlighted was for deaf facilitators to receive training on using existing EGG resources and creating additional games, before applying the method in the classroom with learners. Such training would equip tutors or facilitators with the skills necessary to help learners use their familiarity with various grammatical forms to make generalizations across different structures, opening up possibilities to introduce more explicit, abstract explanations and meta-language about grammar. This training was indeed implemented in late 2021, as outlined in the next section.

Papen and Zeshan (2021) also proposed making EGGs more deaf-friendly by categorizing games by difficulty level and ensuring that the early levels prioritize expressions that have equivalent single-sign translations in ISL. They commented that:

> it seemed easier for students to learn about an abstract expression in square brackets when it had a direct counterpart in ISL. There are individual signs that correspond to some of the concepts, such as [MOVE], [PERSON], [NUMBER], [DO], [QUALITY] and [PLACE]. [...]

When constructing the abstract grammatical frames, we prioritised expressions with such equivalent single-sign translations into ISL for the easiest, entry-level games on the VLE (virtual learning environment). Later on, further expressions were added that do not have single-sign equivalents in ISL but need to be explained.

(Papen & Zeshan, 2021, p. 191)

To support this taxonomy and allow learners to begin with shorter texts that have fewer abstract patterns before moving on to more difficult games, the authors recommended categorizing the games into three levels as shown in Table 7.1.

The process of playing the game and interacting with game materials in different languages and modalities strongly connects the pedagogical practice of EGGs with multiliteracies. First, the entire EGG activity takes place in a bilingual context: learner groups talk in ISL while playing EGGs. For instance, they discuss whether the right structure has been found in the RLE sample, or how the expressions in square brackets should be understood. When sharing their own examples at the end of each game round, they also translate these into ISL. Since the players are deaf, they cannot read out their examples to each other. The modality of fingerspelling also features in these interactions, as they use this modality to 'quote' English verbatim to each other when needed.

Another use of sign language is that players access an online dictionary of semantic categories. When the meaning of a bracketed expression is not immediately clear, players can search the online resource and watch ISL videos explaining these expressions, e.g., the meaning of [MOVE] and what might

Table 7.1 Features of each level of EGG

	Level 1	Level 2	Level 3
Text length	Short, ca. 2 sentences	Medium, e.g., half page	Long, a whole page of text
Number of abstract patterns per game	Mostly 2, exceptionally up to 3	4 or 5	4 or 5
Number of bracketed expressions per pattern	Mostly 1, exceptionally up to 2	Mostly 2, sometimes up to 3	Unlimited
Meta-language about grammar	Prioritize bracketed expressions that correspond to single ISL signs	Bracketed expressions may or may not correspond to single ISL signs	Possibility of using formal grammatical terms (e.g., possessive pronoun, adjective)

Source: Adapted from Papen and Zeshan (2021).

146 *J. Webster et al.*

be subsumed under it. ISL is used strategically as a resource and bridge toward the L2 English.[1]

Finally, the RLE prompts that are the starting point of EGGs are mostly combinations of English text and other visuals, e.g., video stills, pictures, graphics, and comics, so that learners have to integrate the English language components with other visuals that are part of the prompt – having a print-only prompt is rare in the EGG materials. Throughout the game process, these different semiotic resources are mobilized toward learning L2 grammar. Another aspect of using EGGs as part of an overall multiliteracies approach is its relationship to social justice. In their exploration of how multiliteracies pedagogy can be applied to deaf learners learning second and third languages, Papen and Gillen (2022) found that the flexible use of this approach by deaf peer tutors in a collaborative setting could foster students' agency because it values learners' individual preferences, previous knowledge, resources, and experiences. The approach was associated with a clear improvement in ISL skills and an increase in engagement, motivation, and comprehension (Papen & Gillen, 2022; Webster & Zeshan, 2021a, 2021b; Zeshan et al., 2016).

Using EGGs may thus enable deaf signers to exploit multiliteracies methods and ultimately become professionals in deaf education without being forced to confront complicated grammar books or inaccessible courses designed for non-deaf learners. These games could therefore play a role in democratizing the learning process. After field-testing EGGs with deaf learners and deaf instructors, the important next step is to train aspiring deaf professionals in this gamified method. Our present study focuses on deaf trainee tutors learning to work with deaf adult learners.[2]

Reviewing the EGG Training

First, the researchers reviewed the class schedules, sign language videos, Moodle lessons, reports, and feedback from the two rounds of training sessions delivered by Pal and Manavalamamuni in 2021 (see Table 7.2). Six of the

Table 7.2 Summary of data from the two rounds of training[3]

	First batch of training	*Second batch of training*	*Total*
Learners	6 (all male)	6 (3 female, 3 male)	12 learners
Teaching days	10	10	20 days
Trainers' reports	10	10	20 reports
Lessons on Moodle	47 (27 at level 1 and 20 at level 2)		47 lessons
Entries in the semantic/ grammatical dictionary	25 across both batches		25 entries
Feedback from trainees	1 video (70 minutes)	1 video (36 minutes)	2 videos (106 minutes)

trainees took part in the first round from 8 to 18 November, and the other six attended the second round from 22 November to 3 December. All of the trainees in the first round were male; in the second round, there were three female and three male trainees. All were from India except for two of the female trainees, who were from Nepal. On average, the second batch of trainees were more advanced in terms of educational level and knowledge of English.

Though the online learning platform Moodle was employed, both rounds of training were delivered exclusively face to face. During the training, the two instructors introduced the trainees to a substantial number of EGGs as well as video lessons in ISL about various topics in literacy acquisition, multiliteracies, RLE, and pedagogy. The EGG-based lessons on Moodle have several components, namely, the games themselves, extensions for learners derived from the games, and a dictionary of semantic/grammatical terms with explanations in ISL. Trainees also engaged in hands-on activities to learn how to create EGGs and use them to teach.

The training drew from, and built on, EGG lessons and a dictionary of semantic and grammatical terms on the dedicated Moodle platform. The scholar-practitioners' EGGs use abstract semantic categories in square brackets like *[THING]*, *[ANIMAL]*, *[COGNITION]*, *[DO]*, *[COLOUR]*, or *[COUNTRY]*. Each of these categories is explained in ISL in a video of ca. 30–60 seconds in the dictionary (Figure 7.2).

For example, in the definition of the category labeled *[COGNITION]*, Manavalamamuni gives the example sentence *I [COGNITION] this is better* and explains in ISL what 'cognition' means: 'it has to do with thinking, for example, dreaming, learning, forgetting, understanding, such as understanding deeply about science, learning about science'. Some items in the semantic/grammatical dictionary are more specific such as *[FAMILY MEMBER]* while others are quite general like *[DO]*.

Figure 7.2 ISL explanations of abstract categories in the semantic/grammatical dictionary on the Moodle platform

148 *J. Webster et al.*

Figure 7.3 The 'Lunch area' RLE text

An illustrative example of an EGG lesson is 'Lunch area', which has 16 steps, including the RLE text, explanations in ISL, the target structures with abstract semantic categories, examples of extrapolating the structure to form new sentences, and a short quiz with true/false and multiple-choice questions. First, using the RLE text shown in Figure 7.3, the learner would find the structure and then watch the ISL video to find out what the aim of the structure is (Figure 7.4).

Figure 7.4 Pal explains in ISL what *Keep it clean* means (CLEAN STILL-SAME, RUBBISH THROW NO)

Building Deaf Agency through English Grammar Games 149

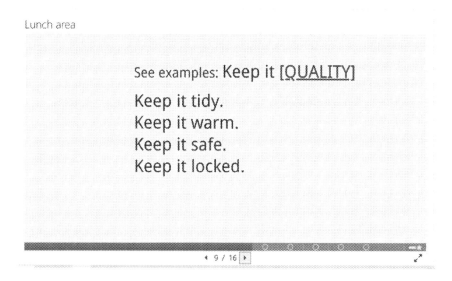

Figure 7.5 Examples of the EGG structure *Keep it [QUALITY]* with a hyperlink to the semantic/grammatical dictionary

Next, the trainee can see examples of the structure (Figure 7.5). The trainee can also refer back to the semantic/grammatical dictionary. In this case, they would click on *[QUALITY]* to be taken to the ISL definition telling them that in this sense, it indicates certain types of adjectives. Then the learner can try the quiz questions (Figure 7.6), the last of which asks them to think of their own examples of the EGG structure.

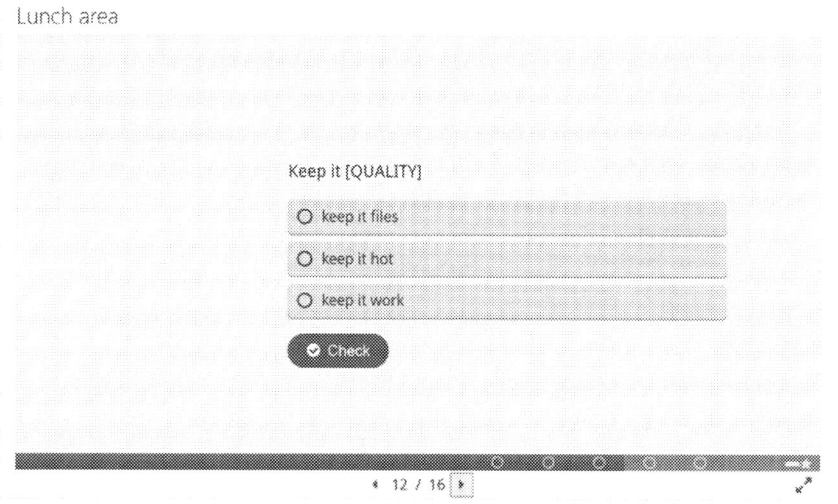

Figure 7.6 One of the quiz questions in the 'Lunch area' lesson

150　*J. Webster et al.*

He goes to the dentist
Nirav went to the restaurant.
She comes to my house.
He meets her at the bus station.
She attend to the class.

Figure 7.7 Sentences generated by trainees on day 6 during the second round of training for the target structure *She [DO] to the [PLACE]*

According to the classroom reports, the trainers explained to the trainees the difference between level 1 and level 2 grammar structures by describing how level 2 EGGs have more bracketed expressions than level 1 EGGs, and level 2 expressions are more abstract (e.g., *[DO]*, *[QUALITY]*) while level 1 are more concrete (e.g., *[ANIMAL]*, *[FRUIT]*). The idea is for learners to begin with the concrete, specific categories like *[BODY PART]* before moving on to broad, abstract categories like *[THING]*. These semantically based expressions are a link to integrate the different language resources that deaf sign language users can mobilize in this context of learning with multiliteracies: the semantic meta-language appears as part of the English constructions but also has translations and explanations in ISL. At the same time, the bracketed expressions are an important key to interacting creatively with the RLE texts, which usually are themselves multimodal, combining print with other visuals.

On day 6 during the second round of training, for the structure *She [DO] to the [PLACE]* (following the RLE exemplar *She goes to the nurse*), the trainees generated the sentences shown in Figure 7.7. They were able to create analogous sentences successfully, altering the subject/agent in some sentences in addition to the bracketed expressions *[DO]* and *[PLACE]*.

However, this example also shows the difficulty of creating the most appropriate generic structure in the first place, which is something the trainers were still experimenting with themselves. In this context, *[MOVE]* would be better than *[DO]* because it is more specific. That the use of overly generic *[DO]* can be problematic was evident in another session with the same target structure, where learners generated incorrect sentences such as *He is working to the railway*. In his interview response, Pal notes accordingly:

> If we compare *[MOVE]* to *[DO]*, *[DO]* is over-general. The word we put in brackets should be narrower, like *[MOVE]*. If we have *[MOVE]*, we can swap in *run, walk, fly,* etc. *[DO]* is too broad for beginners.

However, on other occasions learners were able to produce sentences with minimal errors, as in the sentences shown in Figure 7.8 following the exemplar from the RLE text 'Interesting facts about bears'. This EGG structure uses six

Building Deaf Agency through English Grammar Games 151

Interesting Facts About Bears

- Though bears are large animals, they can run very fast, reaching speeds of up to 35 miles per hour.
- Female brown bears give birth in their dens during the winter. They usually have two cubs at a time.
- The brown bear is Finland's national animal.
- Polar bears and giant pandas are the only bears born with a thin layer of fur. All other bears are born hairless!
- They are born blind and naked.

> Female [COLOR] [ANIMALS] gives birth in their [THINGS] during the [SEASON]. They usually have [NUMBER] [BABY] at a time.

> Female brown bears give birth in their dens during the winter. They usually have two cubs at a time.

> Female black dogs give birth in their kennels during the summer. They usually have a calf at a time.
> Female gray elephants give birth in their jungles during the monsoon. They usually have five calves at a time.
> Female red foxes give birth in their dens during the spring. They usually have four pups at a time.
> Female brown monkeys give birth in their trees during the winter. They usually have an infant at a time.

Figure 7.8 Sentences produced by the trainees during the second round of training, following an exemplar structure found in the RLE text 'Interesting facts about bears'.

placeholders in square brackets; again, the generic /THING/ is not ideal here, but the learners' responses show that they grasped the intended analogies.

A major focus during the training was inventing game-like activities around the EGG method, as competitive games with visual materials have been found to be popular with deaf learners (Manavalamamuni, 2021; Papen & Zeshan, 2021). The EGG process merely provides the linguistic rationale and is not enough on its own to engage and sustain learners' interest; it needs to be

Figure 7.9 Still from video of trainees discussing a competitive EGG activity with Manavalamamuni

enriched by the teachers with activities to make it fun for learners. This was a motivation behind the quiz activities on Moodle as shown in Figure 7.6 above, as well as several competitive activities that Pal and Manavalamamuni trialed during the training. In one of these, Manavalamamuni assigned each trainee a different color marker pen and had them compete to see who could write the most examples of a target EGG structure on the whiteboard (Figure 7.9). Another way to compete was to create the EGG structures in PowerPoint using a different color for each learner.

In another invented game, Pal wrote examples of various EGG structures on slips of paper and spread them out on a table (Figure 7.10). Then he displayed a target EGG structure on the computer screen, such as *[PERSON] and [PERSON]*, and asked the trainees to find an example as quickly as possible that matches the structure from among the slips of paper on the table, such as *Sachin and Hogg*. Whoever could not find an example, or chose an example that did not match the target structure, did not proceed to the next round where a new target structure was displayed. Therefore, the group of players got smaller and smaller until there was one winner.

The trainers reported that several of the trainees found it challenging to try to create competitive activities connected to EGGs. Sometimes these did not correspond to the EGG approach. For example, one group created a card game activity that made use of the numbers on the cards, but not English words. The trainees also found some of the activities introduced by the trainers to be too repetitive, for example, one where they had to take turns adding a word to make example sentences following the target structure.

Building Deaf Agency through English Grammar Games 153

Figure 7.10 Still from video of Pal introducing a competitive activity where trainees must quickly find the papers that show examples that match the EGG structure displayed on the computer screen

Reflections on the EGG Training

After the training files were reviewed by all four authors, a list of five reflective interview questions was prepared by Webster and Zeshan. These were for the two scholar-practitioners, Pal and Manavalamamuni, to each answer independently via a combination of ISL videos and written English in 2023, having had many months to reflect on how to improve the training they delivered in 2021. Being a scholar-practitioner is not the same as doing action research; rather, it means that one is viewing the research as well as the classroom practice in a different light and often through the lens of social justice. As Jenlink (2009, p. 4) describes it:

> The scholar–practitioner's work, in part, is to illuminate and interrogate injustices – such as those created by hierarchies of participation and forms of social control. The scholar–practitioner interrogates social structures and cultural practices that contribute to injustice, bringing democratic practices to bear so as to mediate cultural dominance, political ideologies and asymmetries of power that work to reproduce cultures and social structures that foster injustices and inequities in educational settings.

Therefore, this section discusses the scholar-practitioners' reflections stemming from these five questions and presents a model showing how the use of EGGs facilitates the democratization of teaching, leading to empowerment and ultimately to social justice.

154   *J. Webster et al.*

The first question asked what multiliteracies they used the most and least when teaching the trainees (e.g., signing, drawing, writing, graphs/charts, diagrams, fingerspelling, typing/texting). Pal and Manavalamamuni both predominantly used ISL. The various lessons on topics in language and literacy, which were part of the learning material for this course compiled on Moodle, are also in ISL, with some other visuals supporting the signed explanations.

Pal emphasized the value of using ISL for storytelling and sharing experiences as well as explaining charts, slides, and RLE texts. Manavalamamuni combined signing with writing in English on the whiteboard and showing pictures and videos as visual aids to support the trainees' understanding of the content being presented in ISL. He felt that designing posters in particular helped the trainees to review their learning and retain the content. Manavalamamuni also used fingerspelling and sometimes drew diagrams and gave demonstrations. Pal, on the other hand, identified fingerspelling as the component he used the least. He said the trainees only fingerspelled when new English words were being introduced, and occasionally to explain a newer or less frequent ISL sign that the Nepali trainees did not know. For Manavalamamuni, the multiliteracies skill he used the least was drawing diagrams and charts with symbols such as arrows or circles. He said this was an area he wanted to develop so that he could make more use of relationship diagrams and abstract symbols when explaining topics to learners.

The second question asked the trainers to rate how skilled the trainees were at specific tasks by the end of the training, on a scale of 1 (unskilled) to 10 (very skilled). For the task 'finding RLE tasks on their own', both trainers rated the trainees as having good abilities, with ratings of 7 and 9, respectively. They gave a lower rating of 6 and 7 for 'identifying grammatical structures in the RLE texts on their own'. Manavalamamuni said that the trainees tried to find grammatical structures in RLE texts, but they were able to identify only a few structures. They gave the lowest scores, namely, 5 and 6, for 'creating EGGs on their own'. Pal remarked that this was the most challenging task because even those learners who had ample experience with English were not in the habit of writing in English frequently.

The third reflective question asked what difficulties the trainers had in explaining and/or using the EGG method and how these could be addressed. They spent more time on this question than the other four and proposed a number of solutions to the problems they had encountered. First, they both talked about difficulties in dealing with more abstract concepts. They said while it was relatively easy to swap in concrete or visual examples, e.g., *apple* or *chair* for *[THING]*, the abstract permutations like *happiness* and *enjoyment* were more difficult to swap in. Second, Manavalamamuni asserted that the inclusion of prepositions in an EGG target structure was often problematic, due to the complexity of English prepositions. They said that this issue could possibly be addressed by creating videos in the semantic/grammatical dictionary that define *to*, *at*, *by*, and other such words and hyperlinking the words in the target structure to these videos so that trainees can easily consult the

Building Deaf Agency through English Grammar Games   155

definitions when needed, as has already been done for some bracketed expressions (Figure 7.5). As Pal explained:

> We discussed this problem in the group. If there is a grammatical word like *at* as part of the structure, it would be good if we could click on it and there would be an explanation by video of all the different uses of *at*, i.e. the different ways in which we use *at*. So we would create an ISL video about that, and then the students can understand. Then we could do similarly for *of*. We would have a video so people can understand it and make a link to the sentence at hand. We would have to generate this over time.

Moreover, they noted that all of the EGGs they used during the training highlight structures only at the phrasal level and do not include any morphology such as the suffixes -*ment* and -*ly* which are important for changing word classes, e.g., verbs into nouns or adjectives into adverbs. They asserted that this should be another feature to add to future iterations of EGGs.

The trainers also recommended further criteria for delineating between several different levels of EGG training and building learners' understanding in a stepwise fashion (see Table 2.1). These criteria may include, for example, avoiding structures with prepositions at the beginner stage and ensuring that bracketed expressions are limited to more concrete categories like *[PLACE]*; introducing the more abstract bracketed expressions such as *[DO]* and *[QUALITY]* at the intermediate stage; and changing the bracketed expressions into technical terms like *[ADJECTIVE]* at the advanced stage. As Pal put it:

> If we are working with beginners, we may need sub-categories even for *[THING]*. We would have *[ANIMAL]*, *[CLOTHES]* or *[FRUIT]* instead of *[THING]*. It needs to be clear what we need to replace when there is something in square brackets. Then later, at level 3, the learners should be able to use things like *[ADJECTIVE]*, *[VERB]* and *[PREPOSITION]*, because this is what is used in dictionaries and the wider world. So they start by learning in an easier way, and by the end of level 3 they are able to graduate to technical terms like *[ADJECTIVE]*.

Finally, he suggested making a more pointed reference to the structure and lexical taxonomy of ISL when teaching the EGG approach, for instance, exploiting the fact that ISL signs relating to cognition (thinking, worrying, remembering) are typically located on the head and those relating to emotions (feeling, liking) are located on the chest.

The EGG method as taught by Pal and Manavalamamuni exploits the four knowledge processes of multiliteracies: experiencing, conceptualizing, analyzing, and applying (see Cope & Kalantzis, 2009). The process of applying was the most difficult. The aim is for these lessons to give the trainees enough

156   *J. Webster et al.*

practice that they are then able to find their own RLE text and create their own EGGs in the following session. However, instruction on developing EGGs took much more time than anticipated because the EGG method and its underlying approach were entirely unfamiliar to the trainees. Feedback from the trainers and learners also indicated that hundreds of these games would need to be created in order to deliver viable programs. This is because each structural frame used in a game is based on a specific combination of semantic and grammatical material in context and not on generic grammatical rules.

In response to the fourth reflective question about the trainers' views on the future potential for using the EGG method in a teacher-training program, the two trainers emphasized the novelty of the method and the speed of the learning process. Manavalamamuni commented that:

> Deaf learners struggle to improve their English because traditional methods are not effective for them. I feel that they will be interested in learning the EGG method, as it is new, it can be combined with competitive games, and they only need to spend about two or three months attending the training sessions, after which they can practice on their own. However, to make an EGG-based program, we need many more explanations and examples of the various concepts and we must collect a high number of RLE texts like stories or newspaper articles, including longer texts than what we used in our 2021 sessions. And I suggest that trainees who already know some grammar should be selected as a priority. It is not good for trainees to join the program without any grammatical knowledge.

Similarly, Pal remarked that the EGG method enabled more rapid progress and was more accessible for deaf learners than traditional methods:

> EGGs provide a linguistic rationale that matches deaf people's own way of learning, so it becomes easy for them to make progress. Also, the way in which RLE and EGG practices link with each other is good. With traditional methods of learning to read, deaf people may spend several months practicing and still face a huge barrier in acquiring reading skills. But with EGGs, linked to RLE, we saw progress in only 10 days. This was of course very limited so imagine the outcomes if we were to continue for a couple of years.

Overall, these reflections suggest that EGGs can be a valuable tool in empowering deaf signers to become professionals in deaf education, due mainly to four key features: EGGs are bilingual, multimodal/multiliterate, gamified (Zeshan, 2020), and based on 'real-life English' and semantics. Using EGGs enables trained deaf instructors without any formal background in English language or TESOL to teach their deaf peers because the materials and the

Building Deaf Agency through English Grammar Games 157

game choreography provide an easy access point where formal knowledge of English grammar and literature is not needed. This means there is much potential for the democratization of teaching and learning in this community through the use of EGGs.

Figure 7.11 illustrates the notion that combining the key features of EGGs – that they are bilingual, multimodal/multiliterate, gamified, and based on semantics and RLE – makes it possible to enable deaf signers to professionalize the teaching of English grammar. This professionalization gives deaf people the agency to teach, which in turn promotes social justice. In other words, the question of social justice in this context is the issue of who has the agency to teach. If only hearing people working from grammar reference books have the agency to teach, then barriers and inequalities are being sustained. EGGs contribute to more equity because deaf signers can use them to become professional teachers and develop agencies to teach multiliteracies and make this a more likely career path for deaf people in the future. This in turn gives young deaf people access

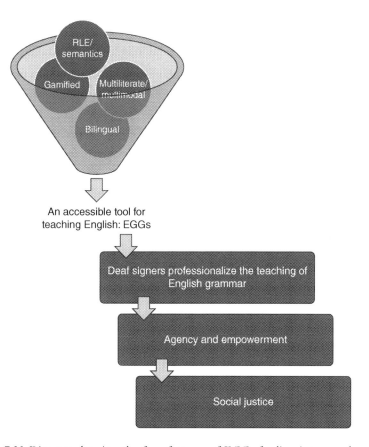

Figure 7.11 Diagram showing the four features of EGGs feeding into a pathway toward social justice

158   *J. Webster et al.*

to multiliteracies learning through visual languages and from teachers who share their deaf identity and who can act as role models to support the educational aspirations of young deaf learners. As noted by Tavares (introduction to this volume), agency necessarily involves actions that contribute positively to the lives of others.

The final interview question asked whether the trainers thought the EGG method could promote deaf empowerment and social justice in the teaching profession. They both suggested that the EGG method contributes to deaf empowerment by enabling deaf trainees to acquire English proficiency and learn how to teach deaf children in the future. Manavalamamuni's view was that by creating an inclusive environment for deaf learners, the EGG method can advance social justice. But to target this more strongly, he said, the training should include content on deaf culture and sign language:

> The EGG method is a good tool for training deaf teachers, but teachers need to be skilled in English and know how to teach methods in a way that adapts to deaf culture and sign language. Because there are various backgrounds among deaf people, it is necessary to make sure all trainees know methods for teaching deaf learners. This could be achieved by adding more content on deaf culture and sign language to the EGG method.

Pal mentioned that the EGG approach could increase social justice by ameliorating the difficulty that deaf teachers in India have when attempting to acquire more advanced English skills at the senior secondary level (class 12):

> It is very difficult for deaf people to pass English with enough marks in traditional courses in India. The main problem is, deaf people struggle to reach the level of class 12. Their understanding of grammar and word classes remains basic, and they have no smooth visual way to acquire advanced English skills. With EGGs this can be different. Deaf teachers can understand English using these square bracketed expressions in a step-by-step way. This can be the trigger that gets them going with further efforts toward English. Rather than taking one or two years to make progress, as in traditional approaches, with the EGG method deaf people can improve their skills significantly in only a matter of months. Even short training courses of only 10 days allow deaf people to begin matching EGG structures to example sentences, understanding English visually and expanding on this cognitive progress by themselves.

Feedback from the trainees supports this view, and one of them commented:

> Learning about EGGs made writing easier for me, because EGGs give a specific format and I can think about how to fit different words into the categories like [DO] or [PEOPLE], instead of trying to follow difficult grammar rules.

Building Deaf Agency through English Grammar Games   159

These two rounds of training are the first small step toward creating a program for deaf people to access. At the time of the training in 2021, Pal and Manavalamamuni did not have experience with delivering training on how to teach children, so it only focused on adults. Going forward, they would include training on how to teach both groups, with a focus on creating multiple varied and engaging classroom activities. Several hundred EGG exercises would need to be produced in order to make a viable course. This could be done through learner groups that share responsibility for creating them, under a sustainable business model. This kind of multiliteracies training for language teachers must be based on continuous and holistic development and ongoing reflection (Warner & Dupuy, 2018) and should involve strategic innovation and engagement with other educational stakeholders including organizations such as India's National Institute of Open Schooling (Akanlig-Pare et al., 2021).

Conclusion

This study has examined training files and interviews with two deaf scholar-practitioners to explore the utility of EGGs as tools for deaf trainee tutors to deliver English language classes to deaf adults. In congruence with an eight-year thread of project work on deaf literacy and multiliteracies (e.g., Gillen et al., 2016; Webster & Zeshan, 2021a, 2021b), the findings emphasize the importance of deaf learners being taught by deaf instructors in their native language, in this case ISL, to strengthen their agency, ultimately leading to greater empowerment, equality, and social justice. The bilingual context and the ISL-based resources on Moodle, most importantly the dictionary of semantic and grammatical terms, mean that the learners' L1 background as minority language users capable of handling a varied semiotic repertoire is respected and mobilized toward L2 learning. This is a hallmark of a pedagogy of multiliteracies. A range of multiliteracies techniques were deployed by the scholar-practitioners, with ISL being predominant. They identified the need to include in the training and resources more grammatical words such as *at* and morphology such as *-ly*. The task of creating EGGs independently was the most challenging aspect for the trainees and would require more time than was available in these two rounds of training.

At the next stage of development, a pedagogical model is needed wherein trainees share responsibility for creating EGGs so that hundreds of these games can be generated. This would facilitate the delivery of viable programs, including EGGs with expressly grammatical words and word endings in addition to semantic categories, and the integration of other activities beyond EGGs to sustain interest and avoid repetition. It would also broaden the collaborative basis, joint ownership, and collective creativity that go well with a multiliteracies approach, especially if trainees could cascade the EGG method to further deaf learners.

On the basis of this study, it is expected that the challenge of planning and delivering extended training on creating EGGs would be highly worthwhile.

160   *J. Webster et al.*

The use of EGGs opens up paths to greater equality and social justice by enabling deaf instructors without any background in English language or TESOL to teach their deaf peers. The materials and the game choreography provide an easy access point where formal knowledge of English grammar and literature is not needed. By contrast, typical training for language teachers is mostly inaccessible for deaf signers, perpetuating the cycle of exclusion from reading and writing. This points to the potential for democratization of teaching and learning in this community through using EGGs.

Acknowledgments

The project 'Peer-to-Peer Deaf Multiliteracies: Research into a sustainable approach to the education of deaf children and young adults in the Global South' (2017–2020, grant reference ES/P008623/1, grant amount £436,000) and its follow-on project 'South-South collaboration in realising the impacts of Peer-to-Peer Deaf Multiliteracies research in India, Uganda, and Nepal' (2019–2021, grant reference ES/T008199/1, grant amount £93,000) were funded by the ESRC and the former UK Department for International Development, which merged with the Foreign & Commonwealth Office on 2 September 2020 to become the Foreign, Commonwealth & Development Office. The authors extend their thanks for this funding and are also grateful to the staff and students at Happy Hands School for the Deaf and its founding institution, the Rural Lifeline Trust in Sonepur District, Odisha, India.

Notes

1 The games can also be played online, which adds a further dimension of interaction with an ICT environment, though the research team does not yet have much experience with the online format yet. In the online version, components of the game layout have to be manipulated by players, e.g., by clicking to uncover a hidden textbox.
2 At the time of writing, authors Pal and Zeshan are also beginning to introduce EGGs to deaf children from age 10 onward at the Happy Hands School for the Deaf, a primary school for deaf children in India where Pal is a teacher. Initial experiences indicate that the EGG method has much potential for working well with children too.
3 The limited scope of this chapter does not permit a detailed analysis of all of these files.

References

Akanlig-Pare, G., Mugeere, A., Singh, R. R., & Zeshan, U. (2021). Disadvantage and marginalisation in special education systems for deaf students in India, Ghana, and Uganda: A comparative analysis. In J. Webster & U. Zeshan (Eds.), *READ WRITE EASY: Research, practice and innovation in multiliteracies, Volume 2* (pp. 119–169). Ishara Press.

Cope, B., & Kalantzis, M. (Eds.). (2000). *Multiliteracies: Literacy learning and the design of social futures*. Routledge.

Cope, B., & Kalantzis, M. (2009). 'Multiliteracies': New literacies, new learning. *Pedagogies: An International Journal, 4*(3), 164–195. https://doi.org/10.1080/15544800903076044

Fan, H. (2018). *Deaf young adults' English literacy development in a peer-supported virtual learning environment.* [PhD thesis]. University of Central Lancashire, Preston, UK.

Gillen, J., Panda, S., Papen, U., & Zeshan, U. (2016). Peer to peer deaf literacy: Working with young deaf people and peer tutors in India. *Language and Language Teaching, 5*(10), 1–7.

Jenlink, P. M. (2009). A scholar-practitioner stance: Practices of social justice and democracy. *School Leadership Review, 4*(1), Article 2. Available at: https://scholarworks.sfasu.edu/slr/vol4/iss1/2

Kelly, J. F., McKinney, E. L., & Swift, O. (2020). Strengthening teacher education to support deaf learners. *International Journal of Inclusive Education.* https://doi.org/10.1080/13603116.2020.1806366

Kusters, A., Spotti, M., Swanwick, R., & Tapio, E. (2017). Beyond languages, beyond modalities: Transforming the study of semiotic repertoires. *International Journal of Multilingualism, 14*(3), 219–232. https://doi.org/10.1080/14790718.2017.1321651

Lawrence, A. J., & Lawrence, A. S. A. (2013). Attitude of student teachers towards using grammar games for teaching English. *International Journal on New Trends in Education and Their Implications, 4*(1), 65–72.

Macedo, D., & Bartolomé, L. I. (2014). Multiculturalism permitted in English only. *International Multilingual Research Journal, 8*(1), 24–37.

Manavalamamuni, D. (2021). The influence of visual learning materials on learners' participation. In J. Webster & U. Zeshan (Eds.), *READ WRITE EASY: Research, practice and innovation in multiliteracies, Volume 2* (pp. 45–86). Ishara Press.

Mestari, S. A., & Malabar, F. (2016). The use of authentic materials in teaching grammar for EFL students (teachers' perspective). *Language and Language Teaching Journal, 19*(2), 125–131. https://doi.org/10.24071/llt.2016.190207

New London Group. (1996). A pedagogy of multiliteracies: Designing social futures. *Harvard Educational Review, 66*(1), 60–92.

Papen, U., & Gillen, J. (2022). Peer to peer deaf multiliteracies: Experiential pedagogy, agency and inclusion in working with young adults in India. *International Journal of Inclusive Education.* https://doi.org/10.1080/13603116.2022.2121433

Papen, U., & Tusting, K. (2020). Using ethnography and 'real literacies' to develop a curriculum for English literacy teaching for young deaf adults in India. *Compare: A Journal of Comparative and International Education, 50*(8), 1140–1158.

Papen, U., & Zeshan, U. (2021). English grammar games. In J. Webster & U. Zeshan (Eds.), *READ WRITE EASY: Research, practice and innovation in multiliteracies, Volume 2* (pp. 173–200). Ishara Press.

Phillips, M., & Shettlesworth, C. (1978). How to ARM your students: A consideration of two approaches to providing materials for ESP. In British Council English Teaching Information Centre (Ed.), *ELT-35: English for specific purposes, milestones in ELT* (pp. 23–35). The British Council. Available at https://www.teachingenglish.org.uk/sites/teacheng/files/pub_F044%20ELT-35%20English%20For%20Specific%20Purposes_v3.pdf

Randhawa, S. P. K. (2005). *A status study of selected special schools for the deaf and identification of intervention areas* [PhD thesis]. Indian Institute of Technology, Roorkee, India.

Richards, J. C., & Rodgers, T. S. (2014). *Approaches and methods in language teaching* (3 ed.). Cambridge University Press.

Stone, A., Kartheiser, G., Hauser, P. C., Petitto, L.-A., & Allen, T. E. (2015). Fingerspelling as a novel gateway into reading fluency in deaf bilinguals. *PLoS ONE, 10*(10), e0139610. https://doi.org/10.1371/journal.pone.0139610

162   *J. Webster et al.*

Tang, G. (2017). Sign bilingualism in deaf education. In A. Lin, O. García, & S. May (Eds.), *Bilingual and multilingual education. Encyclopedia of language and education* (pp. 191–203). Springer International Publishing.

Wang, Q., & Andrews, J. F. (Eds.). (2020). *Literacy and deaf education: Toward a global understanding.* Gallaudet University Press.

Warner, C., & Dupuy, B. (2018). Moving toward multiliteracies in foreign language teaching: Past and present perspectives … and beyond. *Foreign Language Annals, 51*(1), 116–128.

Webster, J., & Zeshan, U. (Eds.). (2021a). *READ WRITE EASY: Research, practice and innovation in multiliteracies, Volume 1.* Ishara Press. Available at: https://library.oapen.org/handle/20.500.12657/51600

Webster, J., & Zeshan, U. (Eds.). (2021b). *READ WRITE EASY: Research, practice and innovation in multiliteracies, Volume 2.* Ishara Press. Available at: https://library.oapen.org/handle/20.500.12657/52174

Zeshan, U. (2020). *Serious games in co-creative facilitation: Experiences from cross-sectoral work with deaf communities.* Ishara Press.

Zeshan, U., Fan, H., Gillen, J., Panda, S., Papen, U., Tusting, K., Waller, D., & Webster, J. (2016). Summary report on 'Literacy development with deaf communities using sign language, peer tuition, and learner-generated online content: Sustainable educational innovation'. University of Central Lancashire, Preston. Available at: https://islandscentre.files.wordpress.com/2016/10/summary-report-p2pdl1.pdf

8 Coming-of-Age Graphic Novels in L2 Education

Reflecting on Social Justice from a Feminist Perspective

Dolores Miralles-Alberola, Margarida Castellano-Sanz, and Agustín Reyes-Torres

Introduction

When considering how to integrate multiliteracies in second language (L2) education in the 21st century, there are two key aspects for L2 teachers to bear in mind. First, there is the transition from thinking about literacy as a single skill that an individual acquires at a particular moment, to considering the term as a plural noun that refers to a dynamic and multidimensional process through which learners develop language skills, multimodal thinking strategies, dialogic attitudes, and social practices (Kern, 2000; Reyes-Torres et al., 2021; Robertson & Hughes, 2012; Zapata, 2022). Second, there is a consideration of how this shift leaves behind the dominant view of the past in which literacy was limited to writing and reading and suggests that literacy development requires a cognitive process connected to social and meaningful environments so that learners can contribute their out-of-school experiences (Duncum, 2004; Kucer, 2014; New London Group, 1996; Paesani et al., 2016). Consequently, integrating multiliteracies in schooling and in L2 teaching and learning represents an opportunity for teachers to address relevant social issues and be agents for social justice.

For almost three decades now, and thanks to the work of the New London Group (NLG), the "understanding of literacy has become fluid" (Bland, 2018, p. 5). Luke (2018) sees two main current trends in literacy education that have reoriented the focus of teachers and teacher educators toward social concerns. On the one hand, genre approaches, such as systemic functional linguistics, would pursue developing learners' personal growth and individualist development by providing the tools to master the ways of dominant cultures and classes, a kind of literacy to help underprivileged individuals succeed within the system. On the other hand, the Freirean vision of literacy through critical pedagogy focuses on social transformation, as "conventional schooling and literacy education have ordained 'cultures of science' among those socioeconomic underclasses" (Luke, 2018, pp. 147–148).

DOI: 10.4324/9781003438847-13

We believe that both approaches can be combined to promote social justice, democratic education, and intercultural competence, as well as to develop students' attitudes, critical cultural awareness, and skills of discovery and interaction (Byram, 1997, 2021). The intercultural coming-of-age graphic novels we have selected for this chapter revolve around memory, identity, and gender in three different ethnic settings. In doing so, they provide teachers with tools to engage students in social justice by giving them the opportunity to discuss specific characters, their ethnic backgrounds, and their cultural roots. Working with the four volumes of *A Girl Called Echo* (2018, 2019, 2020, 2021) by Katherena Vermette (illustrated by Scott B. Henderson and colored by Donovan Yaciuk), *We're All Just Fine* (2023), by Ana Penyas, and *The Waiting* (2021) by Keum Suk Gendry-Kim, L2 students are guided to become aware of issues of identity, culture, and gender. The goal is to expose them to minoritized cultural works in which underrepresented students may also feel reflected in the stories and, on the contrary, learners whose identities are overrepresented may question such dominance.

The Interrelation between Critical Literacy and Social Justice

Critical thinking is embedded in a critical approach to literacy. One way to equip learners with tools to reflect on the world through a critical lens is to engage them in texts and discourses "as a means of bridging time and space, critically understanding and altering the connections between the local and the global, moving between cultures and communities, and developing transnational understandings and collaborations" (Luke, 2003, p. 22). Thus, criticality is an essential tool to promote global democracy and social justice in education which, as stated in the introductory chapter of this volume, has to be informed by diversity and students' agency. Furthermore, following Byram (1997, 2021), criticality is also part of developing intercultural competence. He conceptualizes it as "an ability to evaluate critically and on the basis of explicit criteria perspectives, practices and products in one's own and other cultures and countries" (Byram, 1997, p. 53).

Developed from Freire's philosophy of critical pedagogy (1972), critical literacy has focused on teaching to question dominant discourses and to critically read both texts and contexts. The development of critical literacy contributes to fostering recognition of conformity to hegemonic culture and social structures of power. Janks (2013, p. 227) points out that "critical literacy is about enabling young people to read both the *world* and the *word* in relation to power, identity, difference and access to knowledge, skills, tools and resources." For her part, Reese, a Nambé Pueblo scholar, speaks of Indigenous critical literacies, considering the relevance of encouraging "children to read between the lines and ask questions when engaging within literature: Whose story is it? Who benefits from these stories? Whose voices are not being heard?," she refers to Indigenous children reading within their own cultures. However, it also applies to non-Indigenous children who enter into the stories

Coming-of-Age Graphic Novels in L2 Education 165

from and about Native cultures, as "the larger culture needs to unlearn and rethink how the identities of Indigenous peoples are represented and taught" (Reese, 2018, p. 390).

As Kumaravadivelu (2006, p. 70) indicates, language is not only system but also ideology and it is susceptible to bias, as all texts are ideology-laden (Bland, 2018). Therefore, when selecting materials in L2 education, it is essential to include different experiences from different ethnic and social backgrounds and diverse genders and sexualities but also to start from a critical pedagogical treatment of these materials. In this regard, the three graphic novels selected are deeply rooted in identity, memory, and agency from ethnic and gender perspectives. Social justice is thus shown to be a prominent part of the multiple dimensions of critical literacy, along with disrupting the commonplace, questioning perspectives, focusing on sociopolitical issues, and taking action (Akbari, 2008; Lewison et al., 2002).

While the notion of social justice is associated with John Rawls, who conceptualized the term as a principle from which to examine the social system to make it more just (Rawls, 1971), it is important to note that Rawl's approach "has been the subject of feminist critique for, among other things, neglecting gender altogether, privileging men over women, and, significantly failing to address patriarchy" (Kalsem & Williams, 2010, p. 147). Rawls also used the term, "distributive justice" (1971), which Fraser would later expand as "redistributive justice." On the other hand, the Hegelian concept of "recognition" was further developed by Honneth (2004). Fraser, in turn, advocates a complementary interrelation between redistribution and recognition (1997), which will later be completed with representation, as a three-dimensional vision of the theory of justice (2005).

Social Justice Feminism

Because the characters in *A Girl Called Echo*, *We're All Just Fine*, and *The Waiting* suffer from economic marginalization caused by gender and ideology (redistribution) and cultural domination, as well as identity deprivation (recognition), it is possible to analyze these novels from the point of view of redistributive and recognitive social justice proposed by Fraser (1997). In this sense, considering the positive contribution of critical literacy in students, we understand that social justice in its recognitive aspect implies identity reparation and that redistributive social justice contributes to the provision of agency. On the other hand, in line with Fraser's (2005, 2013) three-dimensional vision of justice theory, representation can be promoted by bringing the memory of these women into the classroom and back into the community.

Fraser (2013) establishes a correspondence between the dimensions of social justice and the different stages of second-wave feminism in a progressive manner, beginning with the claim of redistribution in the 1960s. Joining other perspectives that emerged in this decade, feminism of this era recasts "the radical imaginary" with an initial confidence in *engendering* the socialist imaginary

166   D. Miralles-Alberola, M. Castellano-Sanz, and A. Reyes-Torres

(Fraser, 2013, pp. 3–4). In the 1980s, the movement entered the politics of recognition shifting attention to cultural politics. Finally, Fraser (2013, p. 1) argues for a "reinvigorated feminism" that moves toward representation, along with other emancipatory movements, to regain control of democracy in the face of transnational corporate power. Only representation and redistribution combined could address injustice (Fraser, 2003). However, years later Fraser (2013) would assert that representational justice establishes "criteria of social belonging and thus determines who counts as a member" (2013, p. 95).

Despite Fraser's dialectical connection between social justice and second-wave feminism, the concept as such has been out there since the first wave. In fact, the Social Justice Feminism movement was coined and initiated by Florence Kelley in the early 20th century (McGuire, 2004), which focused firstly on labor reforms (Kalsem & Williams, 2010) to counteract the burdens women faced in the workplace. Parallel to the National Women's Party, created in 1916, which included politically conservative middle- and upper-class women, other feminisms developed incorporating working women (Kalsem & Williams, 2010).

However, taking into account the global transnational macro-corporations and their impact on states' national sovereignty, the social struggles from the 20th century do not appear to be the same as today. These "new spatialities" (Lingard, 2018), which Fraser calls a post-Keynesian-Westphalian framework (2013), require a new approach to social justice. Representation needs to go global, crossing borders to explain to people other folks' cultures and identities, as the three graphic novels selected might help to do, being representations of minoritized groups in various countries: Canada, Spain, and Korea.

The Pedagogy of Multiliteracies in L2 Education: *Learning by Design*

One way to guide L2 learners to become active citizens of the world and promoters of social change is to use multiliteracies approaches paired with social justice (Zapata, 2022). As Healey (2016, p. 16) asserts, "pedagogical frameworks that endorse multiliteracies in the classroom refocus literacy teaching and augment students' social and cultural experiences." The NLG coined the term *pedagogy of multiliteracies* in 1996 with the purpose of adapting literacy to social realities. According to these scholars, multiliteracies transcend the limitations of traditional pedagogical approaches by focusing on learners' linguistic and cultural differences. Moreover, this pedagogical approach enables learners to achieve key goals of literacy: on the one hand, providing access to constantly evolving language, and on the other hand, fostering critical engagement. This pedagogy is based on the idea that language and the meaning-making process are dynamic resources that students constantly remake as they interact with them in a particular sociocultural context. Importantly, this pedagogical trend incorporates diverse forms of representation that delve beyond

Coming-of-Age Graphic Novels in L2 Education 167

language alone, using multimodal resources that integrate the analysis of literary, visual, and sociocultural content.

Moreover, this pedagogy has as a central element called *meaning design* where the textual is also related to the visual, the sound, the spatial, and the behavioral. The NLG (1996) argues that learning is the result of a process of designing meaning from a multimodal text. Three elements are involved in such a process: the Available designs, the Designing, and the Redesigned, which have already been explained in this book's introduction. Therefore, the co-construction of meaning between teachers and students always involves the transformation of the available designs. It is conceived as a cyclical process, since learning is an active process in which learners continuously evolve with the mediation of teachers.

To initiate this process of learning by design, Cope and Kalantzis (2015) propose the Knowledge Processes Framework (KPF) to apply the Pedagogy of Multiliteracies. This framework serves as a guide for teachers to work with multimodal elements. However, it should be noted that it does not establish a hierarchy but is a recurrent process. Menke and Paesani (2019) and Zapata (2022) suggest combining these four Knowledge Processes depending on the learning objectives. The KPF consists of experiencing, conceptualizing, analyzing, and applying (previously elucidated by Tavares in the introduction).

Coming-of-Age Graphic Novels as Multimodal Narratives to Foster Social Justice

While the graphic novels we have selected meet the defining characteristics of coming-of-age stories—also called *bildungsroman*—contrary to the mainstream, all three feature women as protagonists because representation matters (Demitürk, 1986). A *bildungsroman* is a literary genre that portrays a character's growth from youth to adulthood and involves the need to make decisions that are related to family, friends, future, etc.; the time scale is often short; the age of the protagonist is usually around mid-teen; and they traditionally have a boy as the central character (Casey Benyahia et al., 2006, p. 271).

Young adult literature and multicultural coming-of-age stories can provide educators with the materials needed to enhance interest and increase cultural awareness. The use of graphic novels to develop students' critical literacy has gained wide acceptance in language acquisition and has been shown to increase students' motivation to read and engage deeply with texts. In addition, the interaction between text and images is increasingly part of modern media. By integrating text with pictures, graphic novels have the advantage of requiring a lighter cognitive load than traditional full-text novels and can be more visually and emotionally impactful (Barter-Storm & Wik, 2020).

In this regard, graphic novels offer students opportunities to interact with language and with visual, spatial, and multimodal meanings (Castellano-Sanz, 2023). These interactions not only lead to the development of multiliteracies but also serve as the basis for instructional conversations about narratives that convey problematic moral situations in which people must make choices when faced with external pressures. By adopting a critical stance in reading practice, teachers can address social justice issues relevant to students' lives, ask critical questions, and conduct critical discussions of stories to prompt learners to critique the characters and their own social practices, while also questioning stereotypical behaviors (Sun, 2017). Thus, while the readings and discussions that take place in the classroom reinforce students' senses of their identities as learning and thinking readers (Guthrie, 2004), they also have an effect on what is happening in the world in terms of social justice, equity, and cross-cultural understanding.

The following subsections offer an approach to the selected novels in L2 education to provide authentic multimodal texts that reduce barriers to addressing challenging issues of critical literacy and social concerns. In line with new education paradigms that focus on critical and reflective literacy and the concept of social justice, the interest of historically disadvantaged groups is increasingly relevant, and everyday events occurring at the edges and margins finally elicit more attention (Guichot, 2021). In this sense, one of the main claims of the feminist movement is to move out of the suburbs of the main ideological institutions. Through the analyses of these three graphic novels, we aim to improve L2 English teachers' understanding of how to address social justice issues based on the transnational and intersectional visibility of women, as well as the connection to identity, more specifically, during coming of age.

A Girl Called Echo: Echoing Memories within Mirroring Books

In terms of social justice, *A Girl Called Echo* sets an example about the importance of memory and identity (recognition), and also refers to redistribution and representation, as it can be read in terms of Indigenous sovereignty. The graphic novel has four volumes: *Pemmican Wars. Vol 1.* (2018), *Red River Resistance. Vol 2.* (2019), *Northwest Resistance. Vol 3.* (2020), and *Road Allowance Era. Vol 4.* (2021). The series was written by Katherena Vermette, illustrated by Scott B. Henderson, and colored by Donovan Yaciuk. Vermette is a Red River Métis poet, a novelist, a children's literature artist, and a filmmaker.

The series is a historical and contemporary representation of the Red River Métis peoples, portraying "[p]ivotal, and often traumatic, moments (such as the execution of Louis Riel, and government-sanctioned destruction of Metis communities) from an Indigenous focus" (Reese, 2021). The novel constitutes a journey toward recovery and healing. When Echo painfully says she does not "know anything about being Métis," her teacher replies: "Many people don't, but you can learn. You're not any less Métis just because you don't know your history" (Vol. 1, p. 37).

Echo lives with her foster mother. She does not know much about her family history or her Métis identity, but somehow, she reconnects with her ancestors through dreams and visions, triggered by the history lessons at her new

Coming-of-Age Graphic Novels in L2 Education   169

school, where the teacher talks extensively about that part of Canadian history affecting the Métis and their resistance. Through the four volumes, Echo profoundly reconnects with her identity and her forebears: her great-great-great grandmother, Josephine, and Josephine's father, Benjamin. The two women "meet" being a similar age, in their teens, a paradigmatic time for identity crisis, and, by reconnecting with her story, Echo makes peace with her present. She also helps her alienated mother search for the family history and reconnect with her Métis identity. In the last volume, according to Reese, "Echo and her contemporary family healing from whatever trauma led to Echo's mother being in an institution …. And Echo finds that she can decide when she will go to the past, and when she will go home" (2021). Echo appears as a symbolic name, as the echo of her elders' voices vibrating through her and guiding her toward survival and resistance (Reese, 2021). In one of their last encounters, Benjamin tells Echo: "We are inside you, are we not? In your blood. it's something we call blood memory, bone memory. It's powerful medicine. All we have is you" (Vol. 4, p. 29).

Indigenous critical literacies compel instructors who wish to include representation of Indigenous peoples to bring to the classroom Indigenous children's literature that is nation-building oriented, tribally specific, well-researched, and written by Indigenous authors through an unbiased use of language and portrayal of conflict (Reese, 2013). Thus, it is important to consider literary materials written mostly by Natives when it comes to selection criteria, as for decades the representation of Indigenous peoples in literature has come from a non-Indigenous perspective (Cook-Lynn, 1996; Deloria, 1994). It is disconcerting, however, how often it is necessary to clarify in non-specialist contexts that Indigenous literature primarily is produced within Indigenous communities and their members (Miralles-Alberola, 2021, pp. 129–130). To restore Native American/First Nations representation after years of invisibilization, not only the primary works must be of Indigenous authorship but also the bulk of scholarly criticism about them.

As seen, when Fraser talks about representation, we need to take this concept beyond its political dimension of governmental and administrative participation and contemplate the representation of Indigeneity and its legitimacy to speak directly through literature, contributing to the collective memory and imagination of the people represented. *Echo* does that. By reconnecting with the ancestors' voices, this mirroring graphic novel provides an opportunity to bring into the L2 classroom a true and faithful representation of literature.

We're All Just Fine: A Transnational Connection Through Shared Female Experiences

Originally published in Spanish under the title *Estamos todas bien* (2017), this graphic novel by Ana Penyas was awarded with the Spanish National Comic Prize in 2018. The author became thus the first female author to receive this honor. With a narrative oscillating between the past and the present, the story traces the experiences of the author's two grandmothers, Maruja and Herminia, over almost 70 years (the Spanish Civil War, the post-war period under Franco's dictatorship, the transition to democracy, and the first decades of the 21st century). Under the aforementioned dictatorship, patriarchy dominated Spanish society and the place of women was limited to the domestic sphere. Following rules established by dictatorial groups such as *La Sección Femenina*, women were unable to vote, open a bank account, or apply for a passport without their husband's or father's permission (Aramburu, 2019, p. 14).

With an exercise of memory and going backward and forward, Penyas traces not only the traumatic recent Spanish history but also personal and global family histories and tries to overcome the so-called Pact of Oblivion (*Pacto del olvido*) that has been tacit in Spain until the enactment of the Law of Historical Memory (2007) and the most recent Law of Democratic Memory (2022). A graphic novel with a special focus on the details, *We're All Just Fine* is a personal text that follows the autobiographical genre characteristics (Smith & Watson, 2010). While visually documenting past traumas through a local perspective, Penyas reveals global themes of the evolving positions of women in the 20th and 21st centuries, such as the role of women within domestic spheres, gender inequality, or the status of the elderly. As in *A Girl Called Echo*, the author is able to connect with the recovered agency of invisibilized members of the nation, in the redistributive and recognitive dimensions of justice, and also, as in the former novel, such members are well represented.

The mastered use of the collage technique with the addition of original and personal pictures makes this graphic novel a source of identification for a local audience but also resonates with a universal reading. Tracing details all along the graphic novel such as the *lentejas* (Spanish popular lentil stew), Penyas manages to link past and present through familiar memories. Maruja and Herminia represent the historical invisibility of women, graphically seen through the absence of dialogue, which also alludes to memory (Britland, 2022). As Chute (2010, p. 4) notes "the art of crafting words and pictures together into a narrative punctuated by pause or absence, as in comics, also mimics the process of memory." Britland (2022) highlights that despite the fact that some elements might seem local, it also promotes a common understanding among women outside of Spain because it speaks to the larger tradition of the domestic pressures they have historically faced throughout societies, cultures, and times. It is in this sense that *We're All Just Fine* connects to the Spanish reader as to a broader transnational audience, by describing collective, common, female experiences across generations and geographic boundaries.

When analyzing the details and techniques, it is remarkable the use of familiar and personal photographs, which transforms the graphic novel into a documentary. This photographic characteristic echoes Chute's assertion on

Coming-of-Age Graphic Novels in L2 Education 171

the graphic novels as a form of documentary, which helps to witness trauma (2016, p. 136) and transforms Penyas into a historian. As Britland states, the author provides "authentic visuals from the past, reinforcing the idea that she is retelling a true, lived story" (2022, p. 563). Likewise, other global female themes that affect locally Maruja and Herminia are the process of aging and its consequences in a society that has placed elder people in the margins (Freixas, 2013; Morganroth Gullette, 2006). The differences between generations, the increasing involvement of women in social movements, and female empowerment throughout the 20th century can be found in Penyas' illustrations, as well as local events such as the ritual of joining together and having *café con leche* and playing cards as the excuse to develop a broader sense of female solidarity.

The Waiting: Wordless Ink to Approach Controversial Topics

Although *The Waiting* (2020) by Keum Suk Gendry-Kim has been labeled as fiction, it follows the paradigm of personal memoirs (Smith & Watson, 2010). Thus, in this graphic novel, we find pages that alternate between clearly defined scenes, partial images, and total ink stains, revealing that there are some subjects that not only have no words to describe but also no images.

As a great example of a powerful and challenging graphic novel, *The Waiting* begins with the current issue of gentrification and the rising of rentals downtown as an excuse to talk about familiar issues and the always controversial relation mother-daughter. By means of going backward and forward in the story, the reader gets to know a young Gwija (the mother) when, as a teenager, she set out to marry a man she barely knows in order to avoid being forced into sexual slavery After having two kids, the Korean War begins and the family tries to escape the fighting by fleeing south. During the escape, Gwija loses her husband and son in the crowd and, through this very local story, the writer focuses readers' attention on the thousands of families left divided during the Korean Division. As in *We're all just fine*, the protagonist is a young woman (Gwija's daughter from her second marriage). She vows that she will find her long-lost older brother before her mother dies starting thus a coming-of-age journey.

The author's masterful black-and-white drawings and innovative layouts convey a strange sense of longing in this long-invisible account of the Korean War in which thousands of families were separated. Inspired by the author's family account and other historical records, *The Waiting* reveals the longing and resentment suffered by those whose lives were held hostage by the past. Gendry-Kim adopts a non-linear approach that is both radical and naturalistic to illustrate what unfolds in the protagonist's daily life when her family memories and past life were put on hold (Dinh, 2021).

The waiting adds thus another humanizing narrative thread to history. It is a sensitive and understated memoir in which pages alternate between

172   *D. Miralles-Alberola, M. Castellano-Sanz, and A. Reyes-Torres*

light and darkness, and in which the narrative moves very slowly, as to give the reader quiet spaces for reflection. With a graphic style that combines European comic and Japanese Manga, Gendry-Kim delves into a tough narration of loss and survival, through an effective combination of vignettes, to create a dramatic and intense reading, and a very poetic use of visual metaphors. By celebrating the beauty of found-family bonds, the novel mitigates the destructive forces of history. In short, this graphic novel embraces social justice in terms of the representation of disadvantaged minority groups and also in the restoration and vindication of long-invisible women's tough situations.

The Knowledge Processes Framework: An L2 Pedagogical Proposal for *A Girl Called Echo*, *We're All Just Fine*, and *The Waiting*

The Pedagogy of Multiliteracies facilitates students' active engagement with new and unfamiliar types of multimodal texts without arousing a sense of alienation and exclusion (Cope & Kalantzis, 2009). As already mentioned, the implementation of the KPF places students at the center of learning and contributes to creating a supportive learning environment in which they are guided to produce meaning and think critically toward a broader vision of social justice and a specific one of feminism.

In Tables 8.1–8.4, we provide a series of questions to facilitate teachers in the task of designing a reading path to engage learners actively in the discussion of *A Girl Called Echo*, *We're All Just Fine*, and *The Waiting*. The ultimate goal is to guide students in the process of learning by design to develop their multiliteracies and communicate and elaborate their ideas on the concepts of social justice, feminism, and women's rights restoration. As will be shown, we have set four learning objectives for each of the four Knowledge Processes:

Experiencing

As "meanings are grounded in real-world patterns of experience" (Cope & Kalantzis, 2015, p. 4), the questions proposed for this epistemic move aim to promote access to memory and identity through the interaction with the texts. The four learning objectives are:

- To ignite curiosity for the form and content of the graphic novels
- To initiate the connection between the novels and the readers
- To establish scaffolding for deep reading of the novels' cross-cultural contents and feminist perspectives
- To promote access to memory and identity through family and/or community

Coming-of-Age Graphic Novels in L2 Education 173

Table 8.1 Experiencing

A Girl Called Echo	We're All Just Fine	The Waiting
Possible questions and/or tasks:	Possible questions and/or tasks:	Possible questions and/or tasks:
What does "Echo" mean? Do you anticipate any connection between the name "Echo" and the novel?	What are the possible meanings of the title? Who does the pronoun "all" refer to?	What is your interpretation of the title? In what situations can you imagine yourself waiting for something?
What do all four covers have in common? And different?	Who are the characters behind the curtains on the cover? What are their facial expressions like?	Why are the characters on the cover holding a notice? What do you think is written on it? How is their facial expression? Why?
What is the symbol under the title of Volume 4?		
How would you link the meaning of the title with the illustration on the cover?	Who are they staring at?	
	Who do you think will be the protagonist of the story?	Who do you think the protagonist of the graphic novel is?
Look at the biodata on the back cover:		
• Who is the author?	Where do you think the story is set?	Where do you think the story is set?
• Why is her tribal affiliation important?		
• Where is the Métis territory?	Have a look at the back cover: what elements can you distinguish? What do they refer to? Why do you think is there a needle and a thread?	Have a quick look at the back cover: what elements can you distinguish? What words and/or images are highlighted?
What do you think the subtitles of the four volumes refer to? Are the timelines at the end of the volumes related to their subtitles?		

Conceptualizing

For the learners to become "active conceptualizers" (Cope & Kalantzis, 2015. p. 4), the four learning objectives we can aim for are:

- To describe important concepts
- To think about the concepts of motherhood, female family members' teachings, and sorority
- To revise ethnic backgrounds and their implications, whether a majority culture or a minoritized one and link it with other concepts such as translanguaging
- To raise awareness on redistributive social justice from feminist and cultural/ ethnic perspectives

174 *D. Miralles-Alberola, M. Castellano-Sanz, and A. Reyes-Torres*

Table 8.2 Conceptualizing

A Girl Called Echo	We're All Just Fine	The Waiting
Possible questions and/or tasks:	Possible questions and/or tasks:	Possible questions and/or tasks:
Apart from English, what other language/s are present in the novel? Why?	The story starts with a quote by writer Carmen Martín Gaite "...Those classic Penelopes, condemned to sewing, sitting quietly and waiting (...)." What is the relation between the needle in the back cover (and the beginning/ endpaper) and the classic Penelope?	The story starts with a short and direct sentence "I abandoned my mother." Who is the narrator? What's the voice in the story?
Who are the Métis?		
Does Echo feel comfortable with her foster family? Why do you think she is not living with her biological mother?		Where do the women represented in the novel belong to? Urban context? Rural context? What country/culture? How do you know it?
How is sovereignty represented in the novel?	Where do the women represented in the novel belong to? Urban context? Rural context? What country/culture? How do you know it?	What period of time is represented right from the very beginning?
Can you find the Métis flag? What are other symbols that appear in the novel (e.g., on Echo's jacket and T-shirts)?	What period of time is represented?	Have a look at the illustrations introducing each chapter: what is the story about?
What visual hints help us differentiate visions from "reality"?	In what situations can you imagine women waiting for something?	How do you know if the story is settled in the present or in the past?
How are concepts such as identity, memory, acculturation, and assimilation approached in the novel?	How are concepts such as identity, memory, and sexism approached in the novel?	How are concepts such as identity, memory, resilience, and sorority approached in the novel?

Analyzing

For this Knowledge Process, we provide activities to discuss bias and hidden interests in themes and hints that are present in the novels. The four learning objectives are:

- To encourage functional assessment to identify cause and effect, evidence, sequence of argumentation, etc.
- To foster criticality in order to identify bias, hidden meanings, political interests, etc.

Coming-of-Age Graphic Novels in L2 Education · 175

Table 8.3 Analyzing

A Girl Called Echo	We're All Just Fine	The Waiting
Possible questions and/or tasks:	Possible questions and/or tasks:	Possible questions and/or tasks:
What music is Echo always listening to? Why do you think she is always with the earphones in?	What social/critical/cultural message do you think it has, implicit or explicit?	What social/critical/cultural message do you think it has, implicit or explicit?
How does she feel about not knowing anything about the Métis? How does she solve it?	In small groups, can you do a brainstorming on topics represented in the novel by words and/or images?	In small groups, can you do a brainstorming on topics represented in the novel by words and/or images?
Does Echo's biological mother know much about her forebears? How does she solve it?	What colors does Penyas use when describing Maruja? And Herminia? What implications do they have?	Keum Suk gives rhythm to the story by adding different sizes to the illustrations. Pay attention to the full-page illustrations (with or without vignettes).
Do you think Métis are well represented in the novel? What should a good representation contain? Think in terms of stereotypes and clichés.	How are the different contexts (urban/rural) represented in the graphic novel? What feelings can you describe by looking at their representations?	How are the different contexts (urban/rural) represented in the graphic novel? What feelings can you describe by looking at the character's reactions to the different contexts?
Do you think women are well-represented in the novel? Why?		

- To promote the identification of themes and hints that are present in the novels, related to history and the erasure of the memory of colonized/conquered peoples
- To raise awareness on representative social justice

Applying

We propose these novels as mentor texts to create artifacts and/or events (abstract or concrete, through materiality or thought, images and/or words) figuring out ways to understand identity and give back to the community, contributing to the recovery of memory. The four learning objectives are:

- To practically apply knowledge based on learning, whether to test something in "the real world" or to intervene through creativity and innovation
- To promote reflection on identity and memory
- To trigger creative ways to connect with the community
- To help students find ways to raise awareness on recognitive social justice

176   *D. Miralles-Alberola, M. Castellano-Sanz, and A. Reyes-Torres*

As a possible artifact inspired by the mentor texts suggested in this proposal, students will be able to create their own reduced graphic novel using the collage technique. The experience should take place during a workshop in class, creating in community, so although the booklets could be individual—or in groups—students are encouraged to share experiences, ideas, materials, and tools. They can create shapes with scissors and also include their own drawings, photos, and objects. Later, the graphic novels can become part of a temporary classroom library where students can read to each other and share their processes as well.

Table 8.4 Applying

A Girl Called Echo	*We're All Just Fine*	*The Waiting*
Possible questions and/or tasks:	Possible questions and/or tasks:	Possible questions and/or tasks:
Metaphorically, Echo connects with her identity through dreams or visions that she ends up being able to activate and control. Which would be the way in your case?	Memory could be the novel's keyword. A personal documentary to overcome the so-called pact of silence, common within trauma situations. Why is it important to have a feeling of belonging? How is this feeling linked to the concept of identity? How would you represent your family's identity/ies?	Restoration and vindication of traumatic situations are key concepts in this novel. Through the lens of women who suffered in the darkness, the reader gets to know some of the consequences of wars, at a very personal level.
How can we help others connect with identity and memory?		
What is identity to you?		Taking into account that we are dealing with traumatic situations, how can we connect with our family and community's memory?
Think of people you might know whose identitarian selves have to be hidden. Why?	How can we help others connect with identity and memory? Think of people you might know whose identitarian selves have to be hidden. Why?	
What would the story be if it was about you/your family/your community? Would it be a graphic novel? A poem? A photograph? A song? Other ideas?	What personal/familiar objects would you choose to represent your family's story? What format would you use to connect with your family and/or community's memory?	Why do you think the protagonists of the novel kept always their faith in the future?
		How can you relate Gwija's story to other narratives you have read or pieces of news in our daily newspapers?

Conclusion

Schools as a safe space to nurture children have the responsibility to embrace inclusiveness in classrooms, not by standardizing uniformity, but by welcoming differences. L2 teaching is no exception by any means. Pedagogies conceptually anchored in multiliteracies and critical thinking can improve learners' citizenship competence and provide students with new ways to reflect on their life experiences and their identity. To this end, the gift of intercultural multimodal literature provides not only authentic materials but also, and most importantly, authentic representations of non-hegemonic identities and thus, a path to reflect on social justice.

As shown in this chapter, the concept of social justice, from its origins, has been intrinsically connected to the vindication of equality and equity, women's rights, and ethnic recognition, and it has been boosted thanks to the work Nancy Fraser has been carrying out since the 1990s. Her idea of a three-dimensional justice theory where redistribution, recognition, and representation are interweaved has guided us in the proposal of the challenging graphic novels authored by Vermette, Penya, and Gendry-Kim. We have presented them as mentor texts to foster agency, identity restitution, and truthful depictions of lesser represented groups with the hope of encouraging students to empathize with others and embrace their personal history.

The discussion of the female protagonists and their ethnic backgrounds constitute key factors that contribute to Freire's proposal to recover their voices (Luke, 2018). In the hope of providing learners with coming-of-age representations with which they can empathize, our intention with the hemispheric mapping of texts we have outlined, from west to east, is to foster intercultural learning and criticality to invite students to open their virtual school bags (Thomson, 2002) and share their precious stories and memories.

References

Akbari, R. (2008). Transforming lives: Introducing critical pedagogy into ELT classrooms. *ELT Journal*, *62*(3), 276–283. https://doi.org/10.1093/elt/ccn025

Aramburu, D. (2019). *Resisting invisibility: Detecting the female body in Spanish crime fiction*. University of Toronto Press.

Barter-Storm, B., & Wik, T. (2020). Using social justice graphic novels in the ELL classroom. *TESOL Journal*, *11*(4), 1–11. https://doi.org/10.1002/tesj.551

Bland, J. (2018). Introduction: The challenge of literature. In J. Bland (Ed.), *Using literature in English language education* (pp. 1–22). Bloomsbury.

Britland, J. (2022). Transnational female solidarity and gender equality in the comic medium: Pepita Sandwich's *Las mujeres mueven montañas* and Ana Penyas's *Estamos todas bien. Bulletin of Hispanic Studies*, *99*(6), 545–567. https://doi.org/10.3828/bhs.2022.34

Byram, M. (1997). *Teaching and assessing intercultural communicative competence*. Multilingual Matters.

Byram, M. (2021). *Teaching and assessing intercultural communicative competence revisited*. Multilingual Matters.

178   *D. Miralles-Alberola, M. Castellano-Sanz, and A. Reyes-Torres*

Casey Benyahia, S., White, J., & Gaffney, F. (2006). *A level film studies: The essential introduction*. Routledge.

Castellano-Sanz, M. (2023). Trabajar los ODS en el aula de personas adultas mediante textos memorialísticos: género, interculturalidad y multimodalidad. *Aula Abierta, 52*(3), 229–236. https://doi.org/10.17811/rifie.52.3.2023.229-236

Chute, H. (2010). *Graphic women*. Columbia University Press.

Chute, H. (2016). *Disaster drawn: Visual witness, comics, and documentary form*. Harvard University Press.

Cook-Lynn, E. (1996). *Why I can't read Wallace Stegner and other essays*. University of Wisconsin Press.

Cope, B., & Kalantzis, M. (2009). "Multiliteracies": New literacies, new learning. *Pedagogies: An International Journal, 4*(3), 164–195. https://doi.org/10.1080/15544800903076044

Cope, B., & Kalantzis, M. (Eds.). (2015). *A pedagogy of multiliteracies. Learning by design*. Palgrave and Macmillan.

Deloria, V., Jr. (1994). *God is red. A native view of religion*. Fulcrum Publishing. (Original work published 1972).

Demitürk, E. L. (1986). *The female identity in cross-cultural perspective: Immigrant women's autobiographies*. University of Iowa Press.

Dinh, T. (2021). *"The Waiting" is an unflinching portrayal of the separations caused by war*. Book Review published in NPR Books. https://www.npr.org/2021/11/06/1053080537/the-waiting-gendry-kim-review

Duncum, P. (2004). Visual culture isn't just visual: Multiliteracy, multimodality and meaning. *Studies in Art Education, 45*(3), 252–264. https://doi.org/10.1080/00393541.2004.11651771

Fraser, N. (1997). *Justice interrupts: Critical reflections on the "postsocialist" condition*. Routledge.

Fraser, N. (2003). Social justice in the age of identity politics: Redistribution, recognition and participation. In N. Fraser & A. Honneth (Eds.), *Redistribution or recognition? A political-philosophical exchange* (J. Golb, J. Ingram, & C. Wilke, Trans.) (pp. 7–109). Verso Books.

Fraser, N. (2005). Mapping the feminist imagination: From redistribution to recognition to representation. *Constellations, 12*(3), 295–307.

Fraser, N. (2013). *Fortunes of feminism: From state-managed capitalism to neoliberal crisis*. Verso.

Freire, P. (1972). *Pedagogy of the oppressed*. Penguin. (Manuscript of 1968 in Portuguese, first published in Spanish in Mexico in 1970).

Freixas, A. (2013). *Tan frescas: Las nuevas mujeres mayores del siglo XXI*. Paidós Ibérica.

Gendry-Kim, K. S. (2020). *The waiting*. Drawn and Quarterly.

Guichot, V. (2021). Educación, justicia social y multiculturalismo: teoría y práctica en el aula. *Teoría de la Educación, 33*(1), 173–195. https://doi.org/10.14201/teri.22984

Guthrie, J. T. (2004). Teaching for literacy engagement. *Journal of Literacy Research, 36*(1), 1–30.

Healey, A. (2016). Transforming pedagogy with multiliteracies in the English classroom. *Literacy Learning: The Middle Years, 24*(1), 7–17.

Honneth, A. (2004). Recognition and justice: Outline of a plural theory of justice. *Acta Sociológica, 47*(4), 351–364.

Janks, H. (2013). Critical literacy in teaching and research. *Education Inquiry, 4*(2), 225–242. https://doi.org/10.3402/edui.v4i2.22071

Kalsem, K., & Williams, V. L. (2010). Social justice feminism. *UCLA Women's Law Journal, 18*(1), 131–193.

Kern, R. (2000). *Literacy and language teaching*. Oxford University Press.

Kucer, S. B. (2014). *Dimensions of literacy: A conceptual base for teaching, reading and writing in school settings*. Routledge.

Kumaravadivelu, B. (2006). TESOL methods: Changing tracks, challenging trends. *TESOL Quarterly, 40*(1), 59–81.

Lee, J. (2022). Opening up a world and the temporal-normative dimensions: Keum Suk Gendry-Kim's *Grass* as World Literature. In J. Hodapp (Ed.), *Graphic novels and comics as world literature* (pp. 167–186). Bloomsbury Academic.

Lewison, M., Flint, A. S., & Van Sluys, K. (2002). Taking on critical literacy: The journey of newcomers and novices. *Language Arts, 79*(5), 382–392.

Lingard, B. (2018). Miseducation. *British Journal of Sociology of Education, 39*(5), 723–728. https://doi.org/10.1080/01425692.2018.1469244

Luke, A. (2003). Literacy education for a new ethics of global community. *Language Arts, 81*(1), 20–22.

Luke, A. (2018). *Critical literacy, schooling, and social justice: The selected works of Allan Luke*. Routledge.

McGuire, J. T. (2004). Two feminist visions: Social justice feminism and equal rights, 1899–1940. *Pennsylvania History: A Journal of Mid-Atlantic Studies, 71*(4), 445–478.

Menke, M. R. & Paesani, K. (2019). Analysing foreign language instructional materials through the lens of multiliteracies framework. *Language, Culture and Curriculum, 32*(1), 34–49. https://doi.org/10.1080/07908318.2018.1461898

Miralles-Alberola, D. (2021). Native American children's literature in the English language education classroom. In A. M. Brígido-Corachán (Ed.), *Indigenizing the classroom: Engaging Native American/First Nations literature and culture in non-Native settings* (pp. 127–145). Publicacions de la Universitat de València.

Morganroth Gullette, M. (2006). *Aged by culture*. The University of Chicago Press.

New London Group (1996). A pedagogy of multiliteracies: Designing social futures. *Educational Review, 66*(1), 60–93.

Paesani, K., Allen, H. W., & Dupuy, B. (2016). *Multiliteracies framework for collegiate foreign language teaching*. Pearson.

Penyas, A. (2023). *We're all just fine*. Fantagraphic Books.

Rawls, J. (1971). *A theory of justice*. Harvard University Press.

Reese, D. (2013). Critical Indigenous literacies. In J. Larson & J. Marsh (Eds.), *The SAGE handbook of early childhood literacy* (pp. 251–263). SAGE.

Reese, D. (2018). Critical Indigenous literacies: Selecting and using children's books about Indigenous peoples. *Language Arts, 95*(6), 389–393.

Reese, D. (October 29, 2021). Highly recommended! *A girl called Echo, Volume 4: Road allowance era*. American Indians in children's literature (AICL). https://americanindiansinchildrensliterature.blogspot.com/

Reyes-Torres, A., Portales-Raga, M., & Torres-Mañá, C. (2021). The potential of sound picturebooks as multimodal narratives. *AILA Review, 34*(2), 300–324. https://doi.org/10.1075/aila.21006.rey

Robertson, L., & Hughes, J. (2012). Surfacing the assumptions: Pursuing critical literacy and social justice in preservice teacher education. *Brock Education Journal, 22*(1), 73–92. https://doi.org/10.26522/brocked.v22i1.308

Smith, S., & Watson, J. (2010). *Reading Autobiography: A guide for interpreting life narratives* (2nd ed.) (NED-New edition, Second). University of Minnesota Press.

Sun, L. (2017). Critical encounters in a middle school English language arts classroom: Using graphic novels to teach critical thinking and reading for peace education. *Multicultural Education, 25*(1), 22–28.

Thomson, P. (2002). *Schooling the Rustbelt kids: Making the difference in changing times* (pp. 1–18). Allen & Unwin..

Vermette, K., Ill. Henderson, S. B., & Col. Yaciuk, D. (2017). *A girl called Echo: Pemmican wars* (Vol. 1). Highwater Press.

Vermette, K., Ill. Henderson, S. B., & Col. Yaciuk, D. (2019). *A girl called Echo: Red river resistance* (Vol. 2). Highwater Press.

Vermette, K., Ill. Henderson, S. B., & Col. Yaciuk, D. (2020). *A girl called Echo: Northwest resistance* (Vol. 3). Highwater Press.

Vermette, K., Ill. Henderson, S. B., & Col. Yaciuk, D. (2021). *A girl called Echo: Road allowance era* (Vol. 4.) Highwater Press.

Zapata, G. (2022). *Learning by design and second language teaching: Theory, research and practice*. Routledge.

Part V

Practitioner Reflections on Students' and Teachers' Critical Literacies Development

9 Becoming Critically Literate about the Other(ed)

Proposing Disruptions and Innovations to a Portuguese as a Foreign Language Course

Vander Tavares

Introduction

The development of teaching, learning, and assessment methods in second and foreign language (L2) education departed from hierarchical ideologies of language, culture, and knowledge (Macedo, 2019). Such hierarchies framed the monolingual, monocultural, and Western "native speaker" as the best representatives of European languages, for both L2 teachers and learners (Train, 2007). As a consequence of such an ideological matrix, cultural diversity and linguistic variety have been approached vertically and often from a deficit, rather than an asset, perspective. In other words, to look, behave, and speak differently from the "standard" have been considered deviations with profound costs for teachers and learners, including in terms of education and employment. In the context of Portuguese as an international language,[1] these complex patterns have contributed to inferiorizing or invisibilizing certain groups of Portuguese language speakers, especially those from the African continent or of an Indigenous background (Da Silva, 2018).

Drawing on the concepts of critical literacy and critical awareness (Freire, 2018b; Kalantzis et al., 2016), this chapter offers a practitioner reflection based on my past experience of teaching Portuguese in Canada. This reflection offers possible disruptions and innovations to the ideological configuration of a former Portuguese as a foreign language course I taught in a major Canadian city. Such propositions are meant to potentially evoke experiences of becoming critically literate about contemporary injustices between and within groups of speakers of Portuguese in learners of Portuguese as an L2. This chapter begins with an overview of Portuguese colonialism and coloniality, the diasporic presence of Portuguese in Canada, and subsequently the theoretical framework for critical literacies (pedagogies) (Anstey & Bull, 2018). It underscores possible links in L2 education between (pedagogies of) multiliteracies and social justice for minoritized cultural groups in the context of Portuguese as an international language. A discussion on the possible limitations and affordances of this envisioned intervention is presented in the final section.

DOI: 10.4324/9781003438847-15

184   *V. Tavares*

This contribution is grounded in conceptions of reflective practice in L2 education. Farrell (2018) explained that reflective practice occurs "when teachers consciously take on the role of reflective practitioner and subject their own beliefs about teaching and learning to critical analysis, take full responsibility for their actions in the classroom, and continue to improve their teaching practice" (p. 1). In this reflection, I reimagine my teaching in light of my continuous learning as an L2 teacher, including through knowledge, beliefs, and conversations with learners and fellow teachers from over the years. My reflection is based on my attempt to enhance my (future) teaching by connecting the syllabus for the course under consideration to current discussions related to social justice in L2 education, both of which are foregrounded later in the chapter. By relying on the syllabus and memory as sources of information and knowledge, I identify gaps and openings in the Portuguese as a foreign language course, which I now revisit from a multi- and critical literacies perspective.

Portuguese Colonialism and Its Impact: Coloniality

The Portuguese language, as a colonial language, is inextricably interlaced in the history of Portuguese imperialism and colonization. The Portuguese Empire, in its varied iterations over the centuries, was vast and inclusive of territories in South America, Africa, and Asia. In the early 1400s, Portuguese sailors and explorers were financed by the Portuguese Crown to "discover" new places and expand their trade routes initially for financial gains. These two aims were part of a colonial agenda whose overall directive, however, transcended purely financial exploitation. Portugal also set out to "civilize" non-Western peoples through European education, Catholicism, and market development for the benefit of the Crown in times when many European states were changing and expanding their dominance. All such aims depended on the gradual, but forced and oftentimes violent, implementation of Portuguese as a new language and simultaneously on the displacement of local languages and cultures (Tavares, 2023).

Former colonized countries and territories by Portugal spanned across the continents. These include Brazil, Angola, Mozambique, Guinea-Bissau, Cape Verde, São Tomé and Príncipe, Goa (India), East Timor, and Macau. Though these were former colonies of Portugal, not all were embedded in the historical slave trade orchestrated by Portugal. As a result of this and other political processes, Portuguese is now a pluricentric language (del Olmo et al., 2022) among the ten most spoken in the world. However, the various dialects and varieties that constitute the diversity of Portuguese are not viewed horizontally, that is: certain dialects and varieties have been made to hold more social and cultural prestige than others, especially over those spoken by racialized speakers. The differences between the dialects spoken in Portugal are traditionally ignored within the comparative, colonial landscape of the language as racialized varieties and dialects are considered socially inferior, funny, and

Becoming Critically Literate about the Other(ed) 185

ungrammatical for they are not associated with the imagined "European" Portuguese speaker (Severo, 2016).

Although Portuguese colonialism has ended, its devastating impact remains, both materially and socio-culturally, for the former colonies and territories. The abolition of slavery in the nineteenth century did not mark the end of forced and coerced labor for Africans and Indigenous Brazilians who were owned or controlled by Portuguese settlers for several subsequent decades (Kanda, 2005). Such is an example of the early coloniality of power in the domain of exploitation and domination, which has since then become even more complex. Maldonado-Torres (2007) explained that the colonial past has left a visceral impact not only "in the areas of authority, sexuality, knowledge and the economy, but on the general understanding of being as well" (p. 242). Today, in Brazil and the former African colonies, formal schooling remains divisive through its elitist foundation (Tavares, 2023). European epistemology, diffused by Portuguese settlers, has contributed to delegitimizing local and Indigenous knowledges, and by extension, marginalizing those who confront these forms of European coloniality today.

Through language, colonialism and coloniality have also fragmented the sense of cultural identity of the former colonies. Mata (2019) spoke of the colonial trauma left upon the African peoples, which exists in the post-colonial period in the sense that it "modifies and subverts the community and the colonized subjects: they [subjects] could not live (in) their mother tongue without the onus of an inferior status" (p. 212, my translation). Beginning in the colonial era of settlement, the use of native languages was tied to a dehumanization of the individual through a dichotomy: citizen if Portuguese were acquired, stateless if the mother tongues were used. Righteous if catechized into Catholicism but pagan or unholy otherwise (Mata, 2019). Therefore, the Portuguese language has not only displaced but also made identities invisible. Local languages (and cultures) have been assigned a folkloric, exotic, but most predominantly, backward character, even by the African elites today in light of coloniality and modernity (see Nascimento & Tavares, 2023).

Mapping Out the Portuguese Language in Canada

Although immigration to Canada by speakers of Portuguese is not a recent phenomenon, the language itself has only recently received more scholarly attention. In Canada, Portuguese is spoken by first-generation immigrants, heritage learners, and those who have an interest in learning the language for professional or personal purposes, despite being of a non-Lusophone background themselves (Cardoso & Tavares, 2020). Lusophone is the linguistic and cultural term used to characterize and group together speakers of Portuguese as a first or additional language in countries where the language holds official status or in the diaspora. Thus, Portuguese is a multigenerational and multidialectal language in Canada, tied to different immigration histories, social classes, and cultural identities. Based on the latest census, Statistics Canada (2012, 2017)

186 *V. Tavares*

reported that at least 237,000 residents of a Lusophone background classified Portuguese as a first language in the country.

The earliest mass immigration to Canada by Lusophone speakers was led by the Portuguese in the 1950s. This diasporic movement was influenced by changing socioeconomic conditions in Portugal at a time when the country was still under a dictatorship—the longest in Europe in the twentieth century—and by the labor shortage in Canada around the same time. Such trends led the governments of both countries to sign a transnational agreement which resulted in about 6,000 Portuguese workers immigrating to Canada by 1961 (Cardoso et al., 2022). Most of these workers found employment in physically demanding occupations, such as construction and agriculture, and "unskilled" labor, as in the cleaning industry (Giles, 2016). In the 1980s, immigration by Brazilians grew rapidly, particularly by "skilled" immigrants later in the 2000s, contributing to the already-existing linguistic, cultural, and social diversity of the Lusophone "community" in Canada.

Despite the shared language and, to some extent, culture, tensions embedded in power relations also exist within the Lusophone "community" in Canada. Silva (2012) problematized the relationships within the immigrant community from Portugal by explaining that it is "divided between a minority of Mainland Portuguese, whose standard language variety and dominant cultural habitus afford them positions of power, and a majority of Azorean Portuguese, whose ways of being and speaking Portuguese are delegitimised" (p. 59). Similar issues exist *between* Lusophone communities in Canada. Immigrants to Canada from former Portuguese colonies (e.g., Brazilians and Africans) tend to be "excluded from the dominant discourse" about Portugal's culture, history, and language that is disseminated in Canada (Silva, 2013, p. 177). Ideologies of culture and language travel through the generations and also make their way into the Portuguese language classroom, where varieties are seen through monocultural and hierarchical lenses (Tavares, 2022).

Today, Portuguese is increasingly sought out as an international language by non-Lusophone Canadians. Simultaneously, the older Lusophone "community," particularly the one in Montréal, is faced with concern about the future of the language as Canadian-born, heritage speakers construct their identities in a sociolinguistic context where English and French hold more social prestige and cultural capital in comparison to Portuguese, a minority language (Scetti, 2020). Pedagogical innovations in Portuguese as an international language courses have engaged more systematically with the issue of (bi)cultural identity construction for heritage speakers. For example, at York University in Toronto, Dodman et al. (2022) examined the role played by experiential education in bridging learners of a heritage background to cultural and linguistic experiences through work placement, Lusophone literature, museum visits, and guest speakers of a Lusophone background who discuss contemporary topics related to Lusophone immigration to Canada with learners in class.

A Brief Overview of Second and Foreign Language Acquisition Research

Early research, theory, and practice in second and foreign language (L2) education reflected overwhelmingly a psycholinguistic orientation to language acquisition and use. Ortega (2011) explained that "traditional psychologically oriented theories construe knowledge as residing in the mind, assume that learning is an individual accomplishment, and posit that [the] mind achieves learning through environmental stimuli" (p. 168). This meant, among other things, that the social context in which learning occurred received little critical consideration and that the acquisition of an L2 was studied primarily in comparison to the learner's first language. In this sense, the politics embedded in L2 teaching and learning were not a prominent facet of L2 education research for the focus was placed on the learning process and the learner as a member of a fixed sociolinguistic group.

Ortega (2013) identified four major trends in second language acquisition (SLA) research that have emerged since the late 1990s and early 2000s. Epistemological diversity is considered "the most noticeable of trends" for it includes, first, "efforts to dissociate from the quantitative, cognitive, positivist epistemologies dominant in SLA until the mid 1990s," and second, the need to "refocus empirically on variation rather than universals and on individuals as much as on groups" (p. 3). The other three trends may be seen in the growing usage-based research on language and linguistics, methodological diversity in the study of SLA, and the broader range of groups now included in SLA research. These trends have unfolded in response not only to theoretical and conceptual developments in other disciplines but also criticism of SLA research as an exclusive, colonial, and Eurocentric field with the White, Anglophone "native speaker" at the center (e.g., Canagarajah, 2012; Pennycook, 2021).

Of great importance to epistemological diversity, especially in relation to (re)positioning the learner as a whole individual, is plurilingualism. A plurilingual perspective is concerned with a "holistic view of a speaker's plurilingual competence" (Prasad, 2020, p. 903), fusing together the learner's linguistic and cultural knowledges, regardless of "proficiency levels within and across languages" (Chen et al., 2022, p. 2). The basis of this plurilingual competence includes knowledges that have not always been viewed positively in SLA research and L2 education. In fact, these have even been considered a deficit against the learner's own success in the L2. However, plurilingualism recognizes these knowledges as assets and "validates the long existing social phenomenon of flexible language use as documented in many parts of the world" (Chen et al., 2022, p. 2), reinventing the language classroom to equally reflect the social realities of learners. Nevertheless, plurilingualism has also been the object of critique on the basis of its philosophically European-centric motives and goals, reflecting a kind of individual flexibility and mobility characteristic of the European Union (García & Otheguy, 2020).

188   *V. Tavares*

Another change to L2 education inserted in the trends cited previously is the emergence of literacy as plural and multimodal. This change stemmed from the need to rethink what it means to be literate and to develop in learners an understanding that literacy in the L2 is also community-based, situated, historical, and political—a topic discussed specifically in the next section. Learners should therefore be equipped to critically evaluate what *people* mean by written texts, rather than believing that texts have an intrinsic meaning in and by themselves, and "what texts mean *to people* who belong to different discourse communities" (Kern, 2000, p. 2, italics in original). Though this is an important goal for L2 education, it is also a challenging one to achieve. Warner and Dupuy (2018) spoke of the challenges surrounding the implementation of a multiliteracies approach in L2 education, including the lack of adequate training available for L2 teachers and of contextualized, integrated materials that move beyond the focus on grammar and the "culturally neutral" approach.

From Singular to Plural: Literacy, Literacies, and Critical Literacies

Traditional literacy development models in L2 education focused on ("proper") grammar and ("correct") communication. As such, they sought to approximate L2 learners to the imagined "native speaker." Literacies, in the plural, recognize that L2 education should move beyond teaching the grammatical rules of a "standard" or national language and encompass multiple forms of literacy that enable and empower L2 learners to communicate in a variety of social settings, with different interlocutors, through different media and in different modalities (Kalantzis & Cope, 2012). Indeed, literacy can no longer be viewed only as the ability to read and write (and to count) in a decontextualized manner. For Kalantzis and Cope (2012), *multiliteracies* refer to two overarching, yet interconnected aspects of meaning-making nowadays. The authors point to social diversity ("the variability of conventions of meaning in different cultural, social or domain-specific situations") and to multimodality (where "written-linguistic modes of meaning interface with oral, visual, audio, gestural, tactile, and spatial patterns of meaning") as the two pillars of multiliteracies (pp. 1–2).

Literacies in the plural centrally have to do with purpose and context, which are, by nature, dynamic and situated. L2 learners hold membership to multiple social groups simultaneously; however, each social group has and values specific ways of using literacies. Anstey and Bull (2018) refer to literate practices as knowing not only the "what" and "when" of using literacies but also "how." Literacies involve behaviors that are not necessarily shared between social groups. Consequently, literacies also have to do with power, for they give individuals access to and recognition by a particular social group in the form of cultural capital. By the same token, literate practices may be used to marginalize and exclude others. Knowing how and when to apply such behaviors evokes therefore

Becoming Critically Literate about the Other(ed) 189

a certain level of critical thinking in the L2 learner for they are required to "read" the situation and respond appropriately. These important points about literacies hold direct implications for teaching: the L2 classroom functions as a place which both reproduces or confronts dominant literate practices.

The rapid changes to communication brought about by technology have resulted in literacies no longer being language-dominated. Meaning is now made and conveyed through different systems, which creates new expectations for L2 teaching and learning. "Multiliteracies" redefines literacy to be "made up of multiple literacies and multiple literate practices that continuously evolve as local and global society, culture and technology change the contexts in which literacy is practiced" (Anstey & Bull, 2018, p. 17). Two key points emerge here: literacies being responsive to and reflective of growing linguistic and cultural diversity, and literacies interconnecting the local to the global, particularly through technology and globalization. In terms of the latter, literacies—being both plural and multimodal—have epistemological implications for L2 learners, that is: how they come to know something. Knowledge is arrived at and demonstrated differently as literacies evolve (Lotherington & Jenson, 2011). As for diversity, it is critical to remember that diversity is not a "horizontal" concept. For instance, not all forms of linguistic, cultural, and experiential diversity L2 learners possess are acknowledged and accepted in the L2 classroom.

Critical literacies play a role in empowering L2 learners to understand, critique, and transform structural inequality and social injustice through texts. In critical literacies pedagogy, L2 learners are viewed as social agents, political participants, and active citizens. Of notable relevance here is the work of Brazilian educational philosopher Paulo Freire, who confronted the hierarchical nature of education of socializing learners into passive recipients of information (Freire, 1970). Freire coined the term banking education or the banking concept of education (Freire, 2018a) to refer to education that rendered learners "empty vessels" into which encyclopedic and irrelevant information was deposited by teachers in order to keep learners compliant and subordinate. Critical literacies pedagogies emphasize the influence of historical processes and human-made events upon social reality. Freire worked effortfully and continually to ignite this understanding in his learners, who believed that the harsh and unequal social conditions they encountered in life were simply a natural, immutable outcome of the world's natural cycle.

Conscientização is the term Freire used to describe the pedagogical process of developing a critical awareness or critical consciousness in learners. *Conscientização* was about restoring agency, and thus humanizing learners, following centuries of oppression and domination through education by an authoritarian Brazilian government. Freire argued that the development of a critical awareness should lead learners to action; otherwise, education would only be creating a false sense of empowerment and liberation in the learner. He explained that "conscientização implies, then, that when I realize that I am oppressed, I also know I can liberate myself if I transform the concrete situation where I find myself oppressed" (Freire, 1972, p. 5, as cited in Cruz,

2013). Freire spoke from the Brazilian context during a politically turbulent time under the forces of a dictatorship as well as authoritarian and conservative governments in the country. Since this complex political scenario was not completely unique to Brazil in light of post-colonial struggles, Freire's ideas were also adopted in other Global South contexts, especially in Africa.

For Freire, critical literacies pedagogies are encircled within what he termed the problem-posing model of education. Problem-posing education is anchored in dialogue between teacher and learner and seeks to undo the passivity assigned to learners by involving them in their own education (Shor & Freire, 1987). As such, dialogue is a component of a model of education that includes active participation, invites the emotions, reflects the local context, and strengthens democracy. Freire argued that dialogic education was a means to epistemologically align teacher and learner since these two roles had always remained hierarchical. What he meant was that teachers and learners come to better familiarize themselves with the object of study by studying it together in dialogue. Dialogic education departs from the learners' realities for it is concerned with real problems the learners face—lived experience and knowledge become the curriculum (Tavares & Skrefsrud, 2023). Additionally, dialogic education is linguistically constructed through the ways learners use language, rather than the verbose, impersonal, and academic register of language teachers can use as a way to demarcate the boundaries between them (Shor & Freire, 1987).

The Course: Innovating and Disrupting the Curriculum

In the next sections, I will discuss my instructional experience in the context of a Portuguese as a foreign language course for beginners. As a plurilingual teacher of two languages (English and Portuguese), my broader teaching approach has been inspired by a synergy of the theories, pedagogies, and experiences from teaching both languages to different audiences and in different settings. In other words, my teaching, as a single practice, has always been informed by what transpires within the "zone of contact" between my experiences of teaching English and Portuguese (e.g., Tavares, 2022), though my teaching experience is characterized mostly and primarily by teaching English as a second language in Canada. In a nutshell, my reflection surrounds the need for Portuguese as an international language courses to be "reinvented as a space for decolonization, transformation, and the development of critical consciousness" (Gounari, 2020, p. 5). Aiming for such outcomes translates, first and foremost, into a kind of L2 education that goes beyond the study of the formal components of a language.

In this chapter, I will focus on critical literacies in L2 education in the domain of social justice through an emphasis on critical awareness. More specifically, I am concerned with learners' development of knowledge in relation to power relations between the different groups of speakers of Portuguese. These intercultural relations are a product of and contextualized through colonial processes that cannot be separated from ethnicity, race, sex, gender, and

Becoming Critically Literate about the Other(ed) 191

language (e.g., variety and accent). Considering these processes, I am deliberate in choosing to work on content that elevates the cultural *other* within the Lusophone context. My approach relates to a critical language awareness (CLA) perspective, which seeks to "empower learners by providing them with a critical analytical framework to help them reflect on their own language experiences and practices, the language practices of others in the institutions of which they are a part, and in the wider society within which they live" (Clark & Ivanič, 1997, p. 217). However, I do not focus on language variety per se as the object of (critical) analysis.

Portuguese as a Foreign Language: Course Overview

This course was offered twice a year by an institution of higher education in a major Canadian city for beginners with little to no previous knowledge of Portuguese. The course was a stand-alone, credit-bearing course, lasting one academic term (i.e., four months). Over the years, the pattern was that about half of the learners enrolled, on average, would take the course as an elective toward their degree at the college, which offered degree programs in applied arts and technology. Yet, considering the sociolinguistic context of Portuguese in Canada, as described previously, it was common that some of the learners were Canadian-born of Lusophone heritage. The other half was composed of non-degree-program learners: these were typically learners who worked during the day and attended the course in the evenings, being this course the only one they would sign up for. The motivations to learn Portuguese within this group varied: from personal interest and affective relationships with a Portuguese speaker to business-related communicative needs with an occasional work trip to either Brazil or Portugal.

The course was designed for three hours of weekly in-person instruction supplemented by homework and independent study. I used to teach all iterations of this course for several years consecutively. In an attempt to maintain privacy and confidentiality whenever possible, I will either generalize or anonymize information related to the institution. In the course description, developed by the modern languages program at the institution, the first goal of the course is presented as enabling learners to acquire basic skills of fluency to communicate in the language. The second is expanding on learners' cultural awareness through an investigation into the unique customs and characteristics of the different Portuguese-speaking countries around the world. The course syllabus, where the course description could be found, has undergone changes over the years in response to the evolving conversations and research on L2 education. Following the course description, the following learning outcomes are presented:

1 use Portuguese for a variety of purposes and in a variety of contexts;
2 use Portuguese to think and learn in a variety of settings;
3 understand and share one's experiences with others in Portuguese;

192 *V. Tavares*

4 apply the conventions of Portuguese appropriately for the purpose, audience, and context;
5 develop independent and collaborative learning strategies to create practical and imaginative works in a variety of media, in Portuguese.

Although these learning outcomes are broad, they do connect to some of the principles of literacies as plural and multimodal. To begin with, language use being a contextual social practice evokes the principle of literate practices (Anstey & Bull, 2018). This can be seen in the references to the variety of purposes, contexts, and settings involved in using the language. The third learning outcome highlights a tenet of learner-centered theories in L2 education, in which the learner is also expected to think more about their personal, lived experiences as a product of their learning experience—though the "critical" component is missing—and be able to communicate these experiences to others in the language. Finally, the last learning outcome explicitly includes references to not only a variety of media—thus acknowledging multimodality—but also to the imagination and to the expectation that the *learner* will (also) be in charge of their own learning by developing strategies to produce (creative) works in the language. The mention of "collaborative" also makes room, potentially, for diversity to emerge.

Following the learning outcomes, the syllabus presents a section titled "Essential Employability Skills," with eight skills identified. The first skill relates to communicating "clearly, concisely and correctly" in different modalities while considering the needs of the audience. The fourth skill feeds directly into critical literacies by stating that the learner should be able to analyze, evaluate, and apply relevant information from a variety of sources. However, although the link between critical thinking and the workplace is evident, the relevance of critical strategies is clearly not exclusive to the workplace. In fact, most of the learners who have taken this course typically do not end up using the language at work. Finally, the following two skills also connect to multiliteracies: showing respect for diverse opinions, values, and belief systems, and interacting effectively with peers in ways that support the achievement of a common goal. All such skills are often enacted in tandem and considered "21st century skills" for the L2 classroom as the classroom prepares learners for the future workforce (Zapata, 2022).

Further down the document, more specific learning outcomes are presented. The focus here is on the last set of outcomes, titled "Cultural Understanding." Learners should be able to identify where Portuguese is spoken and the "cultural aspects" of the language, such as greetings and introductions. Furthermore, learners should be able to "demonstrate some knowledge of the culture of countries where Portuguese is spoken (e.g., identify famous people, places, typical foods, celebrations)." Here, knowledge of culture surrounds traditional and potentially stereotypical markers of culture (Tavares, 2020). An expectation that learners develop more complex and critical knowledge of Lusophone cultures is missing. The last learning outcome is that learners

Becoming Critically Literate about the Other(ed) 193

should be able to identify and explain contributions from the Portuguese culture to Canada and the world. This point deserves attention: either (1) only the culture of Portugal is of interest or (2) all other cultures (e.g., Brazilian, Mozambican) are of interest but erased and superseded by an overarching "Portuguese" culture. In either case, this is problematic. Nevertheless, this issue was also the point of departure for some of my proposed changes, which I will explain below.

Innovating the Curriculum through Critical Literacies

In this section, I will describe four works of literature whose inclusion in the course could support the aim of innovating the curriculum toward social justice. It is important to note that all four works were written not only by Lusophone authors but also about themes that matter personally to the authors as they have had direct contact with the issues which they discuss and problematize. These works reflect identities of writers from different varieties of Portuguese and geographical contexts—varieties and contexts which have not been traditionally a part of the global, "mainstream" Lusophone cultural discourse—though one work is written in English (see Table 9.1 for a summary). Considering the advanced level of Portuguese used in these works in relation to the level being developed in the course, English would likely come into place to allow me to highlight the main points and promote critical

Table 9.1 Simplified overview of curricular innovations

Works included	Type of source and genre	Place and sociological foci	Awareness of Lusophone power relations (not extensive)
Chiziane (2016)	Blended (fiction and non-fiction)	Mozambique: race, sex, gender, language	Displacement and erasure of local languages and cultures through colonization Racism Slavery
Munduruku (2001)	Blended (fiction and non-fiction), multimodal	Brazil: Indigeneity	Displacement and erasure of local languages and cultures through colonization
Da Silva (2012)	Academic, peer-reviewed (non-fiction)	Canada: immigration, ethnicity, language variety, accent, youth	Legitimacy and authenticity through monolingualism and monoculturalism within the diaspora
Almeida (2015)	Blended (fiction and non-fiction), multimodal	Angola-Portugal: immigration, body, race, sex, gender, youth	Racism Unbelonging

194   *V. Tavares*

discussions around these points with the overall objective of developing critical awareness of power relations within the Lusophony with the learners. This objective is tied to the cultural skills development component of the course.

Paulina Chiziane is a writer from Mozambique who, in 2021, was the recipient of a prestigious literary award called *Prêmio Camões*. This annual award, whose cash value is of about 100,000 euros, is given to a writer who contributes to enriching the literary and cultural heritage of the Portuguese language through an exceptional literary work written in Portuguese. Chiziane grew up speaking Chope and Ronga, two languages Indigenous to parts of Africa, including Mozambique, and learned Portuguese later once she attended a Catholic school. She began her studies in linguistics in university but abandoned them in order to pursue writing. She is the first woman to publish a literary work in Mozambique. Her works are women-centered and deal with themes such as emigration, colonialism/coloniality, democracy, and the patriarchy, among others. Her works are also characterized by a resistance toward the traditional Western genres of fiction writing.

Chiziane's book *O Alegre Canto da Perdiz* (English: The Cheerful Song of the Partridge) foregrounds the beliefs, attitudes, and behaviors of African women during Portuguese colonization in Mozambique. As with her other works, this book (2016) fuses both history and mythology into the story. The book deals directly with racism, as the main character—a Black woman—leaves her poor, Black husband and marries the White colonizer to bear lighter skin children and therefore increase their chances of social prosperity. Racism is obvious in the mother's choice to feed her Black, firstborn child worse food, while the second, from having a lighter skin tone, gets better food. Other central themes are assimilation, love, slavery, and the patriarchy, which Chiziane demonstrates to be an issue also in Indigenous Mozambican cultures. This book, as cultural material, helps to create exposure to issues of gender, culture, and colonization from an underrepresented perspective within Lusophone literature. In particular, this work can afford learners an opportunity to critically examine the role of Portuguese within a post-colonial context and its impact today.

Kabá Darebu is a multimodal picture book written by prominent Brazilian Indigenous author and activist Daniel Munduruku. This short, illustrated literary work (Munduruku, 2001) offers vignettes of the daily life and cultural practices of the Munduruku peoples (to which the author belongs) from the perspective of a seven-year-old Munduruku boy. These vignettes foreground the tribe's ways of living, cooking, playing, and knowing, highlighting an indispensable connection to nature. In the Portuguese language classroom, *Kabá Darebu* can open a window into conversations around why Indigenous cultures have been excluded from the "mainstream" Lusophone culture. Thus, this book functions as a "space" to discuss Portuguese colonization and demystify the "discovery" of Brazil. The absence of Indigenous voices from much of the early discourse about Brazilian society and history has contributed to cementing stereotypes about Indigenous Brazilians, particularly those which frame Indigenous peoples as primitive, backward, violent, and living in nudity in villages (Tavares & Orlando, 2023). This book can also help to confront such stereotypes.

The works of Portuguese-Canadian researcher Emanuel da Silva offer yet another relevant take on the relationships between Portuguese-speaking groups. They tend to focus on the Portuguese language in Canada from the perspective of critical sociolinguistics. In an article about the Portuguese-speaking "community" in Toronto, Da Silva (2012) discussed the different ways in which younger Portuguese speakers attempted to (re)present Portuguese-ness through gala events organized by leaders of Portuguese student clubs and associations. Each of the events experienced varying levels of "success" in terms of their acknowledgment and investment by the local Portuguese community. Gala events which promoted an idealized, monolingual (ignoring English or the Azorean variety), and monocultural materialization of Portuguese culture attracted a significantly larger audience, funding, and media attention. Contrastingly, events which embodied a more hybrid approach to Portuguese-ness were considered less successful.

This work can contribute to making the power relations within the Portuguese "community" in Toronto more evident to learners. This is especially important for those learners, typically Canadian learners of an Anglophone background, who are in relationships with Portuguese speakers in Toronto and may be unfamiliar with the cultural diversity of the "community." Da Silva (2012) noted that the student-led events which were bilingual and de-ethnicized were viewed as a "drastic deviation" (p. 148) from the dominant discourse on what it means to be a (heritage) speaker of Portuguese in Toronto. Da Silva's (2012) work serves as fertile ground to problematize the hierarchies within the Lusophone "community" and the reasons behind the processes of marginalization of varieties of Portuguese that are made inferior, especially in connection to ethnicity and accent. From another point of view, this work also leads to questions about (Portuguese) culture in terms of fluidity, hybridity, and change. It can additionally help to identify ideologies behind cultural attitudes that seek to preserve fixed and exclusive conceptualizations of identity and, by extension, notions of "legitimacy" and "authenticity" within the Lusophone "community."

Still building on the theme of Lusophone identity, the last literary work presented here is *Esse Cabelo* (2015) by Djaimilia Pereira de Almeida. Almeida was born in Angola but grew up near Lisbon. She is of partial African descent and writes about race, gender, and identity, being the recipient of several literary awards. *Esse Cabelo* (English title: That Hair) is Almeida's first book, in which she combines elements of romance and autobiography to tell the story of a dark-skinned and frizzy, curly-haired girl in Lisbon in the 1980s. In the book, themes related to belonging and identity construction are central as the story reveals feelings of outsider-ness in Portuguese society and the impact of colonization on the racial relationships between Portugal and its former colonies. As such, this book connects with the works of Da Silva for they both stimulate conversations about Lusophone immigration and cultural hybridity. However, there are key differences: Da Silva's works focus primarily

196 *V. Tavares*

on language variety, while Almeida's *Esse Cabelo* centers on race and physical appearance. Hair, more specifically, becomes the object of study for complex topics through both text and imagery.

Discussion and Conclusion

I will now engage with the possible limitations, affordances, and connections to multi- and critical literacies based on the reflection I have presented. To begin with, reconstructing the course in the way I have described was not originally planned as a formal action research project in the empirical sense, thereby leading to collection of data. However, in light of my experience of teaching the course over the years (e.g., Tavares, 2022), I believe that these changes would still be necessary for at least two main reasons: first, based on the traditional erasure of minoritized speakers of Portuguese from Portuguese as an international language education and, second, for the fact that many of the students in the course tend to be heritage learners who, like any other learner, bring ideologies of language and culture into the classroom through interactions with family, the media, literature, and so on. Since the Portuguese language classroom is an extension of learners' social worlds (Shor & Freire, 1987), my goal is to promote a meaningful kind of learning experience by inviting topics that have real relevance to learners outside the classroom (Glisan & Donato, 2021).

Critical literacies pedagogy is anchored in diverse pedagogical approaches, including dialogue. Yet, dialogic education is not simply about engaging in *any* dialogue with learners, but one which departs from the learners' realities—the tensions, challenges, and dilemmas they face as whole individuals—and one which leads all involved, both teachers and learners, to unexpected "places" where the answers are not prefabricated: places of uncertainty, discomfort, and of many unknowns (Freire, 2018a). In this course, the sociopolitical issues presented in the works by the four Lusophone authors can be elaborated upon through dialogue and discussion. For L2 learning to be potentially transformative, it has to permeate learners' lives, draw on what they know, and relate to the communities they belong to (Zapata, 2022). Questions posed in the discussions should be aimed at the learners themselves: questions developed to probe and challenge them to relate the topics of social justice to their own lived experiences, knowledges, and perceptions specifically of the Lusophone "community." By doing so, knowledge becomes actively co-constructed by and between learners, wherein personal experience is the common foundation.

Conscientização, or critical awareness, is the hoped-for outcome of my critical literacies pedagogy, though *conscientização* is both a process and a product (Tavares, 2023). By including traditionally excluded voices and perspectives from the Lusophone cultural discourse into the course, I hope to contribute to the development of learners' critical awareness of unequal power relations between different groups of speakers of Portuguese—power relations sustained by hierarchies based on language variety, race, and ethnicity. The Portuguese

Becoming Critically Literate about the Other(ed) 197

language course is a particularly fruitful space for this critical awareness development, since many, if not all, Portuguese language courses are only designed to promote the learning of either "European Portuguese" or "Brazilian Portuguese." Learners must be encouraged to critically evaluate *why* other varieties are left out. As others have argued, *conscientização* and transformation through L2 education are relative and contextual achievements (Lau et al., 2021). In the specific context of this course, I consider the changes made innovative and disruptive since critical perspectives on culture were not included as a learning outcome in the very first place.

Critical awareness flows into and stems from a pedagogy that recognizes and develops multiple literacies in L2 education. In this course, literacy is, indeed, plural: it is about learning not only to read and write in Portuguese but also when, how, and with whom to use the language. The understanding of using Portuguese as a social practice, where *people* use the language to do things, is of central value in the course, despite the beginner's level. Such a value was contextualized through cultural material, drawing attention to the *value* assigned to different literate practices within the Lusophony. Furthermore, the multimodal nature of L2 education should also be evident in this course through the literary works that convey meaning through multiple semiotic systems. Lastly, a pedagogy of multiliteracies connects the local and the global and is concerned with the development of respect for diversity (Cope & Kalantzis, 2016). The global in here is inclusive of more Portuguese-speaking countries and territories, while the local may be viewed as both the Canadian city and the language classroom.

My choice to include those four works was grounded in the hope/aim that learners might come to critically understand and develop an appreciation for diversity in the Lusophony. The focus was therefore on curricular changes as possible pathways to such aims, rather than on the measurement of changes in learners' individual attitudes. It is evident, however, that this kind of pedagogical work requires deep forms of engagement and structural changes so as to avoid framing the cultural *other* as the embodiment of diversity. In conclusion, for L2 learners to be(come) agents of change, they need to confront their own biases and beliefs, about not only the world but also the L2 and its communities. This is one of the tenets of critical literacies pedagogies, which seek to promote "learning about differences in language and power" and "engagement with real-world issues" (Kalantzis & Cope, 2012, pp. 164–165). L2 education that is concerned with social justice must embrace this complex task in ways that are situated, yet disruptive to dominant linguistic and cultural ideologies, political discourses, teaching methods, and emotional comfort.

Note

1 I use "Portuguese as an international language" in order to cover the teaching of Portuguese both as a second and foreign language without a meaningful attention to the political context of instruction.

198   V. Tavares

References

Almeida, D. P. (2015). *Esse cabelo*. Editorial Teorema.
Anstey, M., & Bull, G. (2018). *Foundations of multiliteracies: Reading, writing, and talking in the 21st century*. Routledge.
Canagarajah, S. (2012). *Translingual practice: Global Englishes and cosmopolitan relations*. Routledge.
Cardoso, I., & Tavares, V. (Eds.). (2020). *Teaching and learning Portuguese in Canada: Multidisciplinary contributions to SLA research and practice*. Boa Vista Press.
Cardoso, I., Tavares, V., & Graça, L. (2022). Língua portuguesa no Canadá: Das dinâmicas comunitárias às experiências identitárias. In F. C. del Olmo, S. Melo-Pfeifer, & S. Souza (Eds.), *O que quer, o que pode esta língua* (pp. 53–75). University of Porto Press.
Chen, L., Karas, M., Shalizar, M., & Piccardo, E. (2022). From "promising controversies" to negotiated practices: A research synthesis of plurilingual pedagogy in global contexts. *TESL Canada Journal, 38*(2), 1–35.
Chiziane, P. (2016). *O alegre canto da perdiz*. Caminho Editora.
Clark, R., & Ivanič, R. (1997). *The politics of writing*. Routledge.
Cope, B., & Kalantzis, M. (Eds.). (2016). *A pedagogy of multiliteracies: Learning by design*. Springer.
Cruz, A. L. (2013). Paulo Freire's concept of conscientização. In R. Lake, & T. Kress (Eds.), *Paulo Freire's intellectual roots: Toward historicity in praxis* (pp. 169–183). Bloomsbury.
Da Silva, E. (2012). Heroes or zeros? Portuguese–Canadian youth and the cost of mobilising different sociolinguistic resources. *International Journal of Multilingualism, 9*(2), 138–150.
Da Silva, P. V. B. (2018). *Racismo em livros didáticos: Estudo sobre negros e brancos em livros de Língua Portuguesa*. Autêntica.
del Olmo, F. C., Melo-Pfeifer, S., & Souza, S. (Eds.). (2022). *O que quer, o que pode esta língua*. University of Porto Press.
Dodman, M. J., Cardoso, I., & Tavares, V. (2022). Communicating and understanding *the other* through experiential education: Portuguese language and culture in Toronto. In F. Carra-Salsberg, M. Figueredo, & M. Jeon (Eds.), *Curriculum design and praxis in language teaching: A globally informed approach* (pp. 131–143). University of Toronto Press.
Farrell, T. S. (2018). Reflective practice for language teachers. In J. I. Liontas (Ed.), *The TESOL encyclopedia of English language teaching* (pp. 1–6). John Wiley & Sons. https://doi.org/10.1002/9781118784235.eelt0873
Freire, P. (1970). *Pedagogy of the oppressed*. Continuum.
Freire, P. (2018a). The banking concept of education. In E. B. Hilty (Ed.), *Thinking about schools* (pp. 117–127). Routledge.
Freire, P. (2018b). *Conscientização*. Cortez Editora.
García, O., & Otheguy, R. (2020). Plurilingualism and translanguaging: Commonalities and divergences. *International Journal of Bilingual Education and Bilingualism, 23*(1), 17–35.
Giles, W. (2016). *Portuguese women in Toronto*. University of Toronto Press.
Glisan, E. W., & Donato, R. (2021). *Enacting the work of language instruction: High-leverage teaching practices* (Vol. 2). ACTFL.
Gounari, P. (2020). Critical pedagogies and teaching and learning languages in dangerous times: Introduction to the special issue. *L2 Journal, 12*(2), 3–20.
Kalantzis, M., & Cope, B. (2012). *Literacies*. Cambridge University Press.
Kalantzis, M., Cope, B., Chan, E., & Dalley-Trim, L. (2016). *Literacies*. Cambridge University Press.
Kanda, A. (2005). *Repensar a história de Angola*. Sediou.

Kern, R. (2000). *Literacy and language teaching*. Oxford University Press.

Lau, S. M. C., Tian, Z., & Lin, A. M. (2021). Critical literacy and additional language learning: An expansive view of translanguaging for change-enhancing possibilities. In J. Z. Pandya, R. A. Mora, J. H. Alford, N. A. Golden, & R. S. de Roock (Eds.), *The handbook of critical literacies* (pp. 381–390). Routledge.

Lotherington, H., & Jenson, J. (2011). Teaching multimodal and digital literacy in L2 settings: New literacies, new basics, new pedagogies. *Annual Review of Applied Linguistics, 31*, 226–246.

Macedo, D. (Ed.). (2019). *Decolonizing foreign language education: The misteaching of English and other colonial languages.* Routledge.

Maldonado-Torres, N. (2007). On the coloniality of being: Contributions to the development of a concept. *Cultural Studies, 21*(2–3), 240–270.

Mata, I. L. (2019). Epistemologias do "colonial" e da descolonização linguística: Uma reflexão a partir de África. *Gragoatá, 24*(48), 208–226.

Munduruku, D. (2001). *Kabá Darebu*. Brinque-Book Editora.

Nascimento, A., & Tavares, V. (2023). African and Afro-Brazilian cultural themes as possible paths towards decolonizing English as a foreign language education. In V. Tavares (Ed.), *Social justice, decoloniality, and southern epistemologies within language education: Theories, knowledges, and practices on TESOL from Brazil* (pp. 207–226). Routledge.

Ortega, L. (2011). SLA after the social turn: Where cognitivism and its alternatives stand. In D. Atkinson (Ed.), *Alternative approaches to second language acquisition* (pp. 167–180). Routledge.

Ortega, L. (2013). SLA for the 21st century: Disciplinary progress, transdisciplinary relevance, and the bi/multilingual turn. *Language Learning, 63*, 1–24.

Pennycook, A. (2021). *Critical applied linguistics: A critical re-introduction*. Routledge.

Prasad, G. (2020). 'How does it look and feel to be plurilingual?': Analysing children's representations of plurilingualism through collage. *International Journal of Bilingual Education and Bilingualism, 23*(8), 902–924.

Scetti, F. (2020). Teaching Portuguese as a heritage language in Montreal. In I. Cardoso, & V. Tavares (Eds.), *Teaching and learning Portuguese in Canada: Multidisciplinary contributions to SLA research and practice* (pp. 20–34). Boa Vista Press.

Severo, C. G. (2016). Lusofonia, colonialismo e globalização. *Fórum Linguístico, 13*(3), 1321–1333.

Shor, I., & Freire, P. (1987). What is the "dialogical method" of teaching? *Journal of Education, 169*(3), 11–31.

Silva, E. (2012). Making and masking difference: Multiculturalism and sociolinguistic tensions in Toronto's Portuguese-Canadian market. *Portuguese Studies Review, 20*(2), 59–78.

Silva, E. (2013). Tensões sociolinguísticas na comunidade portuguesa/lusófona de Toronto. In L. P. Moita Lopes (Ed.), *Português no século XXI: Ideologias linguísticas* (pp. 169–191). Parábola.

Statistics Canada. (2012). *Visual Census. 2011 Census*. http://www12.statcan.gc.ca/census-recensement/2011/dp-pd/vc-rv/index.cfm?Lang=ENG&TOPIC_ID=4&GEOCODE=01

Statistics Canada. (2017). *Focus on geography series, 2016 Census. Statistics Canada*. Catalogue no. 98-404-X2016001. https://www12.statcan.gc.ca/census-recensement/2016/as-sa/fogs-spg/Index-eng.cfm

Tavares, V. (2020). Challenging cultural stereotypes in the pluricentric Portuguese as a foreign language classroom. In I. Cardoso, & V. Tavares (Eds.), *Teaching and learning Portuguese in Canada: Multidisciplinary contributions to SLA research and practice* (pp. 164–186). Boa Vista Press.

Tavares, V. (2022). Teaching two languages: Navigating dual identity experiences. *Pedagogies: An International Jssournal, 18*(3), 497–518.

Tavares, V. (2023). A century of Paulo Freire: Problem-solving education, *conscientização*, dialogue and TESL from a Freirean perspective. In V. Tavares (Ed.), *Social justice, decoloniality, and southern epistemologies within language education: Theories, knowledges, and practices on TESOL from Brazil* (pp. 145–162). Routledge.

Tavares, V., & Orlando, I. R. (2023). Developing critical awareness of indigenous languages and cultures of Brazil in EFL education: Children's literature as an entryway. In V. Tavares (Ed.), *Social justice, decoloniality, and southern epistemologies within language education: Theories, knowledges, and practices on TESOL from Brazil* (pp. 35–52). Routledge.

Tavares, V., & Skrefsrud, T. A. (2023). Experiential education, museums, and student teachers' intercultural learning: Reflections on the Scandinavian Romani exhibition. In V. Tavares & T. A. Skrefsrud (Eds.), *Critical and creative engagements with diversity in Nordic education* (pp. 45–65). Lexington Books.

Train, R. (2007). "Real Spanish:" Historical perspectives on the ideological construction of a (foreign) language. *Critical Inquiry in Language Studies, 4*(2–3), 207–235.

Warner, C., & Dupuy, B. (2018). Moving toward multiliteracies in foreign language teaching: Past and present perspectives... and beyond. *Foreign Language Annals, 51*(1), 116–128.

Zapata, G. (2022). *Learning by design and second language teaching: Theory, research, and practice*. Routledge.

10 Critical Literacy for Korean Language Learning and Teaching

Exploring and Expanding Its Possibilities

Joowon Suh

Introduction

Every year in June, Korean language educators from the US, Canada, Korea, and several European countries gather for a three-full-day conference hosted by the American Association of Teachers of Korean[1] (AATK). This year in 2023, at the time of writing, the two most noteworthy words appearing in the conference program are "critical" and "social justice," including diversity, equity, and inclusion (DEI). Witnessing such a focused collective interest in the field of Korean language education was truly exciting. Critical language pedagogy, which encompasses critical literacy, is no longer considered "radical" or "too liberal," whether dealing with Korean as the national language, a second, or a foreign language. With such a welcoming change in the field, one may wonder whether we are using these terms as mere buzzwords in language pedagogy without fully reflecting on them. What would "being critical" really imply in Korean language education? How does, and should, critical literacy pedagogy contribute to the social justice-oriented Korean language classroom?

With increasing awareness of diversity and multiculturalism found in Korean society and language learners of Korean, critical literacy in Korean language education has started to gain long overdue attention, slowly but steadily. Critical literacy, one of the two main axes consisting of the pedagogy of multiliteracies (the other being multimodality), aims to promote critical thinking by emphasizing differing voices and stances represented in texts and challenging social issues addressed in the language classroom. According to Bull and Anstey (2019), the notion of *critical thinking* means "making a discerned judgment" (p. 57) based on one's own experiences and worldviews. It necessarily entails recognizing and understanding linguistic, cultural, social, and political diversity and plurality. Bull and Anstey (2019) further argue that in this sense, critical thinking becomes "a self-directed and self-monitored activity that checks for accuracy, relevance of reasoning, and significance and depth of information" (p. 57).

In critical literacy pedagogy, learners are encouraged to apply their own critical thinking skills to texts by understanding "any other kind of representation of meaning, as a site of struggle, negotiation, and change" (McKinney &

DOI: 10.4324/9781003438847-16

202   *J. Suh*

Norton, 2008, pp. 195–196). In this way, identity has become a focal point of critical literacy pedagogy, encompassing "a person's ways of thinking, communicating and being, based on their life experiences and aspirations" (Kalantzis & Cope, 2012, p. 167). Within this pedagogical framework, the primary purpose of literacy education has expanded to develop learners' critical understanding of social justice, recognize the multiplicity and fluidity of their identities, foster them as *languagers*, agents, and activists, and eventually empower learners. Ultimately, a critical stance allows "learners to participate more fully in society and become active in negotiating equity and social justice" (Brown et al., 2015, p. 158).

This chapter examines how critical literacy is employed and enacted in Korean language education. It focuses on how critical literacy enables learners to actively negotiate and establish their identities in relation to race, ethnicity, nationality, culture, and languages. Through these critical literacy-based instructions, learners are expected not only to understand the complexity of various sociocultural issues but also to negotiate and mediate their cultural, national, or ethnic identities. The discussion in this chapter primarily draws on practices in Korean as a second language (KSL) and Korean as a foreign language (KFL)[2] settings reviewed and examined in the studies written in both English and Korean[3] to provide a more comprehensive picture by reflecting on the changes and transformations of Korean language teaching and learning. The review, however, is limited to the higher education and adult literacy settings since early age and youth literacy studies generally tend to focus more on developmental aspects of literacy education, which is beyond the scope of this chapter.

Critical Literacies in Korean Language Education

Since the early 2000s, multiliteracies pedagogy has gained considerable attention in Korean language learning and teaching in KFL and KSL settings. It coincides with the noticeable changes in Korean society. Korea had long been regarded as homogeneous, with monolingualism being valued. The "purity" of the Korean language used to be, and still is, to a certain extent, a Korean pride, representing unity and oneness. Driven by globalization, mobilization, and technological development such as AI and automation (Yoon, 2018c), diversity and pluralism have risen in every aspect of Korean society. The terms like multilingualism and multiculturalism have started to appear in everyday discourses. With these changes, Korean language education, in need of a new pedagogical framework that can describe and explain such changes, has started to adopt, and adapt to, pedagogies of multiliteracies.

Critical Literacy and Multimodality

According to the New London Group (NLG) (1996), the notion of multiliteracies recognizes the multiplicity of contexts and communication modes and emphasizes both "local diversity" and "global connectedness" (p. 64). The pedagogy of multiliteracies highlights language learners' engagement in dynamic and collaborative meaning-making processes. These core notions of multiliteracies have effectively helped to understand and accentuate the linguistic and cultural pluralism that has been rapidly growing in the learning and teaching of Korean. In the KSL setting, the multiliteracies pedagogy is employed in connection with multicultural, media, and literature literacy with the increase of immigrant workers and international students at universities.[4] In the KFL setting, pedagogies of multiliteracies have widened the perspectives on rapidly diversifying learners while promoting the critical use of multimodal texts in language learning and teaching.[5] In both settings, the notion of *design* (NLG, 1996), defined as what one is expected to do in making and creating meanings, is actively and creatively employed. Through this dynamic *design* process (see Introduction for more detail), learners can be empowered "as designers of learning processes and environments" (NLG, 1996, p. 73). In other words, language learners become "decoders of language" and "users as designers of meaning" (p. 74).

Within this multiliteracies pedagogy, Kalantzis and Cope (2012) define *critical literacy* as "approaches to literacy which focus on texts that communicate student interests and experiences and address challenging social issues such as discrimination and disadvantage" (p. 167). Cope and Kalantzis (2009) suggest that learners can be "being critical" in two ways in a multiliteracy pedagogical context, "to be functionally analytical or to be evaluative with respect to relationships of power" (p. 185). Critical Framing involves both processes. Through these processes, learners are expected to comprehend the contents presented in different text types and appreciate the various voices and stances represented in texts (Suh & Jung, 2021). Kalantzis and Cope (2012) suggest the goals of critical literacy as follows:

- engaging with real-world issues and active citizenship,
- focusing on voice and agency,
- investigating social issues and moral dilemmas,
- addressing discrimination and disadvantage, and
- exploring human differences and social justice.

As stated in these goals, identity and social justice intersect with critical literacy pedagogy. Eventually, these goals establish a transformative pedagogy in relation to "the historical, social, cultural, political, ideological, and value-centered relations of particular systems of knowledge and social practice" (NLG, 1996, p. 86).

Despite concerning Korean as the national language,[6] not L2 Korean, Cheon's (2014) study is worth mentioning here. Adopting a still considered "radical" critical literacy stance, the researcher argues that reading education in the school setting needs to go beyond simple critical reading and be redesigned to reflect sociopolitical dynamics. The study strongly promotes the

204   *J. Suh*

social view of literacy that language use can be deemed as the execution and reproduction of social structure and power. The study further contends that active reading via critical literacy should include social actions to question the dominant social structure and promote social changes and equity. This study is significant in the sense that critical literacy is explicitly and intensely proposed to be adopted for reading education in the primary and middle school curriculum, which may still be the most conservative and slow-changing area in Korean language education.

It is important to note that in L2 Korean pedagogies of multiliteracies, multimodality is often invested as a central pedagogical focus. Recognizing and understanding for whom and for whose interests discourses serve and how they are presented and represented in texts become the core of critical media, digital, and multimodal literacy. This pedagogical focus aligns with Luke's (2013) definition of critical literacy: "the use of the technologies of print and other media of communication to analyze, critique, and transform the norms, rule systems, and practices governing the social fields of institutions and everyday life" (p. 21). In this respect, all classroom practices reviewed in the section that follows, to a different extent, involve critical multimodal literacy, which provides an effective tool to promote identity construction and learner agency.

According to Kalantzis and Cope (2012), *multimodality* refers to "the use of different and combined modes of meaning" (p. 39) through a meaning-making process, which encompasses digital literacy[7] and media literacy.[8] *Multimodal competence*, first proposed by Kress (2003), is broadly defined as "the ability to understand and use the power of images and sounds, to manipulate and transform digital media, to distribute them pervasively, and to easily adapt them to new forms" (as cited in Guichon & Cohen, 2016, p. 515). Therefore, one of the goals of *critical multimodal literacy* is "to foster multiliterate learners capable of consuming and creating a wide range of semiotic systems available to them in a critical way" (Suh & Jung, 2021, p. 131).

Critical Multimodal Literacy in L2 Korean Setting

In the KFL setting, Zhang's (2020) classroom-based study on the critical literacy of advanced Chinese learners of Korean is unique and meaningful in two ways. First, this study explores the critical media literacy competence of Chinese learners of Korean in China, where, according to the researcher, L2 pedagogy remains rather traditional and conservative. Promoting the importance of critical literacy in KFL classrooms in China, the study demonstrates how critical media literacy can be developed and reinforced by encouraging learners' critical thinking in light of their experiences, social roles, and self-reflection. Secondly and more interestingly, using various media texts (e.g., news, TV interviews, advertisements) on a famous Korean poet, Yoon Dong-Ju, the study connects media literacy and literature in a broader critical language pedagogy framework. By incorporating the literary reader-response theory into the critical literacy pedagogy, the researcher argues that the students in this study can achieve even more critical reading of the texts, reflect on their experiences and social values, and develop their creativity. The researcher further argues that the critical literacy framework using poetry and a literary theory allows learners to enact and activate their learner agency in their learning processes.

Jeong and Yoon's (2020) study also deals with the critical multimodal literacy of KSL advanced-level learners. The study examines Advanced Korean II at a Korean university, a general language course carefully designed based on multiliteracies pedagogy. The primary class materials are a wide range of digital media content learners choose for themselves. The research data includes video recordings of three 90-minute classes, 40-minute in-depth interviews with seven participants, student video projects, and the researchers' field notes. The data analysis reveals that learners can understand and critically analyze social changes and biases in Korean society depicted in these multimodal texts by comparing the target language culture and society and those of their own. The study also finds that learners often miss nuanced meanings of Korea-specific multimodal expressions included in the media texts, indicating instructional needs for explicit linguistic explanations and knowledge.

The following studies on critical multimodal literacy are in connection with cultural literacy and multicultural education. Suh and Jung (2021) define *cultural literacy* as "the ability to understand, analyze, and critically engage with diverse cultural practices in today's globalized world" (p. 137). Utilizing clips from the TV drama *Misaeng*, for example, Lee-Smith and Roh (2016) show that through critical analysis of the distinct cultural practices at Korean workplaces, advanced KFL learners widen their knowledge of Korean culture and the language and develop and enhance their cultural literacy. In addition, the learners critically compare Korean and American workplace cultures by bringing their knowledge and experiences as Korean Americans.

Lee-Smith's (2016) study on Korean TV public service announcements (PSAs) is an excellent example of how the semiotic system of PSAs functions as a multimodal text in a meaning-making process initiated by learners while bringing into their knowledge resources and life experiences. Collecting and analyzing the 377 PSAs released between 1981 and 2015, she designs critical multimodal literacy classes in which learners decipher written messages, images, and sounds used in PSAs. In doing so, learners understand not only the linguistic and cultural codes shared by Korean people but also the social and historical contexts in which these PSAs were produced. Through this process, their sociocultural literacy can be developed and enhanced.

Similarly, H-J Kim and J-H Kim (2019) employ PSAs in designing multiliteracy classes for KSL intermediate learners. Using the rich semiotic and multimodal system in PSAs, learners analyze Korean-specific themes and provide their critical understanding of the target culture and society depicted in PSAs vis-à-vis their own cultures. By presenting three stages of multiliteracy lessons (i.e., conceptualization, expansion, and application), the authors demonstrate that Korean PSAs as valuable multimodal texts to promote learners' understanding of diversifying expressions and differences in cultures and societies.

206 *J. Suh*

On a different note, Hong's (2020) study presents the pedagogical roles of critical literacy concerning Korean for Academic Purposes (KAP), the only example of multiliteracies pedagogy used in KAP thus far. In this case study, the author develops a KSL course, *Understanding Korean Culture*, offered to foreign undergraduate students at one Korean university. The course is designed for academic literacy based on multiliteracy pedagogy and ACTFL's 5 Cs (World-Readiness Standards for Learning Languages). Being part of the curriculum for international undergraduate first-year students, the class needs to integrate the characteristics of liberal arts education and language education, and for this reason, critical literacy comes to play an effective role. While learning content (i.e., Korean culture), the students engage in various instructional activities such as group presentations, field trips, and research projects, requiring their critical literacy competence. The study explores and presents the possibilities of pedagogies of critical literacies in content-based KAP instruction.

Despite the strengths of teaching the target language culture in the framework of critical multimodal literacy, Brown et al. (2015) caution that a pedagogical focus on multimodal texts and the teaching of culture using them "frequently stick to 'safe' and accepted generalization about Korean language and culture" (p. 178). Simply employing multimodal texts as instructional materials in class, we may unintentionally propose normative traditionally observed target language culture instead of helping learners to become "problem solvers, active and informed citizens, meaning makers and code breakers" (Brown et al., 2015, p. 178). Ironically, this can undermine the core mission of critical literacy, emphasizing diversity and agency. Keeping this in mind, we should try to incorporate less safe and more "controversial" topics (e.g., social class, political ideology), which can provide our learners with the space that maintains their critical stances and guarantees their agency. After all, social justice intersects with language, interaction, access, equity, power, privilege, and marginalization.

Identity and Agency in Korean Language Education

As shown in the previous section, critical literacy in L2 language pedagogy facilitates learners' critical analysis of and fosters active engagement with multimodal texts based on their experiences, interests, and values. For this very process, learners are encouraged to rely on and actively utilize social and historical contexts in which they are situated and accordingly present their understandings of reality and social justice. By doing so, language learners can demonstrate, negotiate, and (re)construct their identities. Norton (2014) states that literacy should be "not only a skill to be learned but a practice that is socially constructed and locally negotiated" (p. 104). In this sense, Ok (2009), discussing research on L2 identity in Korean effectively summarizes the interdependent relationship between literacy and identity as follows: Literacy is a vital tool for identity representation and construction, and thus, one of the

Critical Literacy for Korean Language Learning and Teaching 207

goals of literacy education is to help learners to represent and construct their own identities.

According to Norton (2014), critical literacy fundamentally focuses on "the relationship between the language learner and the larger social world" (p. 103), which includes linguistic, cultural, social, historical, economic, and political contexts. In these contexts, "learners negotiate and sometimes resist the diverse positions those contexts offer them" (p. 103). Accordingly, critical literacy aims to nurture learners with enhanced agency to take social action in various "sites of oppression" (Crookes, 2022) that they become aware of via multimodal texts. Eventually, critical literacy fosters learners to become active social agents in their community. In this view, literacy practices become "tools or media for constructing, narrating, mediating, enacting, performing, enlisting, or exploring identities" (Moje & Luke, 2009, p. 416).

How is L2 identity then defined and operationalized, whether it is called the *multilingual subject* (Kramsch, 2009), *intercultural speaker* (Block, 2007), or *authentic speaker* (van Compernolle, 2016)? We can first readily agree that L2 identities are not fixed and static but fluid and dynamic, and not monolithic and uni-dimensional but plural and multi-dimensional. From the multiliteracies pedagogy perspective, identities are interpersonal and sociocultural rather than psychological. As Blyth (2018) captures, pedagogies of multiliteracies zoom in on "a critical awareness of language use viewed as a set of social practices that constitute an important part of one's identity" (p. 65).

In Korean language education, changing demographics of learners of Korean are noticed in terms of proficiency levels, learning motivation, and prior target culture exposure, leading to their differing needs and learning outcomes (Lee, 2023). In L2 Korean language education, however, pedagogical attempts to make the connection between critical literacy, identity, and social justice are at a relatively early but promising stage. More in-depth analysis of the practices based on these three complex trilateral points is needed. Such analysis requires more concentrated reflexivity and collective efforts firmly based on solid theoretical underpinning.

This section reviews KSL and KFL studies focusing on identity, agency, and social justice within the multiliteracy framework. For this review, the following questions, proposed by Piller (2016), are enlightening to consider: "How does linguistic diversity structure societies at institutional, local, national, and global levels? How does linguistic proficiency mediate social participation? In short, how is language related to inequality?" (p. 3). Keeping these questions in mind, we specifically examine the three groups of learners of Korean in the following section: marriage migrant women in Korea, KFL college learners in the US, and heritage language (HL) learners (HLLs) of Korean.

Multilingual and Multicultural Voices in South Korea

In the context of globalization and demographic shifts (i.e., increasing aging population, foreign workers, and marriage migrants), Korea, traditionally considered homogenous in terms of language, culture, race, and ethnicity, has become more multilingual and multicultural. This change has posed a salient issue in language education: linguistic minorities with multicultural backgrounds, which Korea had seldom encountered until the late 1990s (Choi, 2021). For instance, according to A. Kim (2018), marriage migrant women who speak fluent Korean are statistically less likely to face social exclusion and more easily integrated into the existing social networks. This finding, although not surprising, not only emphasizes the social impact of Korean language education but also brings to the surface the uncomfortable truth that the Korean language may now work "as a means of exclusion, discrimination, and disadvantage" (Piller, 2016, p. 8) with the prevalent "ideology of linguistic nationalism and one-way assimilation and integration embedded in most education initiatives and reforms" (Choi, 2021, p. 2). Thus, learners' critical awareness of their own experiences concerning power structures (Luke, 2013) through language learning has become even more urgent in multilingual and multicultural contemporary Korean society.

With these changing contexts in mind, the goal of literacy education is expanded to help learners engage in identity construction and negotiation by providing a safe space for multiple, often conflicting, identities without forcing the monolithic mainstream value. In this sense, traditional literacy practices in Korean, which tend to advocate uniform, highly structured, and monolingualism-oriented language ideology, cannot solve the issues. Regarding these imminent sociolinguistic and educational issues relating to diversity and identity, however, most research in the field concerns educational policy and multicultural education. Only a few studies discuss the issues from a multiliteracies perspective or actual classroom practices. Although not explicitly claimed to have adopted pedagogies of critical literacy or multiliteracies, the following two studies offer insights into how L2 Korean pedagogy is changing to accommodate the diversifying learner population in Korea.

Won (2010) is one of the first studies that have employed critical literacy for KSL education for marriage migrant women. The study participants (i.e., 70 married migrant women from 13 different countries) enrolled in a 12-week self-expressive writing workshop are strongly encouraged to bring in and share their experiences as outsiders in contemporary Korean society and express their identities as outsiders. Through various writing projects, participating writers of KSL can reestablish a positive self-image and construct a new form of culturally integrative identity. Also, this study highlights the therapeutic roles of writing activities, which work as a space for communication and healing.

Based on Freire's critical literacy theory, H. Kim and Lee (2018) examine a KSL discussion class with six marriage migrant women at the global center under the Ministry of Justice. They acutely point out the issues with the current KSL classes for migrant women: classes are too assimilation-oriented, ethnocentric, nationalistic, and monolithic. The researchers propose a critical literacy-based, learner-centered Korean language class consisting of problem-posing, dialogues, discussion, praxis, and reflection. The analysis shows that through these processes, learners begin to escape from a "silent culture" by recognizing the problem they encounter. They connect their problems to the social structure by critical thinking and exchanging diverse perspectives, as indicated by the keywords such as autonomy, independence, or agency used in learners' journals in the final reflection stage. As Shin (2022) powerfully contends, the pedagogical goal of critical literacy for learners with multicultural and multilinguistic voices should be "to reveal the unequal distribution of resources and discrimination against the marginalized and to restore their agency by vindicating their lived experiences and contesting the ideological basis for inequality" (p. 105). The practices employed in this study convincingly show that linguistic and cultural minority learners in Korea can significantly benefit from critical literacy pedagogies in which linguistic and cultural pluralism is highlighted and appreciated.

L2 Learner Identity in KFL Classroom

Yoon and Brown's (2017) study on politeness is a great example of how learners negotiate and construct their identities in the multiliteracies classroom. Based on an 80-minute class designed on the theme of *yeyuy* 예의, meaning "manners, etiquette" in Korean, for intermediate-level Korean learners, the study investigates how to express rudeness in Korean through both verbal and non-verbal means. As discussed in the previous section, it is a critical multimodal literacy practice that employs multimodal texts such as TV dramas and shows, aiming to promote the students' multimodal competence. In the class, the students are encouraged to critically engage and analyze various codes and meanings conveyed in the target multimodal texts. They express and construct their identities while discussing their behaviors and perspectives on Korean (im)politeness vis-à-vis the teacher's and other students' views. The researchers demonstrate how the students negotiate their L1 and L2 identities through the meaning-making process of multimodal resources involved in authentic media texts in this short multiliteracy lesson.

Brown et al. (2015), employing visual and printed media sources in a third-year Korean class at a university in the US, are informative in a different sense since the focus of the class is the positioning of foreigners reflected in Korean culture. The pedagogical goals of this class are "enhancing multimodal competence, promoting critical literacy, and empowering students in their negotiation of their identities" (p. 162). The teacher uses clips from the TV drama *My Lovely Sam Soon* (2005, MBC) and the talk show *Annyeonghaseyo* (2013, KBS), which deal with characters of diverse ethnic backgrounds, including a mixed-race person. Based on the four steps of a multiliteracy framework (i.e., situated practice, overt instruction, critical framing, and transformative practice), the students are encouraged to critically analyze the semiotic systems and discourses surrounding the social reality of multiethnicity and multiculturalism in contemporary Korea. The class instruction then focuses on the linguistic and visual elements presented in the texts, contrasting "foreign" and "Korean."

210   *J. Suh*

The analysis of the class demonstrates that the students construct or redefine their identities as either "overseas Korean" or "foreigners" by incorporating their understanding of Korean culture and society and their life experiences. In doing so, they can "explore discourses surrounding different categories of foreigners in Korean society and how they are represented in Korean popular culture" (p. 160) in connection with their L2 identities. The findings of this study convincingly reveal that a multiliteracies approach "encourages students to develop critical perspectives on the target language culture, as well as their own" (p. 178) by activating their learner identity.

Heritage Language Learners of Korean

HLLs have always been a valued but challenging learner group in the KFL setting. Lee and Shin (2008) specifically define Korean HLLs as "those who have an ethnolinguistic affiliation to the Korean heritage but may have a broader range of proficiency from high to none in Korean oral or literacy skills" (p. 154). The differing needs of heritage and non-HLLs have been among the most pressing issues in most Korean language programs at US colleges and universities. HLLs, growing up using Korean within a natural, input-reach setting (i.e., with their parents and relatives), may have limited or no literacy skills while having relatively higher levels of oral proficiency (Lee, 2023).

What often makes the situation even more demanding is that the Korean HLL group has been rapidly diversifying in terms of their backgrounds, proficiency levels in Korean, quantity and quality of cultural knowledge, and learning goals and strategies (Lee, 2023). When dealing with HLLs of Korean, we encounter learners with varying proficiency and cultural knowledge and a wide range of experiences at home and in a community with complex identities. We can now no longer picture a prototypical Korean HLL. As we focus on the linguistic proficiency and repertoire of HLLs, classroom practices rooted in pedagogies of multiliteracies and critical literacies often intersect with the concept of *translanguaging* (Garcia & Li, 2014). Our HLLs are, indeed, "speakers with multiple semiotic resources" (Garcia & Li, 2014, p. 41). All three studies examined below demonstrate the complexity, fluidity, and multiplicity of HLL identity and how HLLs can effectively bring out their "Koreanness" by gaining access to Korean language learning via the critical literacy framework.

Choi's (2015) study, one of the first KFL studies on HLLs' L2 identity construction through multiliteracy practice, explores how pedagogies of multiliteracies adopted in a 3rd-year Korean HL class contribute to the development of a student's HL literacy skills. The study focuses on one participant, Jenny, a college student born in the US with limited Korean learning experiences and literacy development. The analysis of course materials, including all of Jenny's written works, shows that despite her comparatively lower proficiency in Korean, Jenny takes on an "agentive take" (p. 121) on Korean language learning by actively searching for ways to improve her writing and developed "a literate identity in Korean" (p. 122). The researcher argues that Jenny's language learner identity progresses from "an English reader, writer, and storyteller to an emerging Korean literate individual" (p. 124) in her HL.

Choi and Yi's (2012) classroom-based research on the use of popular culture in advanced Korean HLLs offers valuable insights into the role of popular culture in HLLs' literacy engagement and HL identity construction, going beyond its mere use as multimodal class materials. Based on learners' presentations and writing projects, the researchers demonstrate that HLLs in this study draw upon the Korean media and pop culture for their literacy practices and improvement. In other words, Korean pop culture serves "as a contact point for their literacy practice," assists HLLs to "reexamine or strengthen their ethnic identity from a global perspective," and further provides "a window to discuss social issues and explore them" (p. 110) in a critical way.

Jung and Chung (2023) examine a total of 456 writing submissions based on 28 multiliteracies tasks by Korean HLLs enrolled in two separate HL courses at the intermediate-high through advanced-low levels at a US private university. In the meaning-making process via critical literacy, the HLLs in the study actively express their HLL identity by affirming their Korean identity while rejecting the prevalent culture. The analysis also shows that the learners become critically aware of their positions in the dominant community. In these HL classrooms, critical literacy activities bring out their HLL identities and help the learners construct a *hybrid identity* as HLLs by resourcefully utilizing linguistic practices and value systems from both cultures (Suh & Jung, 2021). The study effectively shows that critical literacy pedagogies help HLLs identify and contest the normalized mainstream ideologies and their underlying assumptions by bringing their personalized and localized knowledge to class as a member of a Korean-speaking community. The researchers argue that critical literacy implemented in their HL classes reinforces the view that literacy is indeed a way of being in the world, i.e., identity and agency.

Concluding Thoughts

In this chapter, I have extensively reviewed critical literacy-based research in L2 Korean language education. With increased attention to critical literacy pedagogy, there is still a need for more research concerning identity and social justice from a multiliteracies perspective. Now, we reconsider the same questions posed in the Introduction: *What does it mean by "critical" in the Korean language classroom?* "Being critical" in language classrooms can vary from simple skeptical text reading to taking a full social justice stance regarding texts. Alford and Kettle (2017) contend that instead of a "light touch" approach (i.e., the former), we need to be "engaging learners in robust critical engagement with how things are intentionally represented in texts with associated ideological assumptions and effect" (p. 184). If adopting the more robust version of "being critical," language classrooms become a transformative site to promote social justice and equity as language classroom practices are influenced by all stakeholders' ideologies and conceptualizations of language with regard to what is correct, legitimate, authentic, and dominant (Lee, 2023). We then ask who our learners are in our critical literacy classes. With multilingualism and multiculturalism rising in our learner population, we should be able to extract a more subtle and nuanced understanding of L2 learner identity. By promoting critical literacy through linguistic practices, we should allow learners to freely try out different or hybridized identities and exert their agency (Shin, 2022).

Still, the topics adopted for critical literacy pedagogy in L2 Korean language education remain relatively safe and conservative, often limited to cultural concepts and products, both traditional and modern. Exploring and adopting somewhat controversial and often contentious social justice-related issues in Korean literacy education can be complicated but worth trying. For instance, Block (2014) argues for a *social class* as a crucial construct to examine identity work in L2 learning firmly based on the social view of literacy. I now conclude this chapter by briefly introducing a class in which a social class issue, though implicitly, emerged as a discussion point.

In a high-advanced Korean course at a US university, two 75-minute classes focus on two "national" tragedies: the Sewol Ferry's sinking in 2014 and the Itaewon crowd crush in 2022.[9] In these classes, the students analyze the multilayered characteristics of these collective traumas and to assess the social, economic, and political impacts these two tragedies bring into Korean society. On the surface, these two disasters may come across as freak accidents. However, the aftermaths of these two bring out long-existing tension in Korean society: the victims' socioeconomic status, the conflicting beliefs of what really happened fueled by numerous social media postings, and endless debates on the government's fundamental roles and responsibilities. The topic of social class implied in these two traumatic accidents can lead to a substantial discussion on economic inequality, sub-cultural recognition, and the imparity of political participation and representation (Piller, 2016). Critically aware of multimodal languages used in surrounding discourses of these two disastrous accidents, learners may feel obliged to risk revealing their political affinity in the class, potentially implicating their socioeconomic identities. Not always, but often, such discussion may lead to uncomfortable or even emotional moments (cf., West, 2021) in the classroom.

I here maintain that despite possible or likely uneasiness, we should continue to try out more thorny issues in our critical literacy classrooms to enable learners to develop their positions in understanding the target language culture and society and refine their identities (Suh & Jung, 2021). As Hudley and Flores (2022) powerfully suggest, one of our missions as researchers and language teachers is "a strong political commitment to researching the relationship between language and power with the hopes of positioning this research within broader efforts to dismantle oppression" (p. 151). After all, language represents and transforms the world (Luke, 2013), and the language classroom is not an apolitical space (Kramsch, 2014).

Critical Literacy for Korean Language Learning and Teaching 213

Notes

1 The AATK, founded in 1994, is the single professional organization representing all levels of educators of Korean in North America.
2 Throughout the chapter, the terms *KSL* and *KFL* are used to distinguish the instructional settings. The term L2, as indicated in the Introduction of this book, is also used to refer to an additional language to one's first language (L1), encompassing a second language and a foreign language.
3 The studies written in Korean and published in Korea are retrieved from the Korean databases DBPia and KISS (Korean Studies Information Service System).
4 For comprehensive reviews on Korean literacy education in general, see H-J. Kim (2015), Y. Kim (2020), and Yoon (2015, 2018a). For the reviews of multiliteracies in the KSL setting, see Yoon (2018b, 2018c) and Zhang (2021).
5 See Suh and Jung (2021) for the review of multiliteracies in the KFL setting.
6 In comparison with Korean as L2, it means 국어교육 teaching Korean to Korean citizens residing in Korea.
7 *Digital literacy* is defined as the "practices of communicating, relating, thinking and 'being' associated with digital media" (Jones & Hafner, 2012, p. 13).
8 *Media literacy* commonly refers to "a set of capabilities applied to media messages and experiences" (Scheibe & Rogow, 2012, p. 19).
9 The official death toll of these two disasters amounts to 304 and 159, respectively.

References

Alford, J., & Kettle, M. (2017). Teachers' reinterpretations of critical literacy policy: Prioritizing praxis. *Critical Inquiry in Language Studies, 14*(2–3), 182–209. https://doi.org/10.1080/15427587.2017.1288067
Block, D. (2007). *Second language identities.* Continuum. https://doi.org/10.5040/9781474212342
Block, D. (2014). *Social class in applied linguistics.* Routledge.
Blyth, C. (2018). Designing meaning and identity in multiliteracies pedagogy: From multilingual subjects to authentic speakers. *L2 Journal, 10*(2), 62–86. http://doi.org/10.5070/L210235662
Brown, L., Iwasaki, N., & Lee, K. (2015). Implementing multiliteracies in the Korean classroom through visual media. In Y. Kumagai, A. López-Sánchez, & S. Wu (Eds.), *Multiliteracies in world language education* (pp. 158–181). Routledge. https://doi.org/10.4324/9781315736143
Bull, G., & Anstey, M. (2019). *Elaborating multiliteracies through multimodal texts: Changing classroom practices and developing teacher pedagogies.* Routledge. https://doi.org/10.4324/9781315149288
Cheon, K.-R. (2014). Transformational reading and critical literacy, *Korean Education, 101,* 7–35.
Choi, J. (2015). A heritage language learner's literacy practices in a Korean language course in a U.S. university: From a multiliteracies perspective. *Journal of Language and Literacy Education, 11*(2), 116–133. http://jolle.coe.uga.edu/wp-content/uploads/2015/10/Article-6_Choi-FINAL.pdf
Choi, L.-J. (2021). Educating language minority students in South Korea: Multilingual sustainability and linguistic human rights. *Sustainability, 13*(6), 13–27. https://doi.org/10.3390/su13063122
Choi, J., & Yi, Y. (2012). The use and role of pop culture in heritage language learning: A study of advanced learners of Korean. *Foreign Language Annals, 45*(1), 110–129. https://doi.org/10.1111/j.1944-9720.2012.01165.x

214   *J. Suh*

Cope, B., & Kalantzis, M. (2009). "Multiliteracies": New literacies, new learning. *Pedagogies: An International Journal*, 4(3), 164–195. http://doi.org/10.1080/15544800903076044

Crookes, G. V. (2022). Critical language pedagogy. *Language Teaching*, 55(1), 46–63. https://doi.org/10.1017/S0261444820000609

Garcia, O., & Li, W. (2014). *Translanguaging: Language, bilingualism and education*. Palgrave Macmillan. https://doi.org/10.1057/9781137385765

Guichon, N., & Cohen, C. (2016). Multimodality and CALL. In F. Farr & L. Murray (Eds.), *The Routledge handbook of language learning and technology* (pp. 509–521). Routledge. https://doi-org.ezproxy.cul.columbia.edu/10.4324/9781315657899

Hong, Y. (2020). Lesson planning for general Korean program to cultivate multiliteracies: Teaching "Understanding Korean Culture" to foreign undergraduate freshmen. *The Korean Journal of Literacy Research*, 11(2), 157–187.

Hudley, A. H. C., & Flores, N. (2022). Social justice in applied linguistics: Not a conclusion, but a way forward. *Annual Review of Applied Linguistics*, 42, 144–154, https://doi.org/10.1017/S0267190522000083

Jeong, H.-R., & Yoon, Y. (2020). Practice of multiliteracy education for Advanced Korean language learners: Focused on foreign university students in Korea. *Korean Language Education Research*, 55(5), 32–58. https://doi.org/10.20880/kler.2020.55.5.31

Jones, R. H., & Hafner, C. A. (2012). *Understanding digital literacies: A practical introduction*. Routledge. https://doi.org/10.4324/9780203095317

Jung, J.-Y., & Chung, E. E. (2023, June 15–17). Empowering heritage learners of Korean through critical literacy [Paper presentation]. 28th Annual Conference of the American Association of Teachers of Korean, Philadelphia, PA, United States.

Kalantzis, M., & Cope, B. (2012). *Literacies*. Cambridge University Press. https://doi.org/10.1017/cbo9781139196581

Kim, A. (2018). Social exclusion of multicultural families in Korea. *Social Sciences*, 7(4), 63–79. https://doi.org/10.3390/socsci7040063

Kim, H.-J. (2015). Review of literacy development theory and literacy as Korean language education contents. *The Journal of Korean Language and Literature Education*, 36, 463–493.

Kim, Y. (2020). A study on the current status and future tasks of literacy research in the area of Korean language education. *The Journal of Humanities and Social Sciences21*, 11(6), 3229–3240. https://doi.org/10.22143/HSS21.11.6.226

Kim, H.-J., & Kim, J.-H. (2019). A study on the education of multiliteracies of Korean intermediate learners by utilizing public advertisements. *Teaching Korean as a Foreign Language*, 52, 45–74, https://doi.org/10.21716/TKFL.52.45

Kim, H., & Lee, K. (2018). Action research on subjectivity formation of married migrant women through critical literacy education. *Asian Journal of Education*, 19(2), 543–572. https://doi.org/10.15753/aje.2018.06.19.2.543

Kramsch, C. (2009). *The multilingual subject: What foreign language learners say about their experience and why it matters*. Oxford University Press.

Kramsch, C. (2014). Teaching foreign languages in an era of globalization: Introduction. *The Modern Language Journal*, 98(1), 296–311. https://doi.org/10.1111/j.1540-4781.2014.12057.x

Kress, G. (2003). *Literacy in the new media age*. Routledge. https://doi-org.ezproxy.cul.columbia.edu/10.4324/9780203299234

Lee, J. S. (2023, April 10). Critical pedagogy and sociolinguistic justice in Korean language education. [Invited lecture]. 2023 ACTFL Korean SIG Webinar, Virtual.

Lee, J. S., & Shin, S. J. (2008). Korean heritage language education in the United States: The current state, opportunities, and possibilities. *Heritage Language Journal*, 6(2), 153–172. https://doi.org/10.46538/hlj.6.2.2

Critical Literacy for Korean Language Learning and Teaching 215

Lee-Smith, A. (2016). Pedagogy of multiliteracies for Korean language learners: Developing standards-based (the 5Cs) teaching-learning materials using TV public service announcements. *Journal of Korean Language Education*, *27*(2), 143–192. https://doi.org/10.18209/iakle.2016.27.2.143

Lee-Smith, A., & Roh, J. (2016). Promoting socio-languacultural competence in advanced Korean curriculum: Using Drama *Misaeng*. *The Language and Culture*, *12*(2), 113–142. https://dx.doi.org/10.18842/klaces.2016.12.2.5

Luke, A. (2013). Defining critical literacy. In J. Z. Pandya, & J. Avila (Eds.), *Moving critical literacies forward: A new look at praxis across contexts* (pp. 19–31). Routledge. https://doi.org/10.4324/9780203521861

McKinney, C., & Norton, B. (2008). Identity in language and literacy education. In B. Spolsky & F. M. Hult (Eds.), *The handbook of educational linguistics* (pp. 192–205). Blackwell. https://doi.org/10.1002/9780470694138.ch14

Moje, E. B., & Luke, A. (2009). Literacy and identity: Examining the metaphors in history and contemporary research. *Reading Research Quarterly*, *44*(4), 415–437. https://doi.org/10.1598/rrq.44.4.7

New London Group (1996). A pedagogy of multiliteracies: Designing social futures. *Harvard Educational Review*, *66*(1), 60–92. https://doi.org/10.17763/haer. 66.1.17370n67v22j160u

Norton, B. (2014). Identity, literacy, and the multilingual classroom. In S. May (Ed.), *The multilingual turn: Implications for SLA, TESOL, and bilingual education* (pp. 103–122). Routledge. https://doi-org.ezproxy.cul.columbia.edu/10.4324/ 9780203113493

Ok, H.-J. (2009). Identity and literacy. *Korean Language Education Research*, 35, 361–386. https://doi.org/10.20880/kler.2009..35.361

Piller, I. (2016). *Linguistic diversity and social justice: An introduction to applied sociolinguistics.* Oxford University Press. https://doi.org/10.1093/acprof:oso/9780 199937240.001.0001

Scheibe, C., & Rogow, F. (2012). *The teacher's guide to media literacy: Critical thinking in a multimedia world.* Corwin. https://doi.org/10.4135/9781483387581

Shin, J. (2022). Criticality, identity, and ethics: Toward the construction of ethical subjectivity in applied linguistics research. *Annual Review of Applied Linguistics*, 42, 102–108, https://doi.org/10.1017/S0267190521000179

Suh, J., & Jung, J.-Y. (2021). Literacy and multiliteracies in Korean language learning and teaching. In Y. Y. Cho (Ed.), *Teaching Korean as a foreign language: Theories and practices* (pp. 127–146). Routledge. https://doi.org/10.4324/9780429244384-7

van Compernolle, R. (2016). Sociolinguistic authenticity and classroom L2 learners: Production, perception and metapragmatics. In R. A. van Compernolle & J. McGregor (Eds.), *Authenticity, language and interaction in second language contexts* (pp. 61–81). Multilingual Matters. https://doi.org/10.21832/9781783095315-005

West, G. B. (2021). "Is this a safe space?": Examining an emotionally charged eruption in critical language pedagogy. *Education Sciences*, *11*(4), 1–14. https://doi.org/ 10.3390/educsci11040186

Won, J.-S. (2010). A case study on the Korean writing workshop program for establishing migrant women's identity. *Research on Writing*, *11*, 137–164.

Yoon, Y. (2015). Reflections and perspectives of literacy education in Korea. *The Journal of Korean Language and Literature Education*, *36*, 535–561.

Yoon, Y. (2018a). Convergence of Korean language education and literacy. *Korean Language Education Research*, *53*(1), 39–57. http://doi.org/10.20880/kler.2018. 53.1.37

Yoon, Y. (2018b). Literacy education of multilingual and multicultural Korean language learners. *The Journal of Korean Language and Literature Education*, *42*, 231–256. https://dx.doi.org/10.17313/jkorle.2018..42.231

Yoon, Y. (2018c). The changing global language ecology and the future of Korean language education. *Korean Language Education, 163,* 1–21. http://doi.org/10.29401/KLE.163.1

Yoon, S. Y., & Brown, L. (2017). A multiliteracies approach to teaching Korean multimodal (im)politeness. *The Korean Language in America, 21*(2), 154–185. https://doi.org/10.5325/korelangamer.21.2.0154

Zhang, Q. (2020). A study on the principles of Korean language education for the promotion of critical media literacy: As an example of Chinese learners' media text response. *Teaching Korean as a Foreign Language, 57,* 141–174. https://doi.org/10.21716/TKFL.57.6

Zhang, Q. (2021). Multiliteracies education for Korean language learners in the post-human era. *Teaching Korean as a Foreign Language, 62,* 227–251. https://doi.org/10.21716/TKFL.62.9

Index

Note: *Italicized* and **bold** page numbers refer to figures and tables. Page numbers followed by "n" refer to notes.

AATK *see* American Association of Teachers of Korean (AATK)
Acanfora, F. 77
ACTFL: 5 Cs (World-Readiness Standards for Learning Languages) 206
agency 8–10, 62, 85–86; agency-oriented pedagogy 12, 127, 134; deaf, building 141–160; in ELT classroom 41–56; inspiring 120–135; in Korean language education 206–211; nurturing 101–113; restoring 189
Akimenko, O. 103
Alford, J. 211
Almeida, D. P. **193**; *Esse Cabelo* (*That Hair*) 195, 196
American Association of Teachers of Korean (AATK) 201, 213n1
Annyeonghaseyo (talk show) 209
Anstey, M. 9–10, 62, 188, 201
Applied Linguistics 61
Arcand, J. T.: *Wayfinding* 91, 92
assimilation 2, 76, 194, 208

Baker, W. 41
banking education 2
Bartal, O. 105
Baxter, J. 61
bildungsroman (coming-of-age stories) 163–177
Blackledge, A. 76
Block, D. 44, 68, 73, 212
Blyth, C. 207
Bourdieu, P. 69–70
Brinkmann, L. M. 123
Britland, J. 170, 171
Brown, L. 206, 209

Bull, G. 9–10, 62, 188, 201
Burke, A. 5–6

CBI *see* content-based instruction (CBI)
Charmaz, K. 87–88
Cheon, K.-R. 203
Chern, C.-I. 122
Chiziane, P. **193**; *Alegre Canto da Perdiz* (*The Cheerful Song of the Partridge*) 194
Choi, L.-J. 210
Chung, E. E. 211
Chute, H. 170–171
"Cities in Japan; Linguistic Landscape Project" 104–115, *108*, *109*; Mei 107–114, *113*; Qingxia 107–114, *113*; setting 104–105; students' learning 107
civic engagement 61, 90
CLA *see* critical language awareness (CLA)
Clemente, M. 123
CLIL *see* content and language integrated learning (CLIL)
cognitive linguistics 1
coloniality 184–185
communication 85, 90, 92; challenges 28–29, *29*, *30*; cross-cultural 51; disorders 11, 21, 23, 34–35, 37; at home 31–32; landscape 101; multilingual 103; multimodal 103; at school 31–32; skills 121; technology-mediated 44
communicative conventions, utilizing and challenging 54–55
community analysis 78
conscientização 189, 196, 197

218 Index

constructivist grounded theory 82, 87, 88
content and language integrated learning
(CLIL) 103
content-based instruction (CBI) 103
Cope, B. 3, 63, 74, 82–96, 102, 167,
188, 203; *Adding Sense* 85, 90;
Making Sense 85, 90
cosmopolitan plurilinguals 71–72
critical framing 3, 26–27, 84, 102, 121,
133, 203, 209
criticality 101, 104, 107, 114, 115, 120,
121, 124, 134, 164, 174, 177
critical language awareness (CLA) 103,
105, 122, 135, 191
critical literacy 12, 13, 189–190;
definition of 203, 204; innovating
the curriculum through 193–196;
for Korean language learning and
teaching 201–213; multimodal, in L2
Korean setting 204–206; and social
justice, interrelation between 164–165
critical pedagogy 21, 163–165
Critical Race Theory (CRT) 84
critical thinking 21, 61, 164, 177, 189,
192, 201, 204, 209
CRT *see* Critical Race Theory (CRT)
cultural capital 11, 69, 70, 186, 188
cultural diversity 2, 3, 83, 84, 89, 101,
121, 123, 183, 189, 195
cultural identity 8, 42, 43, 45, 54, 55,
90, 120, 185
cultural inequity 11
cultural literacy, definition of 205
culturally responsive pedagogy 92–93
cultural pluralism 203, 209
Cummins, J. 83
curriculum 10, 13, 35, 36, 84, 85, 95,
102–104, 190, 204, 206; disrupting
190–196; innovating 190–196

Dagenais, D. 123
Danker, J. 23
Danzak, R. L. 10
Da Silva, E. **193**, 195–196
Day, R. 22
deaf agency through teaching and
learning of English Grammar Games,
building 141–160, *142*; 'real-life
English' (RLE) text 143–146, **145**;
reflections on training 153–159, *157*;
training, reviewing 146–153, **146**,
147–153
Dedoose Version 9.2.007 28
deficit 2, 3, 6

DEI (diversity, equity, and inclusion)
114, 201
deliberate invisibilization 76
Deppe, L. 89–90
digital literacy 82, 91, 96, 204; definition
of 213n7
discrimination 8, 10, 65, 70, 75, 77, 92,
93, 101, 111, 112, 203, 208, 209;
linguistic 2; racial 76; social 73
distributive justice 165
Dodman, M. J. 186
Dong-Ju, Y. 204
Dooley, K. 122
Dupuy, B. 188
Dyches, J. 84

Early, M. 83
Economic and Social Research Council
(ESRC), UK 142
economic inequality 212
EGGs *see* English Grammar Games
(EGGs)
elitism 8, 78
ELT *see* English Language Teaching
(ELT)
embodied differences 78
empowerment 6, 8, 11, 14, 21, 22,
36–38, 42, 45, 72, 73, 76, 77, 95,
104, 153, 156, 158, 159, 171, 188,
189, 191, 202, 203, 209
English, as *lingua franca* 62–63
English Grammar Games (EGGs)
12–13; deaf agency through teaching
and learning of, building 141–160,
142
English Language Teaching (ELT):
classroom, learner engagement and
agency 11, 41–56; communicative
conventions, utilizing and challenging
54–55; data analysis 49; data
collection 47; education context
46; learner voice 41–43; materials
analysis 49; materials design 43–45;
participants 46–47, **46**; questionnaire
47, 49; research questions 45; social/
cultural identity, expression of 54;
social justice in 41–42, 55; student-
created materials 47, **48**; teacher
questionnaire 49–50; teaching
materials 50–54, *52*
environmental barriers 22
epistemological diversity 187
equality 73, 159, 160, 177; *see also*
inequality

Index 219

equity 5, 6, 8, 22, 93, 96, 115, 157, 168, 177, 204, 211; negotiating 202; social 42; *see also* inequity
ESRC *see* Economic and Social Research Council (ESRC), UK
exclusion 2, 12, 71, 77, 114, 160, 172; social 63, 208

Falconer, K. 93, 96
Farrell, T. S. 184
FCDO *see* Foreign, Commonwealth & Development Office (FCDO)
feminism: second-wave 165, 166; social justice 165–166
Flores, N. 72, 212
Foreign, Commonwealth & Development Office (FCDO) 142
foreign language acquisition 187–188
Fraser, N. 165–166, 169, 177
Freire, P. 105; on banking education 2; on critical literacy 189–190; on critical pedagogy 21, 163, 164; documentary photography 21; feminist theory 21; *Pedagogy of Hope* 85–86; on problem-posing model of education 190

García, O. 79n6
gender inequality 170
Gendry-Kim, K. S. 177; *Waiting, The* 13, 164, 165, 171–172, **173–176**
generalizing skills 29, 31, *31*
Gillen, J. 144, 146
Gombos, K. 90
"grammars" of semiotic systems 2
graphic novels, in L2 education 13, 163–177; critical literacy–social justice relationship 164–165; *Girl Called Echo, A* 13, 164, 165, 168–170, 172, **173–176**; *Learning by Design* 166–167; social justice feminism 165–166; *Waiting, The* 13, 164, 165, 171–172, **173–176**; *We're All Just Fine* 13, 164, 165, 169–172, **173–176**
Graziano, K. J. 22
Greene, M. C. S. 22, 36
growth mindset 29, *30*

Happy Hands School for the Deaf 160n2
Hardware, S. 5–6
Harré, R. 64, 67–68
Healey, A. 166
Henderson, S. B. 168
Hepple, E. 3

heritage language learners (HLLs) 207, 210–211; definition of 210
hiragana 105, 115n1
HLLs *see* heritage language learners (HLLs)
Hong, Y. 206
Howell, E. 84
Hudley, A. H. C. 212
hybrid identity 211

identity 8–10, 63; construction 9; cultural 8, 42, 43, 45, 54, 55, 90, 120, 185; formation 64; hybrid 211; in Korean language education 206–211; language and 9; literacy 9–10, 143; multilingual 11, 12, 72–74, 76; pluricultural 79; plurilingual 61–79; post-structuralist perspectives of 9; social 43, 45, 54, 55; vulnerability 70
inclusion 2, 12, 96, 107, 114, 154, 193; criteria for participation 24; cultural 5; linguistic 5; social, multiliteracies for 61–79
incompetence 107
Indian Sign Language (ISL) 143–159, *147–153*
inequality 61, 71, 72, 85, 122, 157, 207, 209; economic 212; existential 73; gender 170; social 2; structural 189; *see also* equality
inequity: cultural 11; social 11; sociolinguistic 133; *see also* equity
interactive positioning 64
interculturality 125
International Institute for Sign Languages and Deaf Studies (iSLanDS), University of Central Lancashire 142
ISL *see* Indian Sign Language (ISL)
iSLanDS *see* International Institute for Sign Languages and Deaf Studies (iSLanDS), University of Central Lancashire

Janks, H. 164
Japanese language literacy, characteristics of 105
Japanese linguistic landscapes, for critical multiliteracies 12, 101–116; "Cities in Japan; Linguistic Landscape Project" 104–112; pedagogies of multiliteracies 102–103
Jeong, H.-R. 205
Jung, J.-Y. 211, 213n5

220 *Index*

Kalantzis, M. 3, 63, 74, 82–96, 102, 167, 188, 203; *Adding Sense* 85, 90; *Making Sense* 85, 90
kanji 105, 111, 115n1
KAP *see* Korean for Academic Purposes (KAP)
katakana 105, 115n1
Kayi-Aydar, H. 8
Kelley, F. 166
Kettle, M. 211
KFL *see* Korean as a foreign language (KFL)
Kim, A. 208
Kim, H.-J. 205, 208, 213n4
Kim, J.-H. 205
Kim, Y. 213n4
Knowledge Processes Framework (KPF) 167, 172
Korean as a foreign language (KFL) 202–205, 207, 213n2; classroom, L2 learner identity in 209–210
Korean as a second language (KSL) 202, 203, 205–208, 213n2, 213n4
Korean for Academic Purposes (KAP) 206
Korean language learning and teaching, critical literacy for 13, 201–213; agency 206–211; critical multimodal literacy, in L2 Korean setting 204–206; identity 206–211; multimodality 202–204
Korean TV public service announcements (PSAs) 205
KPF *see* Knowledge Processes Framework (KPF)
Kress, G. 204
KSL *see* Korean as a second language (KSL)
Kubota, R. 71
Kumaravadivelu, B. 69–70, 165
Kurth, J. A. 23, 36

language proficiency 7, 49
La Sección Femenina 170
Lawrence, A. J. 144
Lawrence, A. S. A. 144
learner voice 41–42
Learning by Design 3, 12, 13, 83, 84, 93–95, 166–167; analyzing 4, 102, 113, 119, 167, 174–175, **175**; applying 4, 102, 113, 119, 167, 175–176, **176**; conceptualizing 4, 102, 113, 118–119, 167, 173, **174**; experiencing 4, 102, 106, 113, 118, 167, 172, **173**
Lee, J. S. 210
Lee, K. 208

Lee-Smith, A. 205
Lewis, C. 66, 78
lifeworlds 2, 6, 61, 62, 64, 102, 115, 123
Lin, A. M. 6
linguicism 8
linguistic competence 103, 120
linguistic discrimination 2
linguistic diversity 83, 84, 101, 121, 123, 128, 134, 189, 207
linguistic insecurity 70
linguistic landscapes (LLs): in classroom, L2 learners engaging with 12, 120–135; data analysis 126–127; data collection 124–126, **124–126**; in education 121–122; Japanese, for critical multiliteracies 12, 101–116; in language classroom with young learners 123; lower secondary school 125–126, **126**, 129–132; in pedagogies of multiliteracies 121–122; primary school 125, **125**, 127–129
linguistic pluralism 203, 209
linguistic vulnerability 70
LLs *see* linguistic landscapes (LLs)
LoCALL project 124–126
Lozano, M. E. 103
Luke, A. 77, 163, 204

Maldonado-Torres, N. 185
marginalization 2, 21, 72, 84, 85, 92, 111, 114, 185, 188, 195, 209; economic 165
Martin, J. 9
Mata, I. L. 185
material differences 77–78
McBrien, J. L. 22
meaning design 167
media literacy: critical 204; definition of 213n8
Menke, M. R. 167
Mercer, S. 8
Miller, A. L. 23, 36
Misaeng (TV drama) 205
MLP *see* Multiliteracies Project, The (MLP)
Moje E. B. 66, 78
monolingualism 1, 7, 35, 202, 208
multicultural coming-of-age stories 13, 167
Multicultural Council 90, 93
multicultural and multilingual voices, in South Korea 207–209
multiethnicity 209

Index 221

multilingual identities 72–74
multilingualism 7, 21, 38, 61, 62, 64, 71, 77, 125, 128, 129, 131, 202, 212
multiliteracies: new paradigm 63; for plurilingual identity construction 61–79; skills 62, 142; for social inclusion 61–79; social justice in L2 education through pedagogies of 1–14; theory 82, 85–86; *see also individual entries*
Multiliteracies Project, The (MLP) 87
multimodal competence 204, 209
multimodality, definition of 204
multimodal literacy 63, 177, 209; critical, in L2 Korean learning 204–206
Munduruku, D. **193**; *Kabá Darebu* 194–195
My Lovely Sam Soon (TV drama) 209

National Institute of Open Schooling, India 159
nationality 2
National Women's Party 166
native-speakerism 7
New London Group (NLG) 84, 85, 103, 163, 166, 202–203; 1996 manifesto 2, 83, 101; pedagogy of multiliteracies 1, 3–4, 102
Nguyen, A. 88–89, 96
Nicholas, H. 134
NLG *see* New London Group (NLG)
Norton, B. 9, 206, 207

Ok, H.-J. 206–207
Okwudire, T. 94–96
oppression 8, 89, 189, 207, 212
Ortega, L. 72, 187
Otheguy, R. 7
overt instruction 3, 25, 84, 102, 121, 133, 209

Pact of Oblivion (*Pacto del olvido*) 170
Paesani, K. 167
Papen, U. 143–146
Pavlenko, A. 76
pedagogies of multiliteracies 102–103, 166, 167; components of 3–4; definition of 3; linguistic landscapes in 121–122; panoramic view of 5–6; social justice in L2 education through 1–14; *see also individual entries*
'Peer-to-Peer Deaf Multiliteracies' project 141, 143
Penyas, A. 177; *We're All Just Fine* 13, 164, 165, 169–172, **173–176**

Phillips, M. 143
PHOTO approach 26
photovoice: communicating at home 31–32; communicating at school 31–32; data collection 24–25; engaging with social justice topics 36; exhibit and viewer survey 27; introductory meetings 25; method 23–28; and multilingual disabled students 23; and multilingual students 22; as multiliteracies approach 21–38; as multiliteracies pedagogical tool 35–36; one-on-one photograph discussion meeting 26–27; outcomes 34; participant co-researchers 24–29, **24**, 31–37; peer discussion groups 26–27; photography 25–26; posteriori themes 28–31, *29–31*; priori themes 31; procedures 24–25, **25**; speech-language pathologists, PCRs' perceptions of 33; student feedback, eliciting 36; and students with disabilities 22–23; teaching new skills 36–37; thematic analysis 27–28; as tool for social change 37
Piller, I. 207
plural, literacy in 188–190
pluricultural identity 79
plurilingual capital 61
plurilingual competence 103, 187
plurilingual identity construction 61–79; classroom's multilingual identity(ies) 72–74; data analysis 68; insecurity 69–70; instructional intervention for 66–68; participants 65; pedagogical intervention for 66–68; setting 65; stance, taking 69–70; through positioning and reflexivity, designing 64–65
plurilingualism 4, 7, 70–72, 95, 125, 187
plurilingual selves 66, 74, 78
politics of language 9
Portuguese, as foreign language course 13, 183–197; in Canada 185–186; coloniality 184–185; course overview 191–193, **193**
positionality 88, 134
position-based reflecting model *67*
Positioning Theory (PT) 64–66
powerful literacy 63
pragmatic competence 103, 122
problem-posing model of education 190
psycholinguistics 9
PT *see* Positioning Theory (PT)

222 *Index*

racial discrimination 76
raciolinguistic ideologies 72–73
racism 8, 73, 78, 194
'Raising Learning Outcomes in
　Education Systems' 142
Rajendram, S. 21
Rawls, J. 165
recognition 165
recognitive social justice 84, 92, 96, 165,
　175
redistributive justice 92, 165
redistributive social justice 84, 165, 173
Reese, D. 164–165, 169
reflexive positioning 64
relations of power 62, 66, 73
Ribota, A. 83–84
Ritchie, L. 92
Robinson, B. 89
Roh, J. 205
Roos, J. 134
Rosa, J. 72
Rotich, J. P. 22

Sato, K. 116n7
schoolscape 122
second language acquisition (SLA) 83,
　187–188
second-wave feminism 165, 166
Seed, N. 23
self-advocacy 21, 22, 35
self-construction 69
self-development 64
self-expression 21, 34, 42, 45, 52, 54,
　55, 61, 208
self-reflection 11, 22, 35, 36, 66, 68, 71,
　74, 204
sense-making potentials 85
sexism 8
Shettlesworth, C. 143
Shin, S. J. 209, 210
silent culture 209
Silva, E. 186
Silva, F. 123
singular, literacy in 188–190
situated practice 3, 25–26, 89, 102, 121,
　133, 209
SLA *see* second language acquisition
　(SLA)
SLPs *see* speech-language pathologists
　(SLPs)
SLT *see* speech-language therapy (SLT)
social/cultural identity, expression of 54
social discrimination 73
social exclusion 63, 208

social futures, designing 2–3, 45, 74–77,
　94–95, 203
social identity 43, 45, 54, 55
social inclusion, multiliteracies for
　61–79; classroom's multilingual
　identity(ies) 72–74; data analysis
　68; insecurity 69–70; instructional
　intervention 66–68; multiliterate
　learner 62–64; participants 65;
　pedagogical intervention 66–68;
　setting 65; stance, taking 69–70
social inequality 2
social inequity 11
social justice: action 90–93; criticality
　for 101–116; and critical literacy,
　interrelation between 164–165;
　in English Language Teaching
　41–42, 55; feminism 165–166; in
　L2 education, through pedagogies
　of multiliteracies 1–14; orientations
　in L2 learning 85–86; recognitive
　84, 92, 96, 165, 175; redistributive
　84, 163, 165; social justice-oriented
　pedagogies, L2 education through
　6–8; transpositional grammar, in
　multiliteracies framework 82–96; *see
　also individual entries*
social prestige 186
social turn, in second language
　acquisition 9
sociocultural approaches to L2 learning
　83–85
sociocultural barriers 22
socio-demographic barriers 22
speech-language pathologists (SLPs) 24,
　34; PCRs' perceptions of 33
speech-language therapy (SLT) 11, 24,
　25, 31–34, *32, 33*
Stake, R. E. 87
Statistics Canada 185–186
Stone, A. 143
Streng, J. M. 22
structural inequality 189
student agency 8, 12, 53, 134
student-created materials design 41–56
Sullivan, K. P. H. 123
symbolic differences 78

TESOL 13, 156, 160
thick description method 68
transformed practice 3, 27, 102, 121, 133
translanguaging 4, 21, 173, 210;
　definition of 7; implications for L2
　education 7–8

transpositional grammar 82–96; of agency 88–90; data analysis 87–88; ethics 87; *Learning by Design* 93–95; methods 87; participants 86; participation 90–93; recruitment 86; research sites 86; research study 86; secondary data 87
triangulation approach 68
Turner, S. 90
Tusting, K. 143, 144

Ukita, J. 115n1
Understanding Korean Culture 206

van Langenove, L. 64, 67–68
Vermette, K. 177; *Girl Called Echo, A* 13, 164, 165, 168–170, 172, **173–176**

Vermette, K.168
virtual linguistic landscape project 12

Warner, C. 188
Weber, J. J. 76
Weninger, C. 42, 44
Whitney, J. C. 22–23
Won, J.-S. 208
Woods, A. 84

Yaciuk, D. 168
yasashī nihongo 116n7
Yi, Y. 211
Yoon, S. Y. 205, 209, 213n4

Zapata, G. C. 83–84, 167
Zeshan, U. 144–145
Zhang, Q. 204, 213n4